BUSINESS MODEL WARFARE

The Strategy of Business Breakthroughs

Langdon Morris

BUSINESS MODEL WARFARE

The Strategy of Business Breakthroughs

Langdon Morris

© Langdon Morris 2018

All rights reserved

A FutureLab Book
www.futurelabconsulting.com

ISBN: 9781793031457

Introduction
INNOVATION and DISRUPTION

Innovation is a force of disruption, *intentional* disruption. The innovator's goal is precisely to disrupt the incumbent, to take away market share, and the innovator knows perfectly well that to do this it must be better at something important than the incumbent was.

Business model innovation thereby makes old ways of doing business irrelevant by introducing better value propositions and better experiences for customers, and in so doing it changes the structure of the market while creating competitive advantage.

Business model innovation is also perhaps the most important form of innovation, because it's available to any company of any size, anywhere in the world. All it takes is insight, and the willingness to listen well and try something new.

Since we all know it's better to be the innovator and the disruptor than to be the disrupted, the purpose of this book is to be your guide to successfully competing in the hyper-speed world of new technologies, accelerating change, and brutal competition between business models.

This book is about how business model innovation happens, and how you can make it happen.

Introduction: Innovation and Disruption

Part 1: The Tao of Business Model   7

1   Why Is Business Model Innovation Important?   8
2   Change   10
3   Fear   16
4   Paranoia   18
5   Business Model Innovation   22
6   Behind the Experience   31
7   Experience Design   36
8   Hidden Knowledge   47
9   Innovation Targets   49
10 The Formula   56
11 The Brand   62

Part 2: Innovation Strategy   71

12 The Landscape of Disruption   72
13 The Retail Apocalypse   77
14 The City Transformed   86
15 The Economy Transformed   93
16 Business Model Dominance   121
17 Business Model Platforms   131
18 The Patterns of Change   137
19 It's the Technology…   150

CONTENTS

Part 3: Innovation Leadership   **165**

20   Growth and Maturity   166
21   Creative Destruction   177
22   Innovating the Whole System   182
23   Winning and Losing at Business Model Warfare   195
24   Insider and Outsider   207
25   Core and Edge   210
26   Creative Economy Business Models   215

Part 4: Step into the River   **221**

27   Tool #1: Insight   222
28   Tool #2: Foresight   226
29   Tool #3: The Business Model Map   234
30   Tool #3: The Value Ladder   245
31   Tools #5 & 6: The Canvas and the 10 Types   249
32   Tool #7: Your Business Model Action Plan   256

Conclusion: Winning the War   **259**

About this Book   **267**
Notes   **268**
Index   **273**
About the Author   **278**

COMPANION VOLUMES

This book is part of a growing family of works covering all aspects of innovation, strategy, and branding. Together they address a wide range of important issues that we believe all business leaders should be paying close attention to.

Agile Innovation
By Langdon Morris, Moses Ma, Po Chi Wu

Soulful Branding
By Jerome Conlon, Moses Ma, & Langdon Morris

The Agile Innovation Master Plan
By Langdon Morris

The Brand Bridge
By Jerome Conlon

Foresight & Extreme Creativity
By Langdon Morris

Blockchain City
By Langdon Morris & Moses Ma

Permanent Innovation
By Langdon Morris

The Big Shift
By Langdon Morris

Part 1
THE TAO of BUSINESS MODEL

In many schools of Chinese philosophy, it is understood that there is a profound order which underlies the entire universe, and which brings harmony to nature and to all life. This is called *the Tao*.

Wise leaders act in alignment with the principles of the Tao, while those who do not are likely to bring suffering and ruin to themselves, their dynasties, and to their entire nation.

Today's business world of accelerating change is also subject to the Tao, as there is a specific set of principles that, when followed, may lead to success, and a different set that leads commonly to failure. Too often, however, we see business leaders following the wrong course, and bringing ruin upon themselves and their houses.

Here in Part 1 we examine these principles, and seek to learn what it is that wise leaders must do to bring their enterprises into harmony with the universal patterns and their inexorable processes of change. Our organizing concept for this exploration is that of the *business model*.

Chapter 1
WHY IS BUSINESS MODEL INNOVATION IMPORTANT?
It Differentiates

What do all these companies have in common?

Amazon	Disney	McDonalds	Starbucks
Alibaba	Facebook	Michelin	Tencent
Apple	Fedex	Netflix	Toyota
Bilbao, Spain	Google	Nike	Uber
CNN	Home Depot	Southwest Airlines	Walmart

Of course you know – they're all *business model innovators*. They're also fantastically successful. They've changed the structures of the markets they compete in by figuring out better business models, and those business model innovations then became essential to their success.

In fact, without their business model innovations we probably wouldn't have ever heard much about them, because these were the innovations that caused us to pay attention.

Which is why business model innovation matters so much – in many markets and industries, it's the straightest, surest, and quickest path to success. Conversely, when your competitors come up with the innovations, that's the quickest pathway to your own disaster.

Stated differently, business model innovation matters because it's what...

> **Uber did to taxis.**
> **Amazon did (and is still doing) to retailers.**
> **Google did to the entire advertising industry.**
> **Starbucks did to coffee shops.**
> **Netflix did to Blockbuster.**
> **Home Depot did to lumber yards and hardware stores.**
> **Walmart did to Sears.**
> **Robots will do to human workers, perhaps.**
>
> **It's what winning companies do.**

And it's also what your competitors want to do to your organization, make it obsolete. So it's what you'd better do to them first, by figuring out how to provide better experiences, higher quality, lower prices, better stories, and better organizations that deliver more value to your customers.

All of these are elements of your business model, and innovating it is very much worth talking about, because although it still isn't very well understood, the value and advantages you can create by doing it well are enormous. Success at business model innovation will differentiate your company.

So if there is value for you in gaining a deeper understanding of what business model innovation is, and how to do it, then you're reading the right book.

Chapter 2
CHANGE
It's Relentless

At root, a business model is simply a description of how you make money. It's what you do, create, or provide that your customers pay for. You deliver some sort of experience, product, or service based on organizational and operational mechanisms, you deliver it, and then you brand it.

That's always been true, so it's worthwhile to ask,

> **Q: What's different today?**
> **A: The pace of change is accelerating.**

In the past, even not so long ago, business models stayed the same for years, even decades, but that's no longer the case. Take a look at the graphs in this chapter, and consider what they mean.

The first one shows the growth in share price value of "AAFGM," the big five American technology companies Amazon, Apple, Facebook, Google, and Microsoft, as compared with all the rest of the market, as defined in this case as the S&P 500. It's pretty clear where investors think the future value lies, and if they're right this marks a change in the very structure of the economy.

The second graph is a comparable Share Price Growth graph for stocks in the Morgan Stanley Capital index of developed-nation firms, echoing the enormous divergence between the values of the top five tech companies, Alibaba, Baidu, and Tencent from China, Samsung from Korea, and Taiwan Semiconductor, and everyone else.

Since the whole point of this book it to explore and explain business models, these graphs show with absolute clarity that in the minds of investors technology is the future of the economy, and assuming they're right, then technology will be central to any conversation about business models and business model innovation. (And they are right, by the way.)

The next graph shows a fascinating macro view of the American economy's evolution, the share of the biggest sector during the last 220 years, beginning with the total dominance of economic activity in the pre-industrial economy by farming and finance in 1800, followed by the emergence of transport and particularly railroads at mid-century, and then the dawn of the oil age by about 1920, which of course fueled the development of America's automobile fetish, suburbia, and the development of its consumer culture.

And then around 1960 technology and communications emerged as the dominant sector, although by then the overall economy had become so much larger and so much more diverse that even as it was the largest sector, still it constituted only about 25%

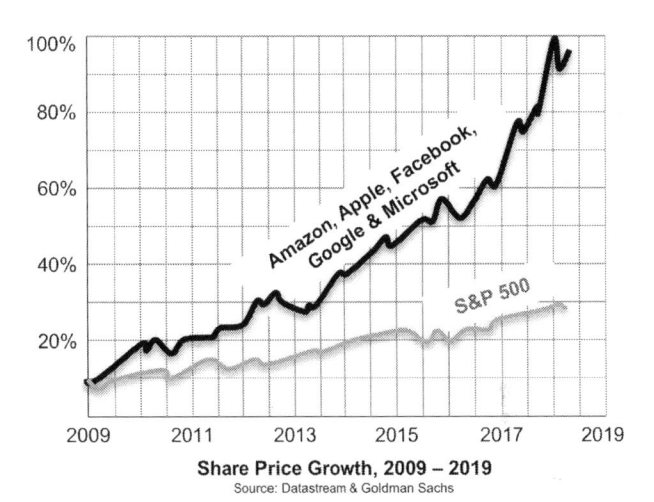

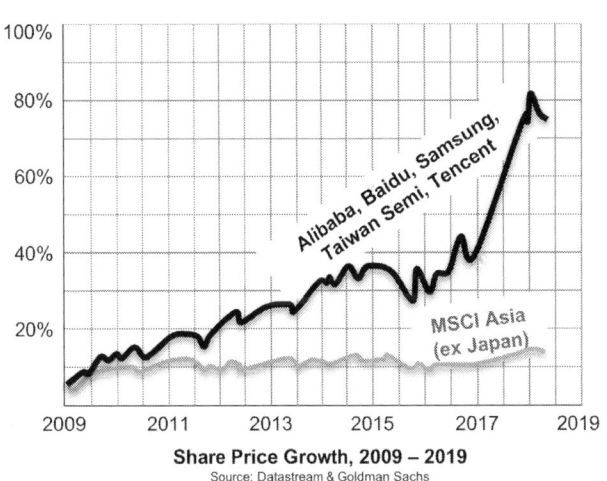

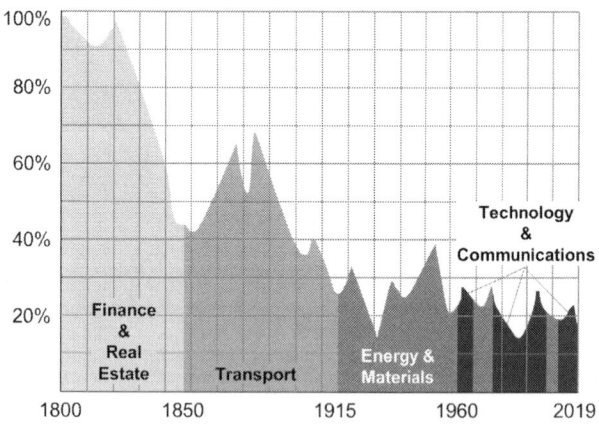

of the total. This evolutionary progression gives the historical context to then consider the fourth graph, the stunning exponential growth of World GDP from 1700 to 2000, an amazing 5000% expansion of economic activity that has become a unified global economy that affects nearly everyone, everywhere.

The next one shows the growth in market of two technology-savvy companies, Walmart and Home Depot, as they have completely blown past two complacent retailers, Macy's and JC Penney, which now languish in the pit of despair of business model stagnation.

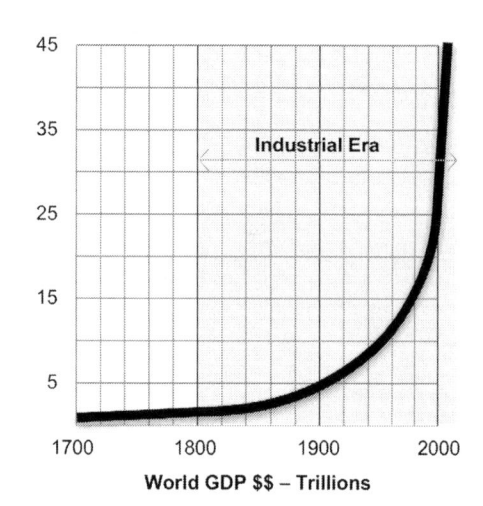

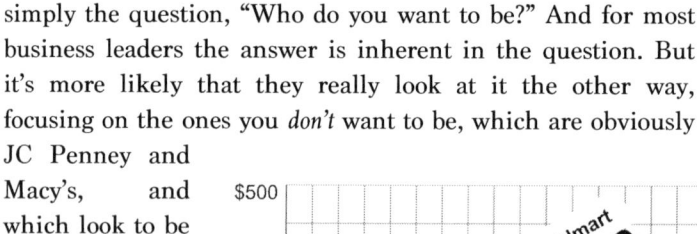

One of the key questions that this graph confronts us with is simply the question, "Who do you want to be?" And for most business leaders the answer is inherent in the question. But it's more likely that they really look at it the other way, focusing on the ones you *don't* want to be, which are obviously JC Penney and Macy's, and which look to be two or three very short steps from the end of their long and storied lives, following Sears and K-Mart into the proverbial dust bin of business history.

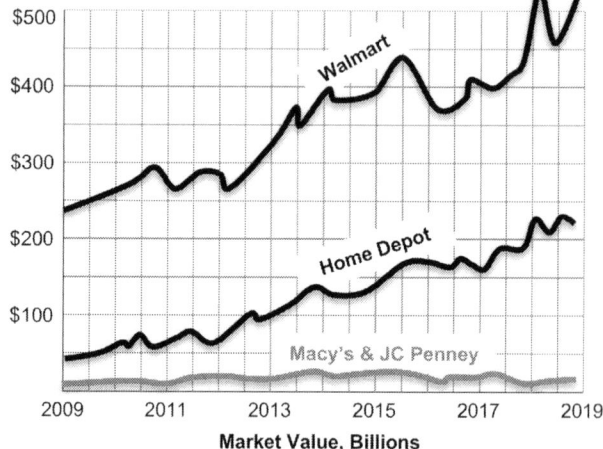

Part 1: The Tao of Business Model

What Walmart and Home Depot have done so well, and what JC Penney, Macy's, Sears, and K-Mart have failed to do, is to innovate their business models.

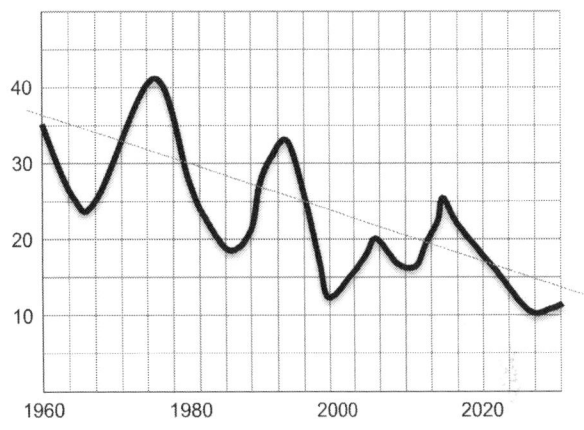

The next graph is a squiggly descending line that shows how vicious the competitive climate has become across all industries during the last few decades, causing the expected life spans of S&P 500 companies to rapidly erode. The average tenure has collapsed from about 35 years to around 15, and it's still shrinking. This is primarily a result of technology, and technology's impact on culture, society, behaviors, expectations, and of course directly as it's applied to products and services.

Thus, just because a company is proudly listed in the S&P 500 or the *Fortune* 500 doesn't mean that it can complacently look forward to a long and happy life. Instead, companies that we haven't yet heard of, and indeed which may not even exist today, will in many cases become next week's industry giants.[1,2]

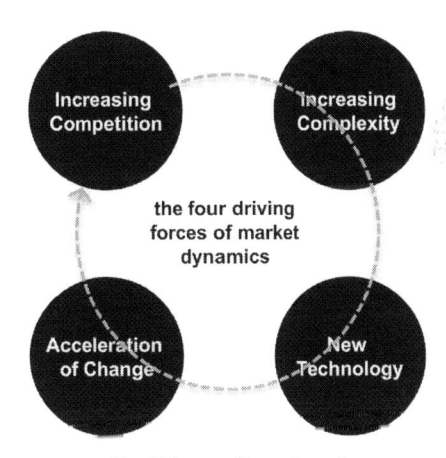

As the context of business strategy is the marketplace in which it is played out, discussions of strategy must begin by considering the character of market dynamics, and these six graphs show quite clearly what's happening today: increasing competition, increasing complexity, the overwhelming

Average Company Lifespan on the S&P 500 Index
Rolling 7 Year Average; Source: Innosight; S&P

the four driving forces of market dynamics

- Increasing Competition
- Increasing Complexity
- Acceleration of Change
- New Technology

The "Change Conspiracy"

13

impact of new technology, all driving the rapid acceleration of change.

While each of these presents its own particular challenge, the impact of all of them acting together significantly compounds the difficulties. You can think of this as a malicious "change conspiracy" which causes the dangers facing each organization to multiply exponentially, presenting massive challenges but also fantastic opportunities.

Business Models and Strategy

In its annual end-of-year issue in which it discusses the possibilities and expectations for the following year, *The Economist* offers dozens of perspectives from many observers on all aspects of society, the economy, business, culture, media, etc., and in the spirit of foresight it offers not just observations, but predictions about what will and will not happen. The editors know full well that many (or most) of their predictions will be wrong, and thus the purpose is not to be right, although it's fun when you are, but to get readers to think about what could, might, or might not happen, and to thereby influence their strategic thinking about their own lives and organizations.

An article by historian Yuval Noah Harari suggests that we should look to our leaders to address three critical issues that are facing all of humanity: preventing nuclear war, stopping climate change, and coping with the disruptive impact of new technologies.[3]

Identifying technology in this way is entirely consistent with what these six graphs show us, that the continuing introduction of new technologies into the market is a highly disruptive force, one not to be underestimated.

There is no doubt that faster planning and faster responses to change are imperative, but lag multiplies throughout large organizations, contributing to the accelerating rate of corporate failure, as leaders show themselves incapable of mastering these very difficult dynamics. This is not the world that most of today's business leaders are accustomed to.

While leaders and companies struggle to adapt, even entire nations struggle to keep their economies viable in the new and demanding framework of global markets, and the parade of failures makes for dramatic stories that are illustrated by sadness, individuals and families struggling to survive the economic and emotional strains, and as more and more companies fail, it's becoming clear that these are no longer unusual events.

Despite the attempts of governments, central banks, and multilateral organizations to address the impacts, it's evident that the forces of change are far stronger than ever before. Turbulence continues to increase, which means that business failures will continue to be common. As they should, managers wonder obsessively deep into the night,

What should we be doing differently?

For one thing, they need to pay much more attention to their business models.

Chapter 3
FEAR
Our Constant Companion

In early 2007 Jim Farley was General Manager of Lexus North America, a position he'd been promoted into because of his brilliant insights about the auto industry combined with his very strong leadership skills. He was a highly original thinker, which he had amply demonstrated as leader of the team that had created Toyota's Scion brand. When they invented it, Scion was a radically new and highly successful business model in the American auto industry (but sadly it collapsed after the global financial crisis of 2008, and Toyota shut it down in 2016).

During the course of our 2007 meeting he recounted the fascinating story of how Scion had been created, what distinguished its innovative business model, and how that business model had been fashioned. Among the many insights he shared was one that I have remembered ever since. Reflecting on the intensely competitive auto industry, he said, "If you're not scared, you're not paying attention."

That was not just his own view, it was the feeling of the entire senior leadership of Toyota in Japan, expressing how they thought about their global business and the competitive threats they faced.

The six graphs in the previous section are of course intended to convey exactly the same thing; there is a lot to be scared of.

Part 1: The Tao of Business Model

The capacity of organizations to adapt to rapid and unexpected change is frequently discussed, but how to actually achieve adaptability is a little understood and poorly practiced art, even as the pace of change continues to accelerate. It takes a few years to design a new car or a new car brand like Scion, even longer to engineer radically new automotive technologies like hybrids and fuel cells, and during that time the entire context can change, rendering all that work obsolete.

As a consequence of these long lead times and of how difficult it is to change a business model that is deeply embedded throughout a long and complex supply chain and a fully entrenched operating model, more big companies are undergoing extreme duress, or going out of business faster than ever before. They just aren't adapting quickly enough. We'll discuss many of them in this book, and their struggles and difficulties. We'll also look at leaders and firms that have mastered this essential art of business model innovation, and are thriving.

> "If you're not scared, you're not **paying attention**."
> — Jim Farley

By the end of 2007 Jim Farley had been recruited to join Ford in a senior marketing position. He quickly rose in the corporation, and it would not be at all surprising if one day soon he becomes Ford's CEO.

Chapter 4
Paranoia
That Too

In a very telling choice, former Intel CEO Andy Grove titled his 1996 book *Only the Paranoid Survive*.[4] So he's moved beyond fear, to an even higher state of agitation. It makes sense, given that Intel competes in the brutal and brutally fast-moving high tech sector, and places multi-billion dollar bets on emerging and unproven technologies.

Grove's book describes the succession of business model innovations that Intel went through during his quite long and very successful tenure, many of them gut-wrenching but utterly necessary, some of the them inspired. Grove refers to these as "strategic inflection points," a phrase that describes those moments when the structure of the market shifts, and you're either left in, or left out.

> "If we get lazy or slow, **we'll be run over** just like anybody else."
> — Reed Hastings

"I'm often credited with the motto, 'Only the paranoid survive.' I have no idea when I first said this, but the fact remains that, when it comes to business, I believe in the value of paranoia. Business success contains the seeds of its own destruction. The more successful you are, the more people want a chunk of your business and then another chunk and then another until there is nothing left. I believe that the prime responsibility of a manager is to guard constantly against other people's attacks and to inculcate this guardian attitude in the people under his or her management."
— Andy Grove

Part 1: The Tao of Business Model

Of course the problems of strategic shifts and accelerating change are two of the most challenging issues facing business and government leaders today, not only in technology, not only in the developed world, but everywhere.

In these turbulent markets, where companies that were once dominant are struggling to survive, leaders are constantly probing to understand what makes the difference between success and failure. Looking at the recent past, we ask what happened to Nokia, Blackberry, Kodak, Sony, Sears, Xerox, Blockbuster, Pontiac, Oldsmobile, Lehman Brothers, and so many other once-great brand names, and we realize that Grove was quite right. Why was GM's Saturn subsidiary a breakthrough in the 1990s, but 100% dead and lying face down in the morgue by 2008? What killed Scion? Change did.

While they were struggling, Walmart, Google, Facebook, Amazon, Fedex, Uber, Starbucks, and Home Depot have grown very successfully, and became widely admired.

Why the difference?

Maybe it's the paranoia. Netflix founder and CEO Reed Hastings recently commented, "You have a lot of paranoia about what's coming next ... and that's an advantage." But maybe it's also the attention to the experience of the customer. Hastings continued, "The consumer has a lot of entertainment options. If we earn more of consumers' time, then we continue to grow. And if we get lazy or slow, we'll be run over, just like anybody else."[5]

There's a story like this behind each business success and every business failure, and someone can probably explain what went right, or went wrong. Sometimes it's the story of a great idea, like Netflix' original business model innovation; sometimes one that succeeded and then failed, like Scion. Sometimes it's a story of insightful management, or

"The changes to the ways television is produced, Netflix says, are in service to the customer ... as long as that customer's aspiration is to watch more Netflix. Hastings explained the company's 2017 decision to eliminate the five-star rating system for movies and TV shows in favor of a simpler thumbs up/thumbs down system. 'Everyone would rate *Schindler's List* five stars and then they would rate Adam Sandler's *The Do-Over* three stars,' he said. 'But in fact when you looked at what they watched, it was almost always Adam Sandler.'

"This is the difference between old Netflix, which was designed to help movie fans expand their horizons beyond Blockbuster, and new Netflix, which is designed to match subscribers to relatable content as efficiently as possible. If Netflix is doing its job properly, the bingeing never stops."[4]

management that failed. But always it's a story about change. Change in technology or the market; change in the economy; change in a product or service that transformed a failure into a success, or vice versa.

Hidden behind many of these changes, or sometimes as a result of them, is change in what customers experience, and as a result, a change in their perceptions and attitudes, and then in their buying habits. Companies soar, or collapse, as a consequence.

While we study the stories to learn about the specific changes, events, insights, and breakdowns in each case, we also look for broader and deeper explanations that show how change applies across industries and the whole of the economy.

Here's one to think about. In his exhaustive account of the 2008 financial crisis and its aftermath, historian Adam Tooze describes the new, post-crisis global economic climate this way:

> "The economic setbacks come suddenly and unexpectedly. We have various words for this – panic, crisis, freeze, implosion, run, sudden arrest, sudden stop, radical uncertainty – and all these descriptions of what has happened or threatened to happen to the global financial system since 2007 point to one thing: the fact that on top of the structural, slow-moving tensions that global integration may generate, it also produces sudden ruptures, events that cannot be fully accounted for or reduced to structural terms, or regulated by law. These crises are hard to predict or define in advance. They are not anticipated and often deeply complex."[6]

Your business model may be disrupted by a competitor's innovations, but it may also be disrupted by a global financial crisis, a geopolitical confrontation, by radical new technologies, or for that matter by a sudden natural disaster or a slower-moving one like climate change. You have to be prepared for all these, prepared to change your business model when (or before) it becomes irrelevant. Which it will, sooner or

Part 1: The Tao of Business Model

later.

Healthy paranoia comes from a sensible awareness of risk, and as changes accelerates then risk rises. Thus, my goal here is to introduce to you a very specific strategic framework that explains how large and small companies can create and sustain market leadership, and the traps they often fall into that prevent them from doing so.

They key I suggest, as you already know, is business model innovation, which is a prudent response to a highly risky world.

Hence, the essential realization for any company's leaders is that it's their business model that matters, and possibly matters most. Consequently, business model innovation *must* shape and drive its approach to the competitive marketplace, as it must also shape how the firm organizes itself to compete for tomorrow.

This is what Intel under Andy Grove did very well, as Intel changed its business model in response to evolving market conditions, entering and exiting businesses and adapting its business model, to remain a leader in its field across multiple generations of technology and a variety of market structures.

> "The biggest risk is not taking any risk. In a world that changing really quickly, **the only strategy that is guaranteed to fail is not taking risks."**
>
> Mark Zuckerberg

This perspective gives us a new and very useful way to think about how to adapt to change, and even better a model for how to create change. Today and going forward what we're talking about is not just competition between companies, but competition in a highly complex and unpredictable world between business models.

Or, in other words, it's Business Model Warfare.

Chapter 5
Business Model Innovation
It's the Experience

It's no exaggeration to say that innovation is one of the most, if not the single most important factor that determines any company's success.

We all know that big changes are arriving every day, and innovation is one of the few productive ways that organizations can cope with them. But innovation isn't easy, which is why there's only one Apple, one Disney, one Alibaba (to mention but three of those listed above). As I will suggest throughout this book, one of the primary reasons that these particular companies are so successful is precisely because they are *business model* innovators.

Why?

Because the essential quality or characteristic that most often distinguishes a great company or a great brand from others is the quality of the experiences that it provides to its customers. And those experiences are what? They're the manifested outcomes of the business model that go beyond just the ostensible product or service to encompass every aspect of the relationship.

And it's because of their excessive attachment to their existing business models that companies become most vulnerable. Because no one wants to mess with success, companies try to prolong the lives of their business models for far too long, and when they keep doing things the same way but competitors come up with new and better ways, then they're in trouble. This is why Jim Farley and Toyota's leaders are afraid, and why Andy Grove and Reed Hastings are paranoid.

The "better ways" involve better experiences – and so business model innovation is all about figuring out how to provide better experiences to customers, and it's obvious what happens when you do that – customers leave the competition and find you.

So while compelling business model innovations can be difficult to devise, companies that succeed at doing so and which implement them well can create amazingly fast, powerful, and enduring returns. In other words, business model innovation is a tremendously effective way to innovate.

The question then becomes,

How do you do it?

This book will introduce you to many perspectives and tools to help you think through your vulnerabilities and opportunities, and I want to mention two of them here as we get started.

1. **From a strategic perspective, the life cycle view of company and industry evolution is exceptionally helpful.**

2. **From the perspective of customers, the experience view is very useful.**

The Life Cycle and Four Types of Innovation

Of course business model innovation isn't the only innovation option available to you, and successful companies don't just practice business model innovation, they do four types.

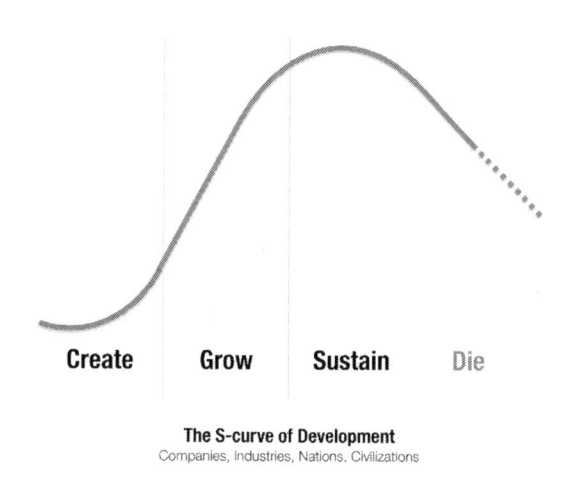

The recognition that there are four reflects the overall life cycle of organizations, shown in the s-curve model that is now a standard way of representing the normal process of development that companies, industries, nations, and civilizations go through during the course of their lives. As the curve shows, they're created, they grow, they sustain themselves for a time, and then they die.

Create Grow Sustain Die

The S-curve of Development
Companies, Industries, Nations, Civilizations

As you can see on the facing page, there's also a specific type of innovation associated with the first three of these stages, and while this is of course a broad generalization, it's nevertheless very helpful in thinking about what type or types of innovation are most relevant for your organization to pursue.

Firms work to create big breakthroughs, new inventions that reframe the market, because when they're successful they can result in fundamental strategic advantage.

They create incremental innovations, typically the easiest ones to figure out, which are often tweaks to existing products and services which they do to protect market share.

As they approach that peak they enter the danger zone, the period of time in which incremental innovation is no longer sufficient and they really have to think bigger than that. But do they instead hesitate, and try to sustain for too long?

When companies and industries reach the peak of their development and can see the frightening downward slope suddenly looming ahead of them, they often find that business model innovations become necessary, and they reinvent themselves. This is what Intel did very successfully at the strategic inflection points.

The Danger Zone
The downturn is coming.
Do we foresee it in time?

As we'll see repeatedly in stories and case studies throughout this book, too many miss the telltale signs and keep pushing incremental change for far too long, thereby making their future suffering even worse.

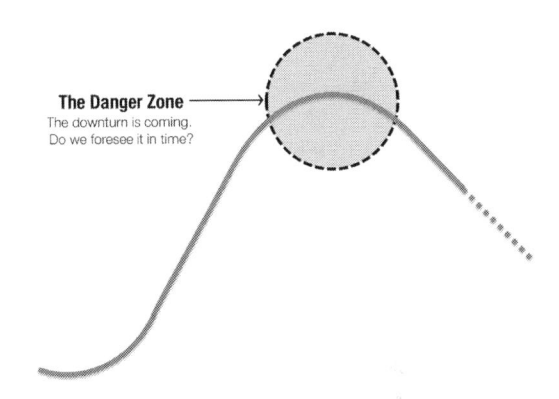

To address this situation, some innovative firms also create new ventures, entirely new companies that bring new solutions to market, and which in the process create new brand identities.

Of the four, there are compelling reasons to focus on business models. They may be difficult to discover, but when you do, they can often be implemented fast and inexpensively, they can create significant differentiation, they can rejuvenate a business, and they can endure because they actually then define a new way of being, which is effectively the next generation s-curve. There are obviously great advantages in doing this, because the new curve implies a new mindset, and it is often exceptionally difficult for competitors to respond effectively precisely because they may not grasp

Re-Invent
Business Model Innovation

Create — Breakthrough Innovation
Grow — Incremental Innovation
Sustain — Has Hesitation Set In?
Die — Too Late to Innovate

← New Venture Innovation →

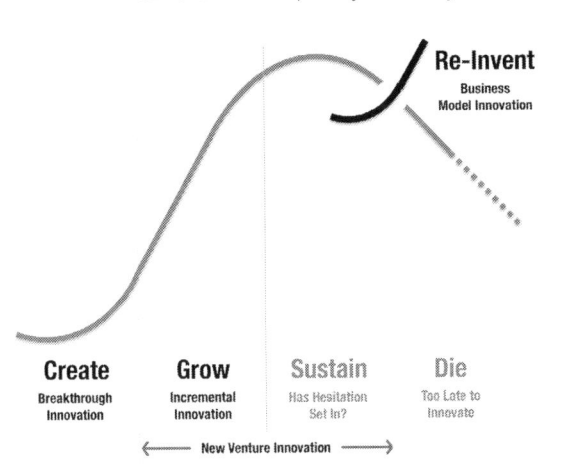

Four Types of Innovation

the essence of that mindset, trapped as they are in the old one.

And happily, you don't have to have a massive R&D budget to innovate your business model, because nearly everything you need to make it work either you already have, or it can be bought on the open market.

But what you desperately do need is **insight**, and for that you have to find new ways to look at your own company, at your competitors, at your customers, and at the new technologies that will either disrupt you or allow you to create better experiences, and thereby to change the business model, to disrupt, to win big.

Elements of a Business Model

A business model consists of four things. First, it's a description of how you make money, as it tells why and how your customers pay for your products and services. But even more important, a business model provides an experience, and that experience is essential to what people pay for. The difference between Saks Fifth Avenue and Walmart isn't just the quality of the merchandise and the prices, it's the way a customer feels because of the service they get, the atmosphere, the vibe.

Similarly, the genius of Starbucks' business model innovation was figuring out how to create a cup of coffee that people would pay ten times more for, and delivering it in a welcoming atmosphere where people are contented to hang out or work for hours, but doing this at really low cost to Starbucks. Part of the genius of WeWork is that they captured the vibe of Starbucks in the design of the office.

The genius of Apple's business model is also the experience, the experience of *using* their devices, and the care and attention that's given to product design and user interface design.

In fact, every company provides or enables or delivers an experience of some sort, and the essence of business model innovation is designing those experiences thoughtfully, and improving on what already exists.

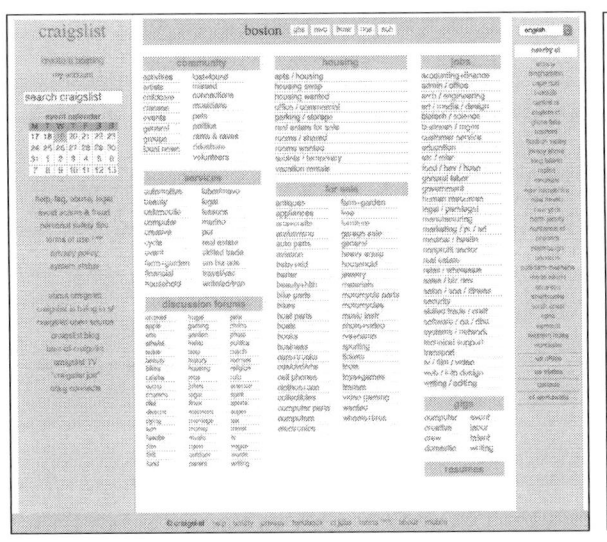

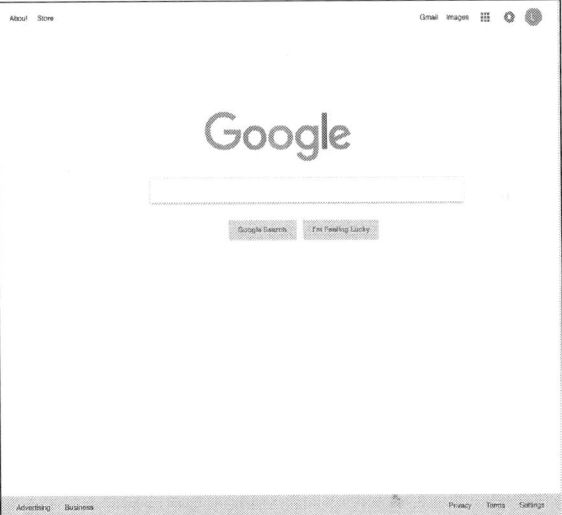

This is pretty easy to see in a retail store environment, but it's just as true online. Compare the Craigslist web page to Google's, and it's easy to see that an online presence can be every bit as experiential as walking into a store. Craig has resisted all efforts to improve the look of the web page, believing that this sparse style – should we call it "1950s newspaper"? – best fits the company's business model. It's a giant list, and it's all about the categories.

Google's simple search page also offers a distinctive experience, and in fact its vast white space has been meticulously designed to convey a very particular message: this page tells you that "it's all about you, and whatever *you* type in the search field."

This has obviously been wildly successful, as Google reports that it did more than 3 trillion web searches in 2017, which works out to roughly 95,000 per second. Clearly people like using their (sort of free) service...

But what makes it possible for any business model to operate? The third element of the business model is whatever goes on inside of the organization that enables it create, provide, and deliver those experiences. We will see in the next few chapters that this is a very long list of possible actions, which for simplicity we organize into four categories, product and services design, technology, supply chain design, and operations design.

The fourth and absolutely essential element of your business model is that it defines how you differentiate (or fail to differentiate) your company.

To summarize, then, the four things that a business model does simultaneously are these:

what is a **business model**?

1. **It's how you make money.**
2. It's how you deliver *experiences* to your customers.
3. It's how you use products, services, technology, supply chain, and operations to compete.
4. **It's how you differentiate your company.**

Then why should you be scared?
Well, what if your competitor comes up with a better business model?
Then what?

Every company has a business model, because it's just a description of "what is." The opportunity in business model innovation is in thinking about "what should be."

Better or Cheaper

So the s-curve model and the four types of innovation that it defines give us a very useful way to think about business model innovation, and explains its strategic significance. Another important framework is embodied in a very simple distinction that has extensive implications, the distinction between "better" and "cheaper."

To illustrate this distinction we use a super simple mapping tool that's really just a field of two essential (and quite explicit) factors of the customer's experience. We label the vertical axis of this market space "customization," which reflects "better" as we go up, and we label the horizontal axis "market size," because as things get less expensive more people can afford them, and so a larger available market. As you can see in the figure, these two axes them compose a market space that we can use as a way to locate any firm, because by definition every firm must offer products or services that have a given quality level at a given price.

To take cars as an example, on the map we can locate a mid-market car in the center, a luxury car toward the top left, and a used car toward the bottom right. What each individual customer is then likely to do is choose the quality level that matches their ability to pay.

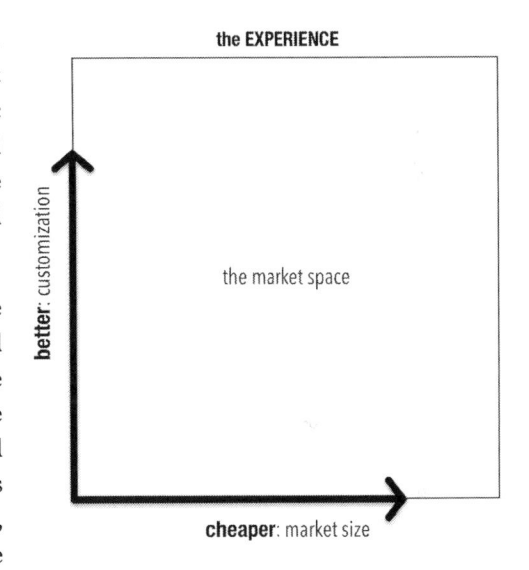

the EXPERIENCE

better: customization

luxury car

mid-market car

used car

the auto market space

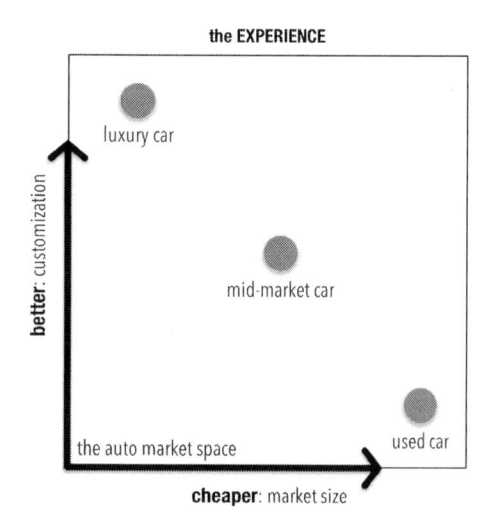

cheaper: market size

This is a simple but very effective way to visualize a set of factors which can otherwise be quite difficult to see. It also simplifies the discussion about business models to its basic essence: it's all about finding the right combination of quality and price.

As we go forward in this book we'll add more levels of detail to the market space map, which will make it even more useful as a tool for analysis and design, but if you want to go into more depth right now, skip ahead to Chapter 29, *Tool #3: The Business Model Map*, page 224.

While the combination of quality at a price is obviously critical, the innovator's role is only half of the equation. Customers are the ones who determine the value of innovations, because they are the ones who pay for them. Market behavior is an aggregate reflection of every consumer's drive to find the most attractive offers, and to maximize value received for cost incurred. As innovation is the process of creating higher value offerings, buyers naturally gravitate to innovative products.

Although "gravitate" is the wrong word. It's more accurate to say that people obsess about innovations, consuming them ravenously. The capitalist system depends for its dynamism on the market's demand for innovation, which history has shown to be insatiable.

The concept of differentiation again becomes critical, because innovation in this context is a matter of coming up with the highest quality at the lowest price. And it turns out that businesses have been incredibly resourceful at coming up with new and better ways to reduce costs and/or to improve quality, and thus the essence of the business model contest is doing this effectively, and repeatedly, as a result of which a firm rises to the top of the heap because it provides the best experience.

Chapter 6
Behind the Experience
It's Complicated

The work required to deliver a business model experience is often exceptionally complex, involving hundreds or even thousands of factors, dozens or hundreds of variables, and in the case of large organizations and complex products and services, vast numbers of people, many partner organizations, and enormous global supply chains.

A typical car, for example, has about 30,000 parts, all of which were designed by someone or a team and manufactured somewhere, and then brought together to one place for assembly, all of which requires a massive effort, and costs the buyer around $30,000.

But that's pocket change compared to a Boeing 787, which has 2.3 million parts (75 times more than the car), and costs $150 - $260 million, 2000 - 5000 times more.

It takes a lot of time and huge amount of effort to work out all the details of a contemporary product, whether it's a car, a plane, or a food truck, a restaurant, a museum, an amusement park, or an ecommerce web site, or even a shirt.

The shirt, your shirt may have been designed anywhere in the world, but it was most likely manufactured in China or Vietnam, or perhaps Honduras or Malaysia (you can check on the label), and then put in a bag, and the bag in a box, the box in a container, the container on a truck, and then a ship, and delivered eventually to the warehouse and then store where you bought it, or directly to you at your home in Sweden or Senegal or Singapore. Yes, it's complex.

In its ever-expanding festival of excess, Amazon reportedly carries more than 560 *million* products (gasp)[7] and the complexity required to organize this vast catalog and deliver to your doorstep the one little $5 thingy that you ordered yesterday is a truly impressive feat of complexity management.

And each element of this experience is part of the company's business model and each was designed.

But wait a minute. Here I am describing a car, an airplane and a shirt as "experiences." Aren't they really just products?

Of course they're products, but they're also more than that, because when we buy and use any product we're having an experience, and it's the experience that matters. In most cases, the end point goal actually was the experience, and the product was just a means to get there.

> "People don't want a drill, they want a hole."
>
> Ted Levitt

Marketing innovator/genius Ted Levitt once commented that people don't want a drill, they want the holes it makes. The drill, as the product, is the means to their end, not the end. He was emphatic about this because product people so often forgot that their product is just a mean to accomplish something else. He coined the clever phrase "marketing myopia" to indelibly convey this misperception.[8]

And people want the hole not because they like to make holes, but because they need them to accomplish something else which the hole enables. The drill is the means to make a hole, and the hole is the means to hang a picture on a wall, perhaps. The drill can be better or worse in terms of its quality, but either ways it's a means, just as the process of buying and using any product is thus a form of experience around which business models should be crafted.

I can buy the same snack food in a gas station quick mart, a grocery store, a Walmart, or on Amazon, and while I'll get the same bag of chips, I will choose one of these four for the specific reasons of price, timing, location, convenience, etc. Buying and using any product embodies an experience, and the company I buy from has to make choices about what the buying experience is going to be like, while the maker has to consider what the using experience is going to be like as well.

Businesses do this every second of every day; business model innovators want to know how can they can do it better, how can they deliver better experiences to you in the process of running their business. Here we're interested in the inner life of your company. In very broad terms we can sort this inner life into four major categories:

1. **Products and services**
2. **Technology** that's appled to operate the business (as distinct from technology products that you might sell)
3. Your **supply chain**, which as we just saw with Amazon, is global and immense
4. And how you **organize and operate** the whole shebang.

products & services	technology applied	supply chain	organization & operations

Most firms work to keep all these factors invisible to customers, as they want them only to experience the bliss of being the customer, and never have to encounter the Rube Goldberg of contortions that's going on behind the scenes.

But that Rube Goldberg contraption is exactly where many fantastic business model opportunities are hidden. After all, it was in the configuration and management of its supply chain that Walmart completely trounced Sears and K-Mart, and generated the business model that now dominates the American mid-market in-store retail landscape. That's what made Fedex so dominant too, the ability to track a package step by step, and never lose one.

But the supply chain innovations were enabled, in turn, by technology, as you can't run a globally-sourced business operation without the high speed internet efficiently connecting the cash registers in all 12,000 Walmart stores to the factories in Asia to the ships at sea to the ports and trucks and bazillions of vendors.

And you've got to have the operation in place to run it all, consisting for Walmart of 42 mammoth warehouses in the US alone, covering more than 50 million total square feet of space, jam-packed with pallet racks from floor to the ceiling 30 feet above, filled with millions of products. Then there's the hiring, 2.1 million employees worldwide, the massive payroll, accounting, training, policies, promotions, etc., etc., and the massive IT infrastructure that's supposed to keep track of it all.

Yup, it's complicated.

But Walmart doesn't want you to see any of that. What Walmart does want is simply for gazillions of customers to stroll into megastores, find just exactly what they want, breeze through one of the 50 cash registers, pay the smiling clerks waiting there, and swiftly be on their way thinking, "Wow, that was easy, and I got such a great deal!"

But it's all the complexity on the inside that enables the lovely experiences on the outside.

And of course it's not always so smooth. When the system breaks down, which it can do perniciously in any number of dastardly ways, then the lovely experience flips. The shelf that was supposed to hold the product you desperately wanted to buy was empty (stock-out, the retailer's nightmare), the price was wrong (sorry, it must be computer glitch), the line at the cash register was soooo long (wrong time of day to do the shopping), the clerk was snippy (she's been on her feet for seven hours already today), the parking lot was a mess, add all that up and maybe next time you'll try Target, or god forbid, Amazon.

Then again, maybe you'll try Walmart's online store, where you can find 35 million products, 300 times more than "mere" 120,000 that you'll find on the shelves in one of its 180,000 square-foot Supercenters.

All this should hopefully make it clear what's going on here – business model innovation is all about providing ever-better experiences to customers by making enhancements or improvements along any one of many dimensions, from price to quality to ambience to service, and delivering that at whatever type or level of experience that is a function of how you've got the thing organized on the inside.

So when your competitor finds a better way which enables them to lower prices, or improve quality, or speed delivery, or make customers just feel better and more valued, then they've figured out how to innovate their business model and enhance the customer's experience, and you've got to respond or face the unpleasant consequences.

Hence, all this work is not optional. You've pretty much got to be innovating your business model on an ongoing basis just to remain relevant.

Chapter 7
EXPERIENCE DESIGN
It's Not by Accident

Since the notion of *experience* is so essential to the entire discussion about business models, ask yourself what company has most obviously mastered the process of applying technology to provide great experiences to millions of people. If you're like me, the one that comes immediately to mind is Disney.

Disney's business success is focused obsessively on creating a very particular type of exceptional experience, and then surrounding that experience with a multi-layered commercial enterprise. The experience itself, whether it's conveyed through a movie, a TV show, an amusement park, a cruise ship, or a branded product, is specifically intended to move the audience/customer beyond the mundane day to day world of everyday reality and into fantasy worlds of past and future, and through that to experience life in a richer way.

There's a well-developed and very explicit philosophy behind Disney's business model, which reflects the genius of Walt Disney himself, and his persistence and determination to bring that philosophy into reality throughout each and every element of his company.

Today the Disney company is surprisingly open about sharing their philosophy, which they do through books, trainings, at their amusement parks, and even in some of their broadcasts.

Part 1: The Tao of Business Model

The five principles that Walt Disney identified as essential to the design of all Disney works are:

- **Start with a great story**
- **Create an immersive and intriguing world**
- **Use the best – talent, technology, media, and materials**
- **Be unique**
- **Make it magical.**[9]

Of course this isn't at all easy to do, or it would common rather than exceptional. It takes a unique combination of vision, talent, leadership, and capital to make this business model work, and as we see in the quote to the right, the determination to overcome all forms of resistance.

At the opposite end of the experience spectrum are the things we do not because they bring us joy and amazement, but because we have to. This is experience-by-necessity, the stuff we know in advance is not going to be enjoyable, like dental appointments, school exams, filling out insurance forms, and moving around crowded cities.

Quite unlike Disney's purpose to enthrall and entertain, the business of Uber and the taxi cab is entirely utilitarian, the simple, important, and often highly annoying need to get from place to place.

The taxi business model dates back at least to 1605, long before there were cars, when you could hire horse-drawn carts and carriages to get from here to there in big cities. In modern times, iconic black taxis in London and yellow ones in New York and red ones in Hong Kong are essential elements in the urban transportation system, vital services that do, however, suffer from easily recognized deficiencies.

New York taxis are also notorious for being dirty and smelly, driven by rude drivers who are gruff and generally unfriendly. Unless you're on a fixed-price route, typically to or from a major airport, you never know

> "The key attribute that has fueled more than fifty years of Disney park innovation in planning, design, storytelling and immersive entertainment was Walt's aversion to the word *no*.
>
> "You never said no to Walt Disney, because he would find someone who was willing to take a chance and try something that had never been done before. That's why we have monorails and submarines and rockets racing through Space Mountain in the dark.
>
> "In the early days of Disneyland, Walt also established a rule for Disney designers: 'I want you to go to the park at least every two weeks and stand in line with our guests.'
>
> "His objective was to understand the guest experience as a road map to what we could do better to enhance it."[6]
>
> Marty Sklar
> Disney Imagineering Leader

what the cost of a cab ride is going to be until the end, and then it often comes as an unpleasant surprise. Sometimes as you sit stuck in traffic going nowhere you can only watch sadly as the amount on the meter rises, and there's nothing you can do.

When you arrive at your destination you fumble with cash or your credit card, and then there's the matter of the tip – should you tip a driver who just grunted at you while you were crammed in the back seat of the smelly cab, and if so, how much?

On top of that unpleasantness, there's all the drama of standing on a corner and trying to wave down a taxi on a cold and dark night, in the rain or snow or wind, and with no cars in sight – here you have all the ingredients of a tedious and highly unpleasant experience, and often outright dangerous one, too.

In many cities, like New York, the taxi industry operates as a licensed monopoly, which enables taxi drivers to do well financially even while providing a marginal or non-existent levels of service with lousy attitudes. New York City limits the number of cabs to about 13,500. It's a classic monopoly.

But couldn't there be a better way?

The two founders of Uber abruptly realized this one day when they themselves were standing in rain and trying (without success) to hail a cab (in Paris, where taxis notoriously disappear when it rains, because, well, who wants to drive in the rain?). There has to be a better way, they thought, with a combination of anger and curiosity, and being themselves computer scientists with iPhones in their pockets, the solution revealed itself crisply and abruptly, a Eureka-like moment of realization – yes, there is a better way!

Ubiquitous mobile connectivity, GPS, so the phone knows where you

Part 1: The Tao of Business Model

are, and which makes it simple to calculate the time and distance to your destination, and so the fare is also known in advance.

Uber's app is the connectivity that unifies the pieces of the solution into a genuine solution, the platform!, and suddenly a taxi is an odd relic of a past era.

Uber thus flipped the entire urban transport business model by creating a digital connectivity platform that facilitates the interaction between driver/owner and passenger, handling routing, booking and payment automatically, all of which happens without Uber needing much in the way of assets, other than its computer code app, and a way to get that app onto your phone. It doesn't own cars or the garages to store them in, and drivers are not its employees.

Yes, it's quite simple, and yet it's also not-simple at all, because being able to see the possibility of this new business model required them to experience profound dissatisfaction with the prevailing taxi model, and have the insight as to how smart phones could enable a new pattern of relationships. And then they had to execute it, which so far has cost billions of dollars, but which has produced a company worth many more billions.

However, ride sharing does not benefit everyone. Recent studies have found that the growth of the ride-sharing industry has led to significant reductions in the use of public transit in many big American cities, increased in greenhouse gas emissions, and a 3.5% increase in fatal car accidents.[10]

In addition, neither Uber nor Lyft are profitable yet, so we can't say for sure how the story will turn out, but clearly the structure of the urban transportation market has permanently changed. In New York City, the license to operate a taxi has declined precipitously in value, from about $1.5 million in the pre-Uber days to around $150 thousand today, a 90%

drop that has caused severe financial distress to the owners of those taxi licenses. But now there are about 40,000 Uber, Lyft, and other ride-sharing drivers on the streets of New York, which means a significant improvement in the lives of people who use them to get around the city, which at one time or another is just about everyone, all 10 million New Yorkers plus the 60 million tourists who visit annually.

But wait. There was a *huge error* in the previous paragraph – did you catch it? I wrote, "we can't say for sure how the story will turn out," which is actually a totally flawed way to look at it. Do you see why?

Because the story will *never* "turn out." It will never be over and done, because even if Uber does make it to profitability one day, the overall rate of change is so fast that there never is and can never be an end state in the ever-evolving market, nothing that should never be considered as permanence. The game now changes constantly, so business leaders must grasp that they can *never* stop innovating.

Ford has of course noticed all this, and it's invested in a partnership with Uber and Lyft with the goal of reducing auto emissions and increasing the efficiency of urban mobility.[11] Ford also invested in one of the major bike sharing companies, Motivate, but as we learn from this comment by Ford's CEO Jim Hackett, it's not about the bikes:

> "What we're doing differently in San Francisco that isn't done in New York is we put telemetry on that bike, so now the bike is pinging data to us. The opportunity is not bikes. That's not why Ford's in it. The opportunity is data, and the data is super valuable because it tells us these invisible paths that people are taking in this complex city in terms of how they want to get around. And there's something else cool about it because we can take that data and we can connect it in ways that our new shuttle is going to connect to the cloud as well."[12]

Part 1: The Tao of Business Model

Yes, "it's all about the data," because the data will tell them where the needs and opportunities are.

To be more specific, though, Hackett's explanation was incomplete because it's actually *not* the data that Ford cares about, it's what the data about how people get around in the city will tell them – the *information* they can extract from it. This requires that data to be filtered – and the *knowledge* that this will provide to help shape Ford's future investments in urban transportation options.

As the figure shows, creating knowledge, which is also called *learning*, is the synthesis of information plus theory to explain it plus experience to validate it. Ford's investment in bike sharing is just the beginning of that chain, from which the company hopes to then create valuable experiences for its customers.

If it's surprising that Ford would invest in a bicycle company, this merely reflects the ways that our ideas about cities and urban transportation are shifting, and the new business models that are emerging. In fact, bike sharing is now a major part of the urban transportation system in many urban areas. New York City's franchise operator is Citi Bike Share, which publishes its usage data, and from which we learn that on a typical day in June 2018, the total distance travelled by all Citi bikes in New York was about 160,000 miles, and about 60,000 trips were taken. In October 2017 a Citi Bike member took the 50 millionth bike ride, and by mid-2018 Citi Bike had 143,000 members, 12,000 bikes in

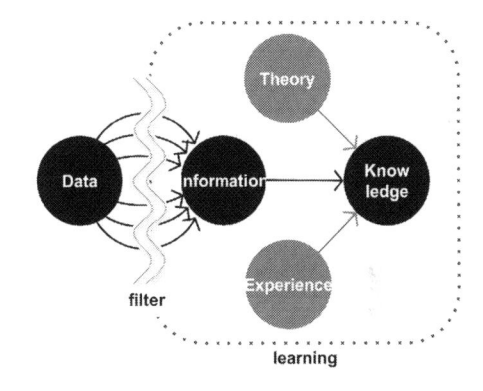

750 Bike Sharing Stations in New York City
(+ 12,000 Bikes)

41

use, and more than 750 stations located throughout the city.

All this infrastructure is of course generating a massive amount of data, helping people to get around, and adding a lovely experiential dimension to life in the city.

Self-driving cars are certainly coming soon and they'll generate even more mountains of data, and progressively all these technology-enabled modes of transportation are radically altering how cities function. Uber and taxis, pedestrians, bikes, buses, subways, and perhaps Hyperloop will soon be part of an integrated urban information-transportation system.

Thus, it's not an exaggeration to say that digital technology is altering the entire industry of "urban transportation" and causing a significant shift in its many underlying business models, which in turn also brings change to the city.

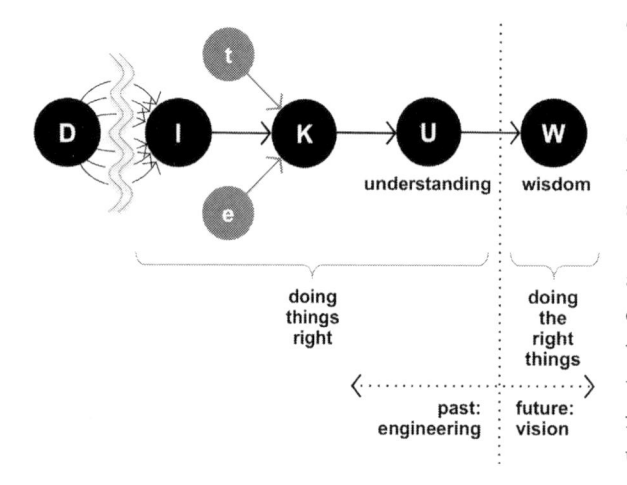

This is the nature of competition that is enabled by technology, changing conditions result from technology that enables us to gather more knowledge and to apply that knowledge to the basic structure of business or urban operations. But as this figure shows, the capacity to apply that knowledge effectively requires of us both *understanding*, which enables us to do things right, and *wisdom*, which help us make the right choices in anticipating a future that is complex and highly uncertain.

And this the essential nature of competition in our times – new technologies arriving constantly, new competitors striving to take market share away from the existing players by using those technologies to disrupt the market, and all this constituting a never-ending cycle of possibility, risk, innovation and change.

And while the study of business model disruption and innovation is not the only way to look at what's happening out there in the marketplace, it's certainly a provocative way, and it's likely to yield many valuable insights that will help you to think about your own business and the evolving dynamics of the industry in which you compete.

What other examples of business model innovation are worth considering? What are some of the most innovative business models that we should take a look at?

Here's an interesting one from the annals of history. Remember what you learned in school about the Vikings, and the way they terrorized Northern Europe for centuries, pillaging and generally wreaking havoc, and causing monks living on the northern coast of Europe to huddle in their monasteries and plead, "From the fury of the Northmen, O Lord, deliver us."

Interestingly, recent research has uncovered what may have been the critical enabling technology that made their long distance sea voyages of conquest business model possible, reaching as far as Greenland and North America. It seems that around 900 AD the Vikings initiated large scale production of tar extracted from wood resin through slow combustion, which was used to waterproof the hulls and windproof the sails of their elegant long ships. This was apparently the critical breakthrough innovation that enabled both long distance trade and the marauding raids through which they conquered half of England and much of Northern France.[13] The technology of tar thus made it possible for a business model innovation that had massive effect across the entire region, and endured for centuries.

Now it's 1200 years later and the English have become the British, but they're still trying to sort out their relations with their European neighbors. This time, though, much of the damage is self-inflicted, in the form of the Brexit fiasco. Because 60% of British GDP results from either imports or exports, the fact that they've chosen to institute significant barriers with their major trading partners is, well, perplexing. And we're not just taking about the high end stuff, the BMWs and French perfumes and fancy Italian clothes. No, Britain also imports about half of its basic food products, leading to concerns about supplies, and leading some to make back-up plans to stockpile essential goods.

So how do we know this? Like the data that's being used by companies to decide where to locate bike sharing stations, or which LCD billboards to buy, and the data on transportation and mobility that Ford and all the automakers now recognize as critical to their future success, so the data on what concerns people comes from sources like Google, which reports a significant jump in searches for the word "stockpile" throughout the UK.[14]

Here we see the fully intertwined business models of nations, regions, trading blocks, and companies, and we can readily observe the actions and reactions like so many ping pong balls flying back and forth as people try to figure what in the world is going on.

The Cinema Experience

Speaking of the interactions between nations, companies, and media, here's a fascinating example from China. The summer of 2018 saw two notable films released into the Chinese market, one of which was a government-made historical fantasy epic, *Asura*, which had the distinction of being the most expensive film ever made in China, at a cost of $113 million. But after earning a paltry and humiliating $7 million in ticket sales, it was pulled from theaters after only 3 days.

In contrast, just a week before *Asura* was released, an independent film titled *Dying to Survive,* which was made for a humble $15 million, brought in a stunning $200 million in box office receipts during just its first weekend, and it topped $450 million within two months.

Movies succeed and fail all the time, but the reason that this is notable is that *Dying to Survive* is the true story of a Chinese man who smuggled cancer drugs into China from India. And why would it be necessary to do that? Because cancer drugs are hideously expensive in China, where in fact 20% of all commonly-used medicines cost more than anywhere else in the world.

Thus, many observers were surprised that a film which is implicitly critical of the government had been allowed at all by Chinese censors, who generally prohibit any form of media that can even vaguely be considered unfavorable. But once the film was out of the can there was no putting it back; within a few weeks of the film's release the Chinese medical administration announced that it had entered negotiations with 18 drug companies, both domestic and foreign, to reduce prices.[15] Life influencing art, which then influences life, the never ending cycle of information feedback loops that largely shape the modern world.

Media companies and filmmakers have business models, drug companies do, and nations have them too, and technology and the information that technology brings are impacting all of them in fundamental ways.

The clash between China's authoritarian government business model and its booming technology sector business model was also recently the source of problems for gaming company Tencent, one of Asia's most valuable tech companies (and one of the Asian Big 5 shown on page 11). Analysts report that there are about 560 million Chinese who regularly play video games, but disturbed by reports in the fall of 2018 about poor eyesight among Chinese youth, President Xi Jinping ordered that changes must be made. In a matter of days, the Ministry of Education introduced regulations to limit the time that children may spend playing video games, and Tencent's stock value promptly dropped by $20 billion. Later in the same month the company reported its first decline in quarterly profits in 13 years, which it attributed to "regulatory interference," pushing its market cap even further down.[16] All in all it was a pretty bad stretch, as the company's market cap fell from $400 billion to $330, quite far off its high of almost $600 billion in February.

•••

I started this chapter by focusing on experience design as an essential element of any business model, and admiring how clearly Disney has articulated the philosophy that puts the customer's experience exactly in its center of focus. Experience is also essential to the success of Tencent, Apple, Uber, and the Vikings too. It's part of Brexit, bike sharing, taxis, film-making, censorship, and medicine. Indeed, it's an essential part of every business model, including yours.

But how exactly do you know what the customer is actually experiencing? To know that, it's essential to discover the hidden, or tacit, aspects of the customer's experience.

Chapter 8
Hidden Knowledge
Everything Speaks

Why would Walt Disney insist that his designers go into the park regularly to experience it as customers did? Because he knew that there can be an enormous gap between what we think it going on, and what's actually happening, and the only way we're going to discover the gap is by experiencing it. The gap exists because "experience" has so many dimensions, and so many of them are hidden, or tacit.

There's a discipline focused on the field of tacit knowledge which is called "ethnography." Ethnography emerged as the branch of anthropology focused on the study of human culture, which seeks to know how it is that cultures come about, how knowledge is transmitted within them, how norms and values develop and change. What ethnographers quickly came to recognize was that many of the most important elements of culture are nonspoken, and that while attitudes and expectations may be deeply held, the reasons why a group holds its beliefs is often lost in time, and only the dos and don'ts remain, the reasons why forgotten.

It's for this reason that in organizations we hear phrases like, "That's just how we do it here..." and why change is often difficult to induce.

Ethnography in business was pioneered at Xerox during the 1970s, when researchers there used these techniques to learn about the interactions

---

Walt Disney understood the importance of attention to detail, and he insisted that every aspect of the Disneyland experience must be well designed.

"Everything speaks"

was a saying of his, meaning that every object, every sign, every flower and tree, every ride, everything matters.

And when you look at every aspect of the customer's experience in this way, you discover, perhaps, how to make magic.

between people and machines. Many of their discoveries were applied in making Xerox copiers so easy to use, and the development of other technologies that I'll discuss below. From Xerox, the practice has spread throughout the high tech world. Intel sent teams of ethnographers to China to study how Chinese used computers, realizing that given the significant differences between the English and Chinese alphabets, computer use might be fundamentally affected.

Kimberly Clark used ethnographic research to learn how babies and their parents feel about diapers, and in so doing exposed a new market that has been worth hundreds of millions of dollars each year to the company. Why "exposed?" Because "diapers" have deep and important meanings for both children and their parents, meanings that had been entirely unrecognized until the researchers began to explore the experiential dimensions of something that happens millions of times each day.

A drug store chain that we worked with was interested in improving their business, so we suggested that perhaps they could think about improving their stores. "What's wrong with our stores?" they asked. "They've been doing fine for years."

After giving them just a little bit of coaching in observational skills, we sent them on a field trip ... to their own stores. The next day they came back shocked, reporting on how bad, and in some cases horrible, their own stores were. After working in them for so long, they simply had become accustomed to it, and failed to see what was right in front of them.

Every business, no matter whether it's a B2B industrial company or a B2C consumer products company provides experiences to its customers, and in the design of these experiences usually offers abundant opportunities for improvement, all the way down the immediate impacts on the business model itself.

Part 1: The Tao of Business Model

Chapter 9
Innovation Targets
So Many Choices

When you ask someone to tell you an example of innovation, most people instinctively think about technology, and they'll pull out an iPhone or Android and say, "this is innovation." Or they might say, "a light bulb," which is the iconic way that new ideas have been represented for a century. And it's true that these are both incredibly innovative, and their amazing charm and usability has made them indispensable.

But it's a mistake to think that innovation is *only* technology, because as we saw above, innovation can create value across so many different dimensions of experience, among which is of course the focus here, the business model.

There are so many possible targets that to sort out what they might be, pretend to be an imaginary and archetypal large organization that sells products and services in many different markets, B2B and B2C, has extensive operations in numerous locations, and operates a predominantly internal support structure, in order to ask …

In how many different ways could our firm innovate?

You could innovate in your core products and services like Apple and Disney, of course, but also in your supply chain, as Apple, Nike, and

Mobile phones have become so important in our lives that the Cambridge Dictionary word of the year for 2018 is "nomophobia," or "no mobile phobia," i.e., "I lost my phone and I'm terrified to be without it."

This product, in other words, has fully captured the mind of the market.

49

Walmart did. You could also innovate in your organization and operations, as Fedex, Southwest Airlines, and Uber did.

The techniques pioneered by Southwest made air travel so inexpensive, while innovations in core operating technology enabled Fedex to create the tracking system that can tell you where your package is at any point on its journey. You could innovate in jet engine design and maintenance as GE has done. Uber's connective platform innovations link passenger, driver, map, and bank, to facilitate nearly-painless urban transit.

All these firms benefitted from their innovativeness: Walmart displaced Sears and K-Mart, Southwest changed the entire air travel industry, Fedex displaced the post office and UPS, and Uber has entirely disrupted the taxi industry.

So how will your company disrupt your competition?

the MEANS:
50 opportunities to improve your business model

products & services	technology applied	supply chain	organization & operations
product / service design user interface functionality product offering product family product life cycle product platforms product availability packaging segmenting sales model R&D innovation process sustainability warranty after-sale service	technology (hidden or embedded) technology (evident) materials connectivity interfaces platforms api apps	sourcing provenance manufacturing distribution system communication automation partners inventory distribution	business structure type capital formation governance IT infrastructure employee / contractor mix insourcing / outsourcing employee experience decision making processes strategy formation process to improve processes administration information flow automation in operations partnering alliances facilities infrastructure facilities effectiveness

As we discussed above, you can focus on reducing costs and thus prices, or on improving quality, or both. Your means for doing so will likely involve one or more of these 50 innovation opportunities.

What's the first thing that jumps out to you when you see this list?

The thing I saw was that the vast majority of these opportunities do *not* involve new technology embedded into products. Thus, despite the widely-held mental model that "innovation is an iPhone," this shows that innovation is definitely not limited to technology-in-the-product.

Indeed, one the key lessons of business model warfare is that technology innovation by itself has rarely been sufficient to ensure the future for any organization. Nokia, to go back to that sad story, owned mountains of great new technology, and in its halcyon days as the world's leading cell phone maker it was also one of the world's greatest technology innovators. Its massive R&D budgets were the envy of companies worldwide.

But Nokia's collapse is one of the most effective messengers for an important lesson, which is that it's not a question of *how much* you spend on innovation, but rather the *process* you use to manage the effort that matters most. Booz & Co. research has shown repeatedly that spending a lot on R&D is no guarantee of future business success:

> "Yearly R&D spending among the world's 1,000 largest public corporate R&D spenders hit a record high of US$638 billion in 2013, according to Booz & Company in its annual Global Innovation 1000 study. However, despite the sustained overall increase in R&D budgets over the last decade, this year's findings show once again that higher spending doesn't guarantee bigger payoffs. Indeed, the 10 most innovative companies financially outperformed the world's top 10 spenders, despite actually spending significantly less on R&D."[17]

The 10 most innovative companies financially outperformed the world's top 10 R&D spenders, despite spending significantly less on R&D.

Interestingly, this is the case even when innovative technology *is* at the core of the offering.

A good example is Xerox. Chester Carlson's technological innovation was a stunning breakthrough, and a testament to his insight and persistence. The Xerox story is also testament to the difficulties of forecasting the market for genuinely new products. Many industrial giants of the day, including IBM, Kodak, and GE rejected the opportunity to acquire Carlson's technology at a bargain price because they just didn't see that it had much value.

Why did they not see it? Because they were thinking from the framework of the current mindset, and were unable to see how the future might be different from the present.

When Carlson finally did find a partner, it was the tiny Haloid Company that stepped up to help perfect and market Carlson's innovation. However, they soon found that getting the technology to market entailed far more than simply building new machines that worked.

Instead, the success of Haloid-become-Xerox in its early years was largely due to, yes, its business model innovation. That innovation was its approach to distribution: it leased the machines on a per-use basis, instead of selling them outright. Why? Because they didn't know that they needed to make copies – they'd never had that option before. Leasing per use removed the buyer's risk and put it on Xerox. After all, if customers didn't use the machines they would pay nothing.

But they did use them, and soon they came to utterly depend upon them, all possible because the brilliant business model insight, which had also propelled Xerox into the top echelon of American business. Without shifting the risk onto itself, its pathway to market penetration would probably have been much slower.

Ironically, Xerox became so huge and so dominant that the US government became worried that it was approaching monopoly status, and through court action forced Xerox to share its valuable intellectual property, which marked the beginning of its slow demise.

The importance of reducing customer risk was not lost on other astute business leaders, however. Think about these applications and extensions of the same basic model: Apple now rents its phones for a monthly fee, and guarantees in return that you'll get the latest and greatest phone ahead of everyone else. And did you know that Michelin rents tires? That's right. Airlines no longer have to buy tires for their aircraft, as Michelin rents them, the basic cost calculated on a per-landing basis, as that's where tires suffer the majority of their wear. Working this way shifts costs from an airline's balance sheet to its P&L, and thus reduces capital costs in a very capital-intensive business.

GE does the same thing with aircraft engines, and in fact airlines can rent the entire plane if they want to.

Working this way transforms a product into a service, which is an important category of business model innovation. They even do it in the paint industry, as PPG now operates the paint shops inside many GM auto factories, relieving GM of the need to maintain state-of-the-art knowledge in paint and application technology. Instead, PPG supplies the paint, the equipment, and the staff who operate inside of GM factories.

GM's paint purchases used to be done based on competitive bidding, in which GM's goal was to reduce the cost of paint, and so PPG was forced into a commodity bidding trap with its competitors, where the pathway to success was only down. By switching the model, PPG offers a service and accepts the risk, reduces GM's total cost and its risk while assuring a guaranteed service level, but can innovate and find savings and efficiencies to make the entire agreement a win-win.

How can your organization benefit from this way of thinking? Where are you being forced into a downward pricing spiral, a commodity trap, and how can you flip that around to create a service opportunity instead?

Shifting Generations of Technology

Did Xerox top management believe that the market was stable, and that their incumbent competitive advantages would persist? No, they were smarter than that, but legal action, i.e., an inexorable external power (the government) forced their hand, and now another generation of top managers has the task of rebuilding the company.[18]

Xerox was not complacent, and thus the problem was *not* that Xerox failed to recognize the importance of innovation. In its boom days the company generously funded technical R&D that surpassed the efforts of most other companies. For example, it created the legendary Palo Alto Research Center in the heart of Silicon Valley in California, PARC, and staffed it with brilliant scientists, technologists, and ethnographers, and from it sprang an amazing series of breakthroughs in many dimensions of technology.

For good reason, PARC attained the status of legend in Silicon Valley. It was at PARC, in fact, where the personal computer as we know it today was invented, an amazing and foresighted result, quite accurately called visionary.

And even as the company entered its period of decline, it was still producing astonishing technological breakthroughs. It's Docutech printing system, for example, was a self-contained digital printing plant and bindery that did what no copier had done before.

But within a relatively short time Xerox competitors had machines that matched or surpassed the Docutech, which illustrates one of the most vexing problems associated with technological innovation: In today's environment, technology is one thing that a determined and adequately-financed competitor may readily replicate or bypass. Patents offer useful but limited protection, and sometimes they simply provide stimulus and insight for others determined to be still more inventive.

Thus, a focus on technology breakthroughs to the exclusion of other aspects of innovation is misplaced. Given the complexity inherent in today's technologies, you simply can't count on being able to out-R&D the market on a consistent enough basis to sustain a competitive advantage. Sooner or later, and probably sooner, every technology meets its match or its superior, and it's probably coming from a competitor.

But for the brief interval while a particular technology is superior, it can be the basis upon which to build something of truly critical importance: strong relationships with customers through well-designed experiences. Innovation efforts must therefore address the creation of new approaches that help strengthen the bonds with customers, and to do so they should leverage whichever of the 50+ dimensions listed above might provide differentiation of the experience.

The quality and characteristics of the customer's experiences are the core elements of business model value. There are dozens of ways that experiences can be shaped by what goes on inside of an organization, and so what we have arrived at is the outlines of a formula for business model innovation, which we will consider next.

Chapter 10
THE FORMULA
Yes, There Is One

Does your firm have a business model today? Of course it does, because *every* firm has a business model. Is it a happy or sad one?

In *Anna Karenina,* Tolstoy wrote, *All happy families are alike; each unhappy family is unhappy in its own way.* In other words, there is but one way to be happy, through love and kindness, but there are many root causes of family misery, from cruelty and abuse to mental frailty, poverty, disease, premature death, business failure, crop failure, adultery, and external events like wars, pogroms, droughts, etc. etc. Tolstoy saw that there are so many pathways to misery, and so few that sustain a family's happiness across the generations.

Interestingly, and the reason this is worth remarking on, is that the situation with business models is exactly the opposite. It the successful (happy) business models that are unique, while each unsuccessful (unhappy) business model suffers from exactly the same shortcoming.

> Successful business models always leverage some uniquely exceptional quality or characteristic that brings value to and enriches the experiences of customers.
> **But failures inevitably fail for exactly the same reason,** which is that customers simply turn away because they find a better offer elsewhere.

The failure of any business thus reflects at root the failure to innovate, failure to recognize change, and the inability to respond to change adequately or appropriately.

And today as we see that yet another massive wave of new technology is about to crash across the global marketplace, what with artificial intelligence, blockchains, machine learning, self-driving cars, robots, quantum computing, etc., etc., all arriving immanently, we must therefore anticipate that every existing business model of every existing business is thoroughly and utterly subject to disruption. This is a stark warning about the need to innovate.

Wouldn't it be *so* incredibly helpful if there were a formula to explain all this, to simplify it and make it useful in practice? And indeed there is, a simple, three element framework:

1. **Outside:** The company provides **experiences** to customers through the delivery of products and services. The current quality of those experiences is today's reality; making them transformatively better is the **vision**.

2. **Inside:** The factors inside the organization make this delivery possible. These can be many and varied, including the product or service itself, the supply

the business model innovation formula

inside	bridge	outside
products & services		**a business model is how you deliver experiences to your customers**
technology applied	**channels** / **ways of communicating** / **brand**	
supply chain		through products & services
organization & operations		
the MEANS	the STORY	the EXPERIENCE

chain, the operations, and technology.
These are the means.

3. **The Bridge:** And then the way that a company communicates this value proposition to customers through marketing and branding, which are the messages and means through which the company communicates.
This is the story.

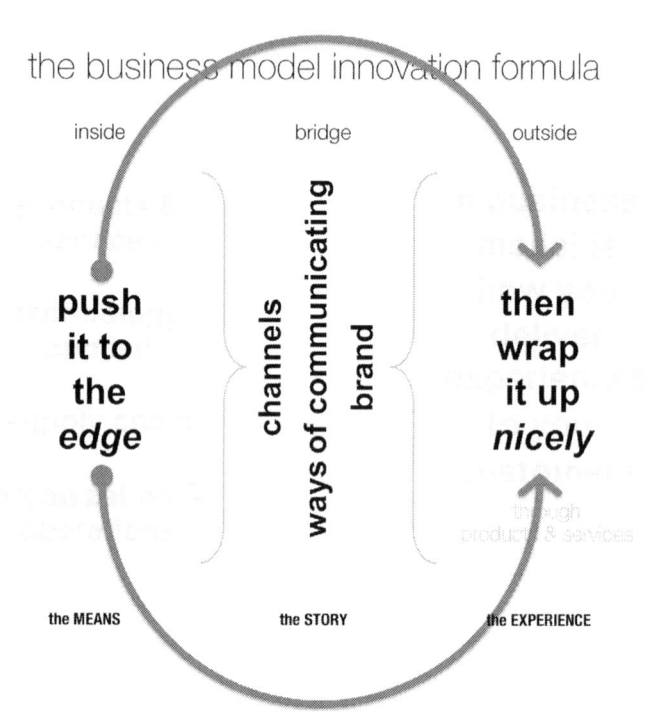

This formula for business model innovation immediately gives us three essential questions to ask about our own business model, and how to improve it:

1. What's the best possible experience that our customer can have? (vision)
2. How can we organize ourselves to deliver that? (means)
3. What's the best brand identity to represent it? (story)

the business model innovation formula

inside — bridge — outside

push it to the *edge* — channels, ways of communicating brand — **then wrap it up *nicely***

the MEANS — the STORY — the EXPERIENCE

We also observe that the most successful business model innovators tend to focus obsessively on *one particular aspect* of their business means, and develop it innovatively and far beyond what's been done before. That is, *they push it to the edge,* the absolute limit of possibility, and in so doing create an entirely new capability that they then leverage to define or enable an exceptionally better value proposition for their customers.

Let's look again at some of the companies we've already been discussing to see how this applies: where did they push it?

Amazon: The company's determination to leverage its core technology into every aspect of the customer relationship.

Apple: Obsession with the user interface design created an ease of use that is the basis for nearly everything else that Apple has accomplished.

Google: Obsession with creating user traffic on its platforms has driven two decades of growth.

Southwest Airlines: Obsession with reducing operating costs enabled an entirely new business model and created three decades of exceptional growth and success.

Walmart: Obsession with supply chain optimization is the foundation of its global retailing empire.

The word "obsession" shows up in each one for good reason, and in fact in each of these examples it's a dual obsession. On the inside, it's the obsession to optimize some aspect of operations; on the outside it's the obsession to optimize the customer's experience.

Getting there may not be easy, though. Southwest Airlines had to endure a near-death experience during its startup stage before a core element of its eventually-successful business model became clear; it took Google years to figure out how to make money; Amazon and Uber are still losing money, and Apple was moribund as late as 1997, and it was only in about 2005 that its many decades of persistence began to pay off.

How does this work in practice? Business model innovators often begin with these questions simultaneously at the forefront of their thoughts:

The first is simply, What would make the customer's experience better? Answering this question well requires a detailed understanding of the tacit dimensions of the user experience.

The second is, How can we achieve that? This is the means.

The third question then focuses the compelling story, the critical importance of branding.

16 business model innovators

	inside the MEANS	bridge the STORY	outside the EXPERIENCE
AMAZON	Web programming	Every product in existence	Free 2 day delivery
APPLE	Interface design	Best user experience	Elegant usability
CNN	Cable TV	24 hour news	Live drama all day long
COCA-COLA	Secret formula	Love	Caffeine + sugar
FACEBOOK	Web programming	Connect to the world	Friend me!
FEDEX	IT + an airline	Absolutely positively	They delivered on time
GOOGLE	PageRank	Best search results	Best search results
HOME DEPOT	Scale	More saving, more doing	Low price; long line
IKEA	Supply chain	Not expensive	Furnish my home
NETFLIX	Web programming	Watch what you want	Choose + binge
NIKE	Design + outsourcing	Be Like Mike	I am Mike
SEARS	Been around forever	Middle America	Time forgot this place
SOUTHWEST AIRLINES	Cost removal	Low cost travel	I arrived
STARBUCKS	Ideal coffee house	Consistent high quality	$5 caffeinated luxury
UBER	App connectivity	Better than a taxi	It was better
WALMART	Supply chain	Lower prices every day	My full shopping cart

Yes, the table is of course a simplification (and possibly an over-simplification), but isn't it interesting anyway? Do you agree with all the labels I've chosen? Perhaps not. But it does convey some important ideas that you need to think about with respect to your own business model:

- **Can you articulate what your business model is about clearly and concisely?**
- **Does it tell a story that matters to your customers?**
- **Can you deliver on the promise?**

Notice that nowhere on the chart is the story or the experience actually the technology itself. Thus, it becomes clear that the importance of new technologies is that they're *the means* through which new and better experiences are delivered, but they should rarely be the focus.

Mediocre marketers sell technology. But people buy the hole, not the drill, so skilled marketers sell the hole.

That is, the best business model innovators figure out how to deploy new technologies in order to create better experiences for their customers, while the non-innovators push technology without considering what it means for their business model, or how their business model should be designed to create optimal experiences.

If you look at the up-and-down history of retailers like Best Buy, this is one of the key lessons. They originally designed their stores as temples for people to come and worship technology, which immediately got them commoditized, and soon squeezed by Amazon and Walmart. To turn the business around they had to make it experiential and thus interesting, which they did by turning the stores into brand bazaars, collections of interesting shops in one big box. To complete the turnaround they're now developing the new brand identity, an essential element of all business models.

Chapter 11
THE BRAND
Expressing Your Soul

Since any brand is basically a promise, it's essential to be clear about what you're promising and on your capacity to deliver on the promise as well.

Our colleague and branding genius Jerome Conlon compellingly explains it this way:

> "In many organizations, the brand identity derives, as it should, from the aspirational or inspirational core values of a founder's personal passions, which leads to the creation of high-value products and services. Such a foundation can also lead to a positive work-life climate and values that become powerful sources of strength that can endure for years, decades, or longer. Many companies, however, maintain only a functional brand identity, focusing on the mundane and largely ignoring these heart-centered human qualities and possibilities. Such brands may signify a firm's trademark, but they do not inspire familiarity, praise, admiration, or loyalty, for they appeal to physical needs, convenience, or logic only, but not to deeper human emotional needs of the different constituencies they touch. Basic functional brands offer little soul depth and don't provide meaningful detailing of character, persona, or purpose beyond the functional."[19]

This is obviously a critical theme for us to consider since the brand is the story you tell about your business model.

Here are four examples of brand + business model showing how four companies have evolved their business idea and the story they tell about it over time, Apple, Adidas, 23andMe (the home genetic test kit company), and Sears.

Apple

Founded in 1976 by Jobs & Wozniak, Jobs had it in mind from the beginning to transform the world. But he was forced out of the company in a power play by CEO John Sculley in 1985. Apple soon floundered, and Jobs was invited back as the company's savior in 1997. From there you know the story of its resurrection, as Jobs recreated the company at its first strategic inflection point with the iPod, and then the iPhone, which turned it for a time into the world's most valuable company. But it's now a one-product show, and its fortunes depend far too much on the one.

Apple under Tim Cook looks uncannily like Microsoft under Steve Ballmer, but unless Cook can develop a much more diverse portfolio of strong revenues, his tenure will be marked by the amazing growth of the iPhone, its peak, and then its (tragic) decline. Apple is thus approaching another strategic inflection point, and will have to reinvent itself by around 2025 to avoid a sad fate.

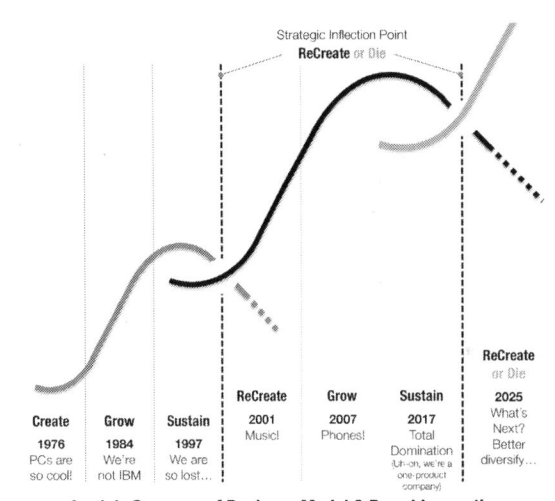

Apple's S-curves of Business Model & Brand Innovation

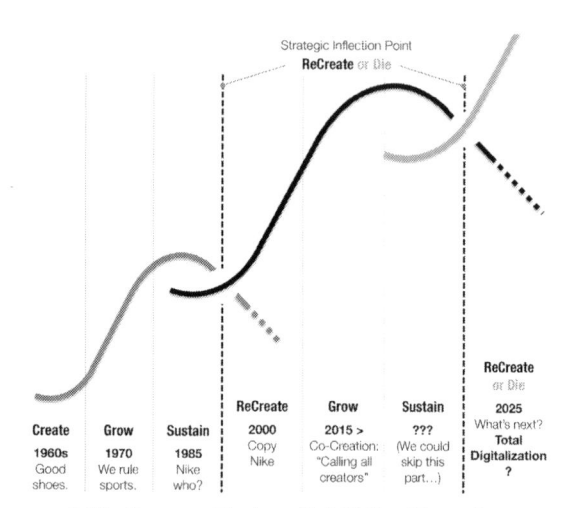

Adidas

Adidas dominated the global athletic shoe market for decades, but by 1985 Nike's marketing innovations began to transform the structure of competition. By the time the first Nike Town store opened in 1990 Nike had entirely refashioned the entire industry by redefining the relationship between the customer and the brand, a transformative approach (that Jerome was a major part of) which left Adidas far behind. It was only when Adidas began to copy Nike that its fortunes turned around, thus showing how a follower can sometimes catch up, although it wasn't particularly fast about it. But during the last couple years Adidas has moved effectively by fully embracing the concept of co-creation, and recognizing that its future lies with the Creative Economy in which it is now an exemplar in its marketing strategy and brand identity. It's moved beyond athletes to include artists in its orbit, but like Apple, that position, too, will have to be reinvented soon given the intense competition in this market.

From creativity and customization one next step forward may be into more totally immersive digitalization, but this is just one possibility among many that the company may choose to pursue for its future brand identity and business model. We will discuss Nike, Adidas, and branding in greater depth below.

Adidas S-curves of Business Model & Brand Innovation

Phase	Year	Description
Create	1960s	Good shoes.
Grow	1970	We rule sports.
Sustain	1985	Nike who?
ReCreate	2000	Copy Nike
Grow	2015 >	Co-Creation: "Calling all creators"
Sustain	???	(We could skip this part...)
ReCreate or Die	2025	What's next? Total Digitalization?

Strategic Inflection Point: ReCreate or Die

23andMe

23andMe sells genetic test kits in the consumer market, which means that it's a high tech company in life sciences. If you send them a saliva sample they'll determine your entire DNA sequence, which will reveal your ancestry heritage. Although it was founded in 2006, it's been a long startup process, as the market and the technology are developing together.

After years of discussion and negotiation with the US Food and Drug Administration about the validly and efficacy of its analysis, it's also now beginning to offer insight into your genetic predispositions toward certain diseases. As the science of genetics continues to advance, this implies a third generation brand identity for the company based around the promise to reveal to you not only the genetic past of your ancestry, but your health future, your destiny. It's science fiction, realized by science, another classic business concept in which scientific progress, regulatory scrutiny, and market acceptance are evolving together, step by step.

If you were to ask the founders when they started the company 13 years ago where they would be today, surely they expected their company to be much more developed, but the adoption curve has been exactly the opposite of the iPhone's, a long and slow process.

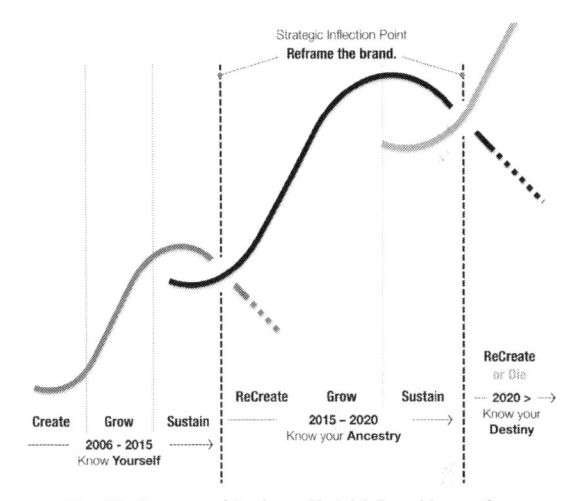

23andMe S-curves of Business Model & Brand Innovation

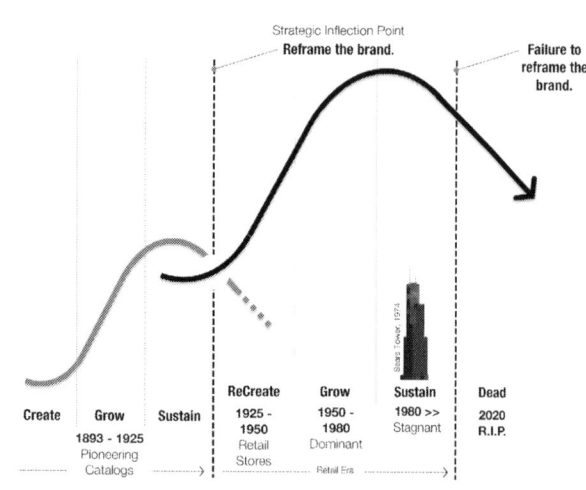

Sears

You already know the story of Sears; this is what it looks like on the s-curve model, two hugely successful business generations, and then decades of negligence that lead to the collapse of the company due to its disregard for the reality of a changing marketplace. It is not a unique story, but it is iconic.

At its peak around 1974 the company expressed its overweening pride by building what was for a time the world's tallest building, Sears Tower in Chicago, but it sold the tower in 1988 and moved back to the suburbs as the contraction began.

That would have been the ideal time to launch its third generation business model, but there was no third generation as their attention was on protecting the old one, not on pioneering a new one. In reality, the only reason the company was able to hold on for so long was because of very creative finance by its hedge fund owner Edward Lampert, and because during its time of strength it had assembled a hugely valuable real estate portfolio, which, although it's worth much less now that the Retail Apocalypse (see Chapter 13) has arrived, still constitutes a significant asset that will find other uses now that Sears itself is gone.

Sears S-curves of Business Model & Brand Innovation

•••

Each of these examples is prototypical in its way – the company that soars on a hit product, but then what? The fast follower that surpasses its target. The edgy tech startup that develops more slowly that the business plan said it would, and the failed old line company that failed because ... it was unapologetically so old line.

The idea that I want to make sure comes through with each of these four examples is that each company offers a certain type of experience to its customers, that this is enabled by its means of operation which are mostly if not totally hidden from view, but that what is fully evident is the brand positioning, the story. And as Jerome points out, the stories that we resonate with most strongly are those that address not just our mundane or functional needs, but our soul qualities, ideals, and highest aspirations. It is in the soulful companies that we have the most trust, and it is with these companies that we forge the most lasting relationships.

But even when we do love them, that love can fade faster than a desert pansy if the company fails to live up to its promise, or if a competitor finds a way to make itself more attractive. The four s-curve stories emphasize the huge significance of the critical strategic inflection points, at which it's essential to recreate the product, service, experience, and/or the brand itself. Failing to do so carries heavy consequences. Thus the question, "Can you manage *this*?"

We could chart another dozen or two companies on their s-curves, but doing so would soon be repetitive. What's important instead is for you to map your own company and your competitors to gain insight into your own past, present, and future. And the question on which to focus is ...

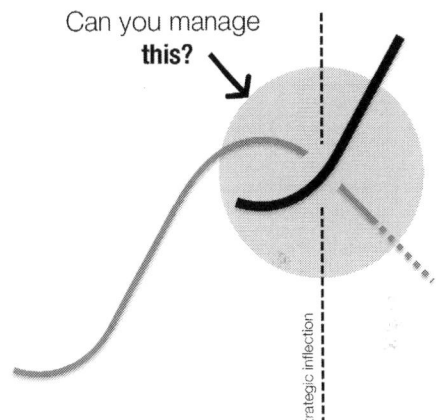

Where are we?

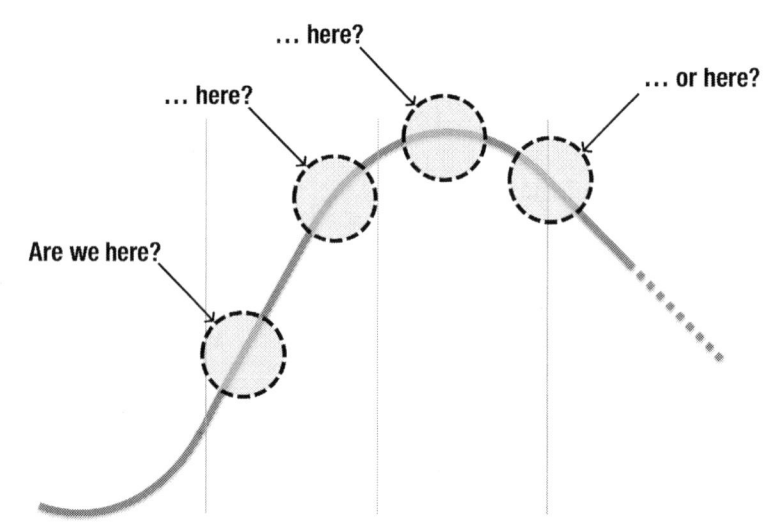

Are we here?

... here?

... here?

... or here?

The right strategy depends on where are you on the S-curve of development
(But sometimes it's not so easy to know.)

Yes, to make the right decisions you've got to know where you are, recognizing also that companies with multiple divisions or which compete in diverse markets won't be in just one place, as each part of the business will have its own developmental curve, and thus its own specific situation to address.

All the topics and questions that we've presented here should be considered for each one, which should result in a diverse and robust portfolio of strategies and business models that will strengthen the whole.

Part 1: The Tao of Business Model

•••

We're now at the end of Part One. So far we've defined what we mean by business models, introduced all the basic concepts of business model innovation, and discussed some of the key thinking tools that we use to understand present reality and future possibilities. We've considered the s-curve with the four types of innovation, the business model map with its axes of quality and price, the 50 possible internal targets, and the formula that describes business model innovation as an effort consisting of "the means, the story, and the experience."

All together, your field of action looks something like this:

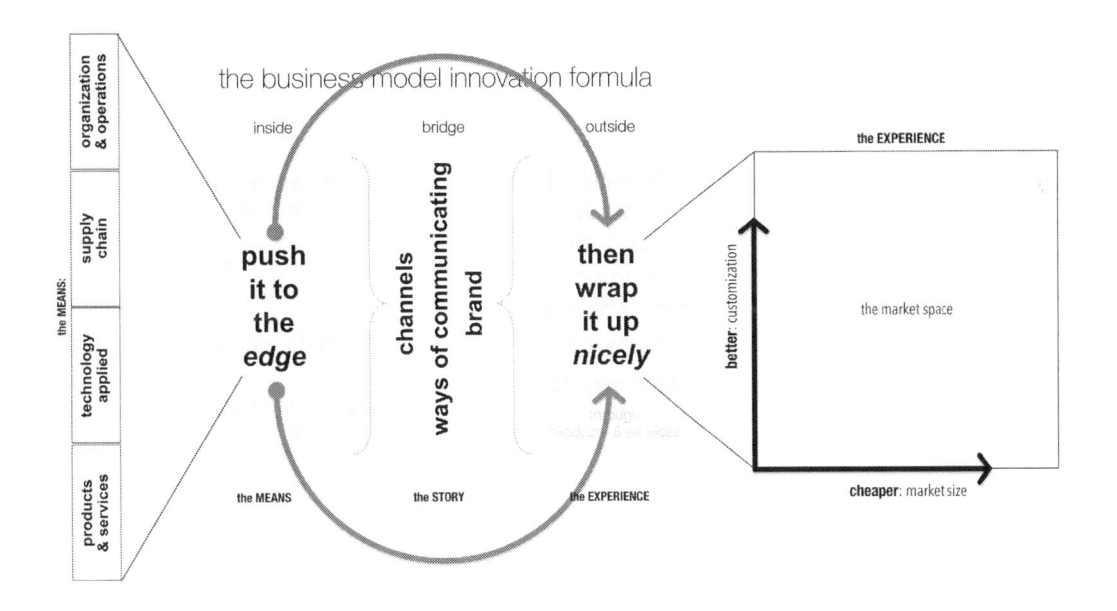

Next, in Part 2, we will engage in a detailed discussion of the external landscape in which you and your firm will be innovative, the crazy world of exponential change that's driving such incredible competition in the marketplace, and which offers so many threats and such amazing opportunities. This is the vital realm of Innovation Strategy, an essential and existential domain in which your skills as a leader will prove so critically important.

Part 2
INNOVATION STRATEGY

Grandpa told Peter that beyond the farmyard gate was dangerous meadow, and of course he was right. There were wolves out there. But what Grandpa didn't realize is how clever Peter could be, and Peter didn't realize that he ought to be afraid.

You, too, are very clever and resourceful, but you know better than Peter , as you know that you perfectly well ought to be afraid, just as Jim Farley and Andy Grove and Reed Hastings know it too.

But you also know that your fears should not control you, and that fear or not, you'll have to venture far beyond the safety of the farmyard and into the deep, dark forest, where you will be obliged confront the wolves and other dangers waiting there. Peter used a rope to capture the wolf; you will use innovation, and to plan your approach to innovation you will apply well-reasoned innovation strategy, which we will discuss in this section.

Chapter 12
THE LANDSCAPE OF DISRUPTION
It's Imperative

There's a business, or maybe more than one, whose innovative thinkers are working right now to take away your share of the market, and innovation is indeed their weapon of choice.

What is your best response?
Innovations of your own, of course.

In fact, innovation may be your only possible valid response.

However, innovation is a term that means different things to different people, and since it's a critically important concept, we'll pause here to define it carefully.

We note, first of all, that the word "innovation" refers to an attribute, a process, *and* a result. No wonder people get confused ...

Innovation is a process that happens somewhere in your organization, although it always begins in someone's mind. The result of the process may be an insight, a new idea, a product, a strategy, a new or improved business process, or even a better new business model. It may be sparked by a question, a theory, or just a fear.

Whatever causes it to come forth, one of the qualities that will distinguish the new thing is its *innovativeness.* This innovativeness refers to its distinctiveness, its originality, perhaps its usefulness, and most importantly its potential value.[20]

The label "innovation" also refers specifically to that new thing itself that the innovation *process* has produced.

To be considered an innovation in business, the result of this effort must be increased value along at least one dimension of the experience, in the form of new or improved quality, functionality, or customization, reduced cost, a price increase (good for the seller), a price decrease (good for the buyer), better margin for the seller, or some combination of these.

According to this definition, not every new or different idea qualifies as an innovation. In fact, only a small percentage qualify, specifically those that address quality and/or price. If it's not better, or cheaper, or the means to achieve one or both, then it's probably not an innovation.

Innovative ideas by definition create value for their users and valuable competitive advantage for their owners, as well as economic rewards.

However, even innovations that have only minor impact on the market can be significant and critically important, especially if they help a company to provide its customers with superior experiences. In this context innovation can be used to defend, to block competitors from gaining our share even as it can also be used to attack.[21]

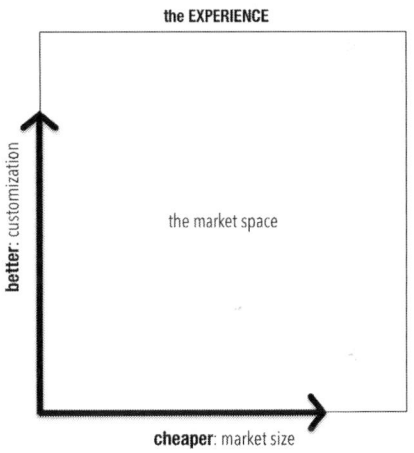

Hence, the approach that Peter Drucker labeled as "fast-follower" is a useful defensive strategy to overtake the growing effectiveness of a competitor's offering.[22] For example, Netscape Navigator had a strong head start in the browser market by the time of its IPO in 1995, but Microsoft's Internet Explorer became a fast follower and quickly overtook Netscape, forcing it to seek refuge as a subsidiary of AOL in 1998. Microsoft became a habitual fast follower, while AOL then grew dominant for a short time, acquired Time-Warner, and then itself collapsed into near-irrelevance before being reinvented, and then getting acquired by fast-follower Verizon in 2015. (Verizon also acquired Yahoo, which had also fallen from pioneer innovator into irrelevance due to its inability to keep up with the rapid pace of innovation.)

While these aspects of innovation and the innovation process occur in the life cycles of individual companies, innovation is also a significant factor in macroeconomics at the level of nations and the economy as a whole, and the s-curve model is an exceptionally useful way of looking at it.

Economists know that it is *only* through this journey of innovation that real economic growth occurs, because the underlying economic impact of innovation is to make resources more productive, which literally *creates* wealth for society. Hence, innovation is crucial to the economic viability of cities, regions, and nations.

Nevertheless, when discussing innovation the focus should remain on individual companies because it's their work that drives the economy forward. Thus, just as innovators drive microeconomic change in specific markets and macroeconomic change in economies, it is innovators who trigger disruption in their search for commercial success and competitive advantage. Most companies that are widely admired today attained success and envy precisely *because* they innovated. Through their innovations they brought structural change to their markets; their motivation was to gain advantage, and they succeeded in doing so by addressing the needs of customers.

As people never stop trying to optimize their situation, they never stop looking for ways to make life better, and as new technologies create new options and possibilities, behaviors are never fixed or static. The aggregate of individuals changing their view leads to changes in the macro context, and if you're not paying attention your company can get shoved aside. As Jim Farley reminds us, "If you're not scared, you're not paying attention," while Andy Grove suggests that what you need is paranoia.

Inherent in the dynamics of market demand is the process that drives competition through innovation. The waves of change launched by innovators are countered by competitors who innovate in order to defend their existing positions, or to attack with ambitions of their own.

It's an endless positive feedback cycle that serves only to drive the process of change still faster and more widely throughout the economy. Accelerating change and the convergence into the marketplace of so many competing innovators who wish to leverage so many new technologies results in greater complexity for all, a landscape of acute danger, astonishing challenge, and monumental opportunity. We label this *positive feedback* not because it's good, but because more begets more. "Positive feedback" is a term that refers to how systems are regulated. Systems that have built-in self-controls have "negative feedback," which isn't bad, it just means that they balance themselves, while positive feedback leads to constant acceleration.

Most physical systems have inherent limits – your heart can only beat so fast, an engine can only spin so fast (and it has a device on it called a 'governor' to keep it from destroying itself), a factory can only produce so much output, and your brain can only process so much information at once. But non-physical systems are

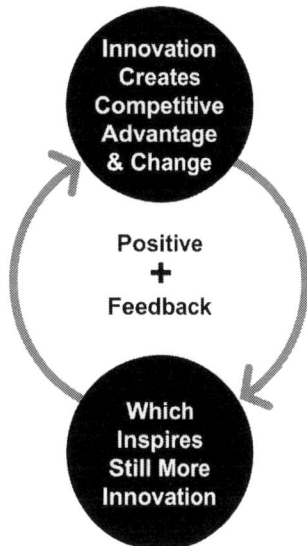

> Global currency transactions in 2016 averaged $5 trillion a day, up from about one trillion a decade before. Transactions take a variety of forms, including pure speculation as well as lending and trade finance, i.e., purchases of goods and services across borders.
>
> Note that currency exchange, which is subject to positive feedback, is about 22 times greater than global GDP, which at about $220 billion per day is a physical process and therefore subject to negative feedback.

different. Knowledge can grow apparently without limit, there may not be any limits to innovativeness, and no one actually knows if there is a limit to how much money can whirl through the global economy on a daily basis (see sidebar).

Systems subject to positive feedback accelerate, and if nothing stops them they break; systems with built-in negative feedback mechanisms tend towards balance, or equilibrium. Innovation-driven markets are positive feedback environments, as they do not seem to be subject to limits.

And since innovation is not subject to any natural limits, and it never stops, any enterprise that intends to survive must innovate. Furthermore, innovation itself is the only defense against innovation by others; through innovation you may catch up if you are behind, or even take the lead.

Thus, we see clearly that the future of every firm is determined largely as a function of its ability to innovate effectively, and that failing to innovate when competitors do so is often fatal. Innovation is therefore a mandate, an absolute requirement for survival.

And it's a problem, a thorny and even wicked problem for enterprises, because managing the innovation process is one of the most challenging issues they have to manage. It's extraordinarily difficult to do well, in part because, as with top management, R&D organizations are often focused on the wrong objectives, on protecting existing market share in the existing structure of the market rather than anticipating how the market is going to change, and preparing for the new conditions.

With too much focus on optimizing for today and not enough focus on what will change tomorrow, organizations fall into the trap of short term or backwards-looking thinking, which leaves them exceptionally vulnerable to change. In no market is this easier to see than in retail.

Part 2: Innovation Strategy

Chapter 13
THE RETAIL APOCALYPSE
Happening Now

Sometimes the sheer volume of information in the *Wall Street Journal* can be completely overwhelming, but the insights it provides about the evolving business and economic landscape makes it a tremendous resource for strategists and innovators. I realized recently that the entire newspaper could easily be renamed the *Wall Street Disruption Journal*, because so many of its stories describe how change is forcing companies into crisis by developing new business models, or report on their failures to adapt.

THE WALL STREET DISRUPTION JOURNAL

The retail industry was one of the first to feel the disruptive impact of the internet, and then it was thrashed again by smart phone mobility, and then by the 2008 crisis, and now Amazon, Walmart, Apple, and China's Alibaba are among the companies leading the next tsunami of disruption and transformation, and are the subjects of the next avalanches of *Journal* coverage.

Which we see clearly in the November 12, 2018 edition of the *Journal*, where it was reported that Alibaba recorded a record $30.8 billion in sales on its tenth annual "Singles' Day" event, far exceeding sales in the

US on Black Friday and Cyber Monday combined.

The name Singles' Day comes from the date, 11/11, and its solitary implications in the highly number-conscious Chinese culture. It's a sort of Chinese anti-valentine's day celebration of the lone individual, which Alibaba first co-opted in 2009 into its online retail extravaganza now as known as *Global Shopping Day*. It was an event created essentially out of nothing, an event for the sake of having an event, but now it's quite something indeed.

Statistics on Alibaba's Singles' Day are stunning. Salesforce reports that in 2018, $1 billion of orders were placed in the first 1 minute and 25 seconds, breaking 2017's record time of 2 minutes, 1 second. Sales totaled $10 billion after only the first full hour, and through the full day orders were placed from 230 countries. Products were available from 180,000 global brands, and in total more than 1 billion orders were received.[23]

Consider for a moment the massive infrastructure that's necessary to pull that all off successfully, and you realize that it's completely amazing that the internet didn't crash. The Alibaba website has to scale massively to handle the huge volume of traffic, while its logistics infrastructure has to be ready for the tsunami of resulting boxes that have to be delivered globally - imagine what's involved in processing 1 billion orders, packing 1 billion boxes, and delivering 1 billion packages! To get a sense of what the means in terms of scale, consider that Amazon ships about 5 billion items to its prime members in an entire year.

Walmart is struggling to catch up, and while its online sales increased by 43% from 2017 to 2018, it's a distant third at about 4% of total US ecommerce. For 2018

2017			2018		
Amazon	43.1%	$194	Amazon	48.0%	$242
eBay	7.6%	$34	eBay	7.2%	$36
Apple	3.8%	$17	Walmart	4.0%	$20
Walmart	3.3%	$15	Apple	3.9%	$20
Home Depot	1.4%	$6	Home Depot	1.6%	$8
	59.2%	$266		64.7%	$326
	100.0%	$450		100.0%	$505

US Retail Ecommerce Sales
The Top 5 Sellers; $ billions
Sources: eMarketer; Statista
These numbers are estimates. Figures vary according to who's reporting.

as a whole, Walmart expects sales of about $20 billion, which is still $11 billion less than Alibaba's one day total for November 11.

This explosive growth of ecommerce is having a devastating effect on retail stores, of course, and also on the shopping malls that house them. Indeed, more than 6400 American retail stores closed in 2016-2017, and at least 3600 more followed in 2018.[24, 25]

It's a brutal, total wipeout.

When the store that closes is a major department store it has a drastic impact on the mall where it was located, because the impact cascades from the larger stores to the smaller ones that depend on the big anchors for their traffic, creating a pervasive downward spiral. This is the very bad aspect of positive feedback, a runaway collapse.

The dumbbell shaped design of the classic suburban mall is a physical expression of the importance of the department stores at each end, and when the anchors close it usually means death to the shops between. As a result, 105 million square feet of American retail space shut down in 2017, a number greatly surpassed in 2018.[26]

And in a subtle if brutally ironic twist, the Euclid Square Mall in a Cleveland suburb closed in 2016, but then Amazon bought the site, tore down the mall, and turned it into a 1 million square foot distribution warehouse, as it also did with the nearby Randall Park Mall as well.[27]

Sears' long slide into irrelevance and bankruptcy

US Retail Store Closings 2016 – 2018
(Partial List)

Sears	2600
Toys R Us	735
Mattress Firm	700
Subway	500
H+R Block	400
Payless ShoeSource	400
Teavana	379
Ann Taylor	268
Benton	256
Best Buy Cell Phone	250
Macy's	220
Gap/Banana	200
GNC	200
K-Mart	200
Starbucks	180
Walmart	154
JC Penney	150
Foot Locker	110
Brookstone	102
Michael Kor	100
Orchard Supply	99
Chipotle	65
Abercrombie	60
Lowe's	57
Victoria's Secret	20
J Crew	20
Fresh Market	15
Kroeger	14
Lord + Taylor	<u>10</u>
TOTAL	**8,464**

continues as it looks to sell off its best locations, but who will buy them when there is a massive glut of vacant retail space already on the market?

It's obvious now that the root of all this disruption has been the internet, followed by the high speed internet, and then the mobile internet, and while the incumbent retail giants ignored the threat in the early days, from its very beginning Amazon founder Jeff Bezos understood that the changes his company was pioneering in the retail landscape would leverage fundamental shifts that were only then just starting to appear in the structure of the market. This is of course exactly what business model innovators search for, opportunities to exploit new market forces so they can dislodge the incumbents.

Bezos understood the direction in which things were headed before nearly anyone else, and he shaped Amazon to leverage these changes. At a Legg Mason investor conference in 2003 he remarked, "The proliferation of perfect information on the internet will enable people to do price checks on things, when they're in physical stores, not just when they're online."

This was years before smart phones, but he already recognized what future mobile phone technology would enable consumers to do, even though this wasn't even close to true at the time. That is, he understood the longer-term, macro perspective on the evolution of mobile and web technology, and he correctly anticipated both the technology that would emerge and the behaviors that it would enable.

At the Legg-Mason conference he went on to make the compelling prediction, noting that, "The balance of power is going to shift to the consumer, which has huge implications."

Huge indeed. This is exactly what Singles' Day is all about. What Bezos had recognized was that the very nature of price competition was changing. In the pre-internet world, consumers who wanted to shop based on price had to carefully check the ads in the newspaper, patiently call stores and ask them to check prices (and then wait interminably on hold), or physically journey from store to store to see the actual prices posted on the shelves. It was all tedious, time consuming, and even after doing all that you still weren't sure if you were getting the best price.

When online retail enabled price comparisons at home, this completely altered price-shopping behavior, and high speed mobile internet took this one step further, and very much in the consumer's favor, enabling buyers to compare prices wherever they were, whether standing in the store and looking at the items on the shelf that they want to buy, or in their kitchen, or riding the bus to work. A shopper in a Sears or Target store could ask, "Is this cheaper at Walmart? Let me check," and get the answer instantly.

This meant that getting customers into the store no longer was a guarantee of making sales, and in fact many shoppers went into stores to check out new products, but then went home and bought them online for less. As Bezos predicted, stores have to have the right product, *and* they have to have the right price.

Bezos continued, "Companies that have historically been great marketing and advertising companies will have to change. If they spend 70% of their time shouting about their products, and 30% of their time, energy, and dollars creating their products, that may over a long period of time flip-flop." In other words, he realized that sales and branding hype would be replaced by hard-core price and quality shopping in all

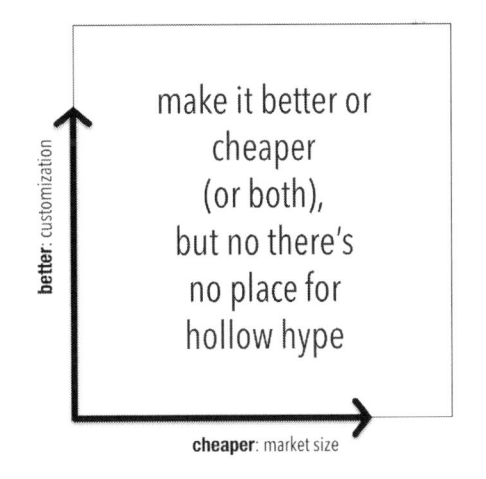

better: customization

make it better or cheaper (or both), but no there's no place for hollow hype

cheaper: market size

markets, and if retailers resisted the change they might flip all the way into bankruptcy.

This turned out to be a stunningly accurate prediction about the shift in consumer behavior that has punished retailers like Macy's, JC Penney, Sears, Lowe's, and so many others so badly, while Amazon and Alibaba have been incredibly proficient at exploiting this new technology, pioneering a new business model that has radically disrupted the entire retail landscapes across both North America and Asia, and now worldwide.

For retailers, things will never be the same.

Today we all understand how the online retail business model works, but someone had to figure it out first, and that was Amazon. Its complex and multi-faceted business structure consists of many elements – the web site, customer ratings, wish lists, the marketplace for third party vendors, the used books, the warehousing, the shipping, the returns, discounting, and all that was in place even before two day delivery and Prime and streaming TV and Kindle and Fire, and before the company was using 100,000 robotic warehouse workers, and before Amazon starting opening its own retail stores, and before it created Amazon Web Services, the world's leading business-to-business web services company, and before it bought Whole Foods,[28] and, and, and.

It's been an amazing parade of innovation, and it's all been about the business model. It's also been an apocalyptic disaster for Amazon's competitors.

Interestingly, the whole ensemble of Amazon services defines an entirely new relationship between a company and its customers, and of course this is exactly the intent. It enables many new and different experiences and transactions, the results of which have transformed the global retail

When Amazon bought Whole Foods in 2017, notes PayPal CEO Dan Schulman, "it was like the Pearl Harbor of the retail industry. It woke everyone up that things are fundamentally changing."

But how did they manage to stay asleep for so long?

landscape, and not coincidentally made Jeff Bezos one of the world's richest people.

Amazon and Alibaba have changed the business model of an entire industry, one that constitutes and major portion of the entire economy. Amid all the changes they've pioneered, we can concisely express it this way. In the old model, consumers went to the products; in the new models, products go to consumers. It's a profound inversion.

How transformative has it been? Credit Suisse predicts that 20 to 25% of American shopping malls will close between 2017 and 2023, and that's on top a great many that had already closed.

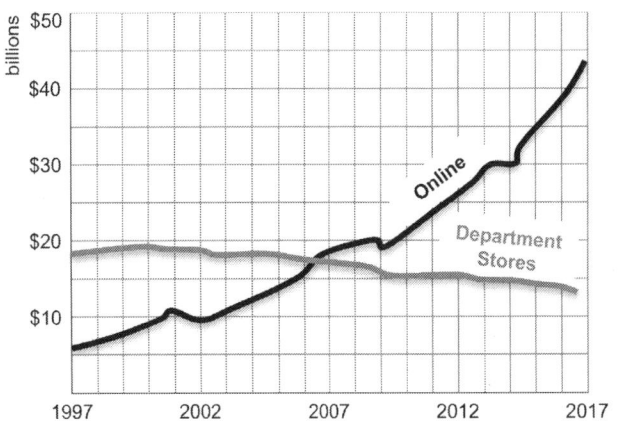

US Retail Sales: Online vs. Department Stores
Source: US Census Bureau; BMO Private Bank

No, it's certainly not an exaggeration to call this a retail apocalypse, and as the big stores collapse one by one, the smaller stores that depend on them have to get creative, or they too disappear.

Meet Bruno Palessi

Discount shoe retailer Payless ShoeSource has been feeling the sting of the apocalypse too. The company filed for bankruptcy in 2017, and immediately closed 400 of its 4400 stores. It's likely that the purpose of the bankruptcy filing was simply to get out of those 400 leases on stores that were underperforming, and guess where they were located? Most of them were in failing malls that had already lost one or more of their anchor department store tenants. And so we see the ripple effect.

In its reorganization plan, Payless determined to carry on, and in 2018 it was still in business and conducted an interesting and very revealing experiment. Payless created an imaginary Italian designer named Bruno

If you want to see what a retail apocalypse looks like in haunting photos that have a decidedly surreal and post-abandonment feel, check out the online publication *Business Insider* from July 7, 2018 entitled *50 Haunting photos of abandoned shopping malls across America* by photographers Seph Lawless, Mike Kalasnik, and Chris Cognac.

Palessi, and outfitted an empty retail store in a high end mall in the LA suburb of Santa Monica, California as the Palessi outlet. (They had lots of vacant stores to choose from.) They stocked it with their own low-cost products, but upped the prices from the normal $30 - $40 range to the stratospheric range of $200 - $600. Customers, who came by invitation, raved.

"It's just stunning. Elegant, sophisticated and versatile," said a woman, as she held a pair of floral stiletto heels. "For me to experience this as an Italian designer is amazing."

They were, in other words, completely fooled by the location, the décor, and the fawning, overdressed sales staff into thinking that $30 shoes were exclusive Italian designs worth ten times more.

When they'd completed their purchases, customers were invited to the back of the store where they were let in on the prank. Most laughed. Said one, "We wouldn't have ever known. We were really convinced. They had us fooled, like completely." [29]

Like, yes. It was a clever marketing ploy by the Payless team, and a courageous experiment as well. Customers got to keep the shoes, and they got their money back too, as the point wasn't the sales, it was all about repositioning Payless' web site. Like Singles' Day, it was a fabricated event.

While only a tiny fraction of Payless customers will ever see "Palessi's" creations and its chic store, the purpose of the ruse was to get attention and promote the company's online business.

> "The shopping experience on payless.com is different from the store. It's the fastest-growing piece of the business," said Payless Chief Marketing Officer Sarah Couch. "The stores are an incredibly valuable part of the business, but the digital side is the focus of the campaign."

The Palessi story evokes many dimensions of the changing retail environment, including the relationship between the store environment and ecommerce, the meaning of a brand, and the value of a product as perceived and as influenced by the store environment itself.

Do shoppers know the value of the things they buy? Perhaps not always, but then who's to say what is or is not valuable? What does it mean that a product sells for $30 at Payless and the same product sells for $300 at Palessi?

Singles' Day, perfect information, the radical transformation of an entire market sector, and a new set of relationships between vendors and customers, these are key aspects of the wrenching transformation of the retail sector, one of the most visible disruptions occurring today, but far from the only one, as we will examine in the next chapter.

Chapter 14
THE CITY TRANSFORMED
National and Urban Business Models

Just as companies have business models, nations and economies have them also, and so do regions and cities. For example, while the economies of most major oil producing nations operate according to classically extractive economics as highly exploitative and often highly destructive to the environment and are also subject to disruptive boom and bust cycles, a manufacturing economy functions quite differently, while an agricultural, finance-based, high tech or tourism-based economy different still.

Eighty percent of Great Britain's $2.5 trillion GDP comes from services and trade, while a miniscule 1% comes from agriculture, and the rest from manufacturing. This is the national business model of a trading nation, but that's been thrown into upheaval by the Brexit vote, and the situation is approaching chaos as the date on which the divorce will be finalized, March 29, 2019. (If you're reading this after March 29 then you know what occurred, but as I write it's still 2018, and the outcome is very much in doubt.)

Brexit is a strangely compelling example of self-inflicted business model disruption, as it poses the question, "Are you in favor of 'stay' or 'leave' for the UK?" The expected outcomes of two positions embody very different national business models that have broad implications for taxation, trade, employment, currency, migration, etc., and so for economic growth, security, and perhaps most of all for national identity. What kind of country are we? a citizen of Britain might ask. And what kind of country do we want to become?

Posed in a blatantly economic fashion, we could ask, What's the value proposition behind Brexit?, and we'd immediately see that it's not about the money, it's about national identity. Under every conceivable forecast Britain will lose huge amounts of money because of Brexit, but those in favour have chosen pride over pocket book.

Britain's established business model as a proud empire has taken a beating in the minds of many British from the EU's regulations on immigration and trade, a sense of pride and independence that led to the Brexit vote, and because of which Britain's economy will likely suffer as the drama unfold, even after the divorce date has passed.

Since we're on the topic of national business models, we might also ask what kind of nation China wants to become. With its growing economic might and massive budget surpluses earned as it became the world's dominant manufacturing hub, China has a business model too, one that certainly has global repercussions. It's got to do something with all the excess capital its manufacturing industries are producing, so it's become a major global investor. For example, in recent years China embarked on a $50 billion buying spree in Brazil, purchasing oilfields, mines, ports, and power grids, among other major assets. Not everyone in Brazil feels so good about this, though, as it led Brazil's newly elected president, the nationalistic Jair Bolsonaro, to angrily accuse the Chinese of "not buying in Brazil, but buying Brazil," a critical difference that he felt was offensive and, if nothing else, something he could get Brazilian voters riled up about.

Bolsonaro didn't mention that China is also Brazil's number one trading partner, with nearly twice the import-export value that it exchanges with the US, and nearly three times more than it trades with its immediate neighbor Argentina. China buys huge quantities of Brazilian soybeans, iron ore, oil, and copper, and thus Brazil's leaders can hardly afford to alienate their number one customer. In the world characterized by globalized commerce, things quickly get quite complicated, your friend can also be your enemy, and nothing is simple.

The Bilbao Effect

And just as nations have business models, so do cities. Bilbao, Spain, for example, was trapped in a cycle of decline as the industries that had formerly been its economic anchors gradually shrank and then collapsed, leaving the city with a weak economy and a dispirited population. In a bold and innovative move, the city negotiated with the Guggenheim Foundation to open a new art museum there, and then hired architect Frank Gehry to design a stunning building for the dramatic site by the city's central river. Gehry recalls, "They said: 'Mr Gehry, we need the Sydney Opera House. Our town is dying.'"[30]

In 2017 the Bilbao Guggenheim attracted 1.3 million visitors, and serves as the anchor of Bilbao's revival as a tourist destination for the northern Spanish coastal region.

This transformation has been so influential that it now has a name, "the Bilbao Effect," which describes the combination of iconic architecture and cultural institutions to promote civic

Guggenheim Bilbao

regeneration. It's a new business model, one so effective that dozens of art museums are not under construction worldwide, many designed by the star architects of our era, and characterized by daring designs and soaring public spaces. (The "star architect" is also a new business model.)

But it might have been named "the Sydney Opera House Effect," though, as that magnificent building was really the first of the world's modern cultural landmarks that came to be so closely associated with its city that you can hardly ever now see a photo of Sydney without the billowing sails of the opera house roof soaring beside the Harbour Bridge.

The lyric sails of the iconic Sydney Opera House

There are dozens of museums under construction around the world now in cities from tiny Aspen, Colorado to giant Beijing, a veritable explosion of investment in culture, most of them aspiring to capitalize on this new urban business model of "culture + tourism," and to replicate the Bilbao Effect for themselves.

Of course culture is but one of many factors that shape a city's business model. In the US cities of Detroit, Pittsburgh, and Cleveland for example, their economies were based on heavy industry that employed millions. When those industries went through major changes, or collapsed entirely, then of course the cities that depended upon them also suffered. Detroit, for example, lost two-thirds of its population as the US auto industry contracted from 1995 to 2008, 65,000 homes were foreclosed due to the 2008 mortgage crisis, and the city had to spend $195 million to tear down 140,000 abandoned houses even as its tax base had shrunk by $300 million. Now there are vast stretches of open fields where a thriving city once was.[31]

Detroit's pain is continuing, as GM announced that its massive Hamtramck assembly plant will close in 2019, meaning the loss of another 1800 jobs. In its perverse version of corporate double-speak, GM's press release of November 26, 2018 refers to the shutdown of the plant as "unallocation," meaning that no autos will be "allocated" for assembly there, nor at another Detroit plant, nor in nearby plants in Warren, Ohio, and Oshawa, Ontario Canada. GM also announced plans to lay off 25% of its entire executive staff, which it claims will "streamline decision making."[32]

Can Detroit develop a new business model that will enable the city to reinvigorate itself, or is it on a downward slide to oblivion? As of right now, no one knows.

Financialization

New York City was also once a major hub for manufacturing, particularly in clothing, but when production shifted to Asia starting in the 1970s the city nearly went bankrupt. It remained in social and economic shock until the globalization of the finance industry rescued it in the 1980s with massive and high-paying employment in banking and investment. Indeed, globalization of the world economy has had a massive impact on cities everywhere, as the leading ones have become essential hubs for management, coordination, and finance, a process sometimes referred to as "financialization."

Sociologist Saskia Sassen notes, "The sharp growth in the globalization of economic activity has raised the scale and complexity of transactions, thereby feeding the growth of top-level multinational headquarter

Part 2: Innovation Strategy

functions and the growth of advanced corporate services."[33] The increasing demand for these services has direct impact on urban form, urban concentration, and urban employment, all key elements of the urban business model. She goes on to observe that, "We are seeing the formation of a new urban economy," in which super-profits from finance and investment devalorize manufacturing, with the result that even though employment in finance is quite small compared to that in manufacturing, the urban system becomes more and more organized around finance, to the detriment of manufacturing companies and many workers.

This trend also lends itself to urban density. Sassen notes, "Firms in highly competitive and innovative lines of activity and/or with a strong world market orientation appear to benefit from being located at the center of major international business centers, no matter how high the costs," and thus we see strong demand for housing and offices in London, New York, Shanghai, Dubai, Singapore, Tokyo, and all the world's major centers of trade and finance.

This concentration is a partial explanation of the Brexit vote, as the London financiers who benefit from globalization were unanimous for "stay," while the rural manufacturers were for "leave." Similarly in the US, support for Democrats tends to come from cities, while rural regions tend to favor Republicans.

This shows how intertwined politics, society, economy, and business models have become, and surely the complexity expressed by these relationships is only going to increase.

Speaking of complexity, urbanization, and business model transformation, in 1980, Shenzhen, China, was a town of about 30,000 people, while today it is the central hub of southern China's manufacturing industry, and home to more than 10 million. China's economic revolution, its embrace of the business model of the globe's manufacturing hub, has brought new wealth to millions of Chinese.

But with the booming economy and population have come massive pollution of water and air, congestion, and just living close to waterways is hazardous. "My family doesn't dare open our windows," said a resident who has lived near the Longhua River for years. "Our throats are sore, our eyes burn and our noses itch. And then there's the mosquitoes."[34] At present about 930,000 tons of untreated waste water is discharged into local rivers every day, while in Detroit the waste water treatment plants have an abundance of excess capacity, the roads are not so congested, and since the big plants have closed the air has gotten much cleaner.

The interaction of economy, environment, and innovation weaves a very complex landscape in which business models play a fundamental role. New York, London, Bilbao, Sydney, and Shenzhen all have unique business models, as do the UK, China, and Brazil.

Indeed, each city and each nation tells own story of development and change, and as cities are now the essential centers of creation and trade for the global economy, macroeconomics and urban design intersect to formulate business models and stimulate business model innovations. In all of these settings and in every possible form of economic situation, business models continue to play a decisive role in business and economic outcomes, and all these business models are in the process of being changed or even entirely transformed by the impact of technology, which we examine next.

A significant side effect of China's explosive industrial growth has been the parallel growth of pollution of the country's air and water. The Chinese government is addressing the problem of water pollution with an interesting business model innovation, assigning local officials to oversee waterways, and making them responsible for keeping them clean.

There are now more than 1.1 million designated "river chiefs" in China, each with the duty to remove trash and identify industrial and civic polluters.

The chiefs not only have the duty, they are also accountable to local citizens; the name and mobile phone number of nearly every river chief is posted on a signboard adjacent to the waterway for which they are responsible.

The Economist, December 15, 2018.

Chapter 15
THE ECONOMY TRANSFORMED
No Industry Left Behind

If you peruse any source of news in addition to *The Wall Street Journal*, whether print or online, you'll also find a steady flow of coverage about business model innovation, endless stories about companies and industries in ascent or descent, about nations and their economies struggling with change, and established companies trying to adapt to changing conditions. Startups seek to introduce those changes by altering the structure of the market, to disrupt, while others wish to survive, and in nearly every business model story in every newspaper, magazine, blog, web site, or news broadcast, the root of the disruption saga comes back to technology.

Technology does drive disruption and is therefore frequently (although not always) the essential enabler of new business models. So if you're concerned about your business model (and you ought to be) then you have pay close attention to the development of emerging technologies and their implications not only for how your company operates, but for how the entire market operates.

To get a sense of how this is unfolding, in this chapter we survey how change and technology are impacting across a wide diversity of 16 industries: Banking, insurance, real estate, entertainment, energy, employment, education, privacy, manufacturing, materials, aviation, space, home improvement, tourism, sports apparel and health care. It's clear from this diverse list that no industry is left behind, and it's also clear that there are important patterns emerging. What thoughts and insights do these examples inspire for you?

Banking

The entire banking industry has been very sensitive about its business model for the last decade, ever since the global financial crisis of 2008 revealed how badly they were being managed. As the crisis unfolded the biggest banks got bailed out at a cost of many billions of dollars, while many homeowners were wiped out, and some nations including Greece, Ireland, Italy, and Spain were very hard hit.

The industry persists despite the fiasco because the economy cannot function without lending, and as the economy continues to globalize it's evident that scale matters. That is, as banks grow larger their capacity to support economic activity and fund the business models of many types of industries is fundamentally enhanced. Consequently, it's worth noting that European banks lack scale, and that this will impact significantly on their future success: "Europe's banks have global reach but not a big, integrated domestic market. The top four lenders are 50% smaller than the top four American firms and 66% smaller than the top four Chinese ones. As banks digitize, the fixed cost of staying at the top is rising: JPMorgan Chase will spend $11 billion on technology this year. European banks will struggle to keep up."[35]

This is, surely, a business model problem-in-the-making, one that arises as a consequence of Europe's basic continental business model as a collection of separate nations. The lack of a unified domestic market is an inherent characteristic of the European Union, so while the aggregate economic power of the EU is nearly on par with North

America and China, its fragmentation is a business model challenge that is inherent in the EU structure.

Keeping up with JPMorgan's technology investment, the massive $11 billion of spending, is also a business model problem for its competitors. The automation of finance is a business model in and of itself, but what can you buy with $11 billion? A lot of artificial intelligence, a lot of predictive analytics, a lot of risk management, and a global platform to support extensive growth.

Massive technology investment is now table stakes, a basic cost of competing in the global banking business; if you can't make the table stakes, you can't play in the game. This will drive business to the winners, making them larger, thus showing how the big get even bigger and leave the others behind. Here we see yet another instance of "positive feedback," spinning away in banking as in so many other sectors of the economy.

So what will happen to the banks that fall behind? They will likely get caught in the downdraft of reduced capacity, and so slip further behind. The smartest ones will also search for new business model opportunities that are not reliant on hugeness, so they will develop world-class expertise in essential services, and personalization, in the hopes that the larger banks cannot match them.

One such niche opportunity is in American mortgage banking. Today the largest firm originating home mortgages in the US isn't a bank at all, it's Quicken, a technology firm that does much of its business through its web site and a phone app. This is clearly a different business model, one that is technology-dependent, and certainly one of the reasons that JPMorgan is spending so much money on tech.[36]

Insurance

Like banking, the insurance market is highly competitive, very conducive to scale-oriented business models, and also able to support many niche-oriented firms. For example, some insurance companies now offer services that are not part of their core business, but which enhance it in interesting ways. British insurer Aviva installs sensors on water pipes at its customers' homes to detect even tiny leaks, thereby avoiding expensive claims before greater damage occurs.

Brazilian firm Porto Seguro offers its clients access to locksmiths, electricians, and taxis as a way of fostering customer loyalty (how did they pick those three services?), while French firm AXA provides annual health check-ups for its heath insurees. China's UnionLife embeds real estate services in its policy by guaranteeing its policy holders a place in a home for the elderly, while the American firm State Farm offers discounts on home monitors for the elderly.[37]

Each of these examples demonstrates the combination of risk-avoidance, which is of course essential to all insurance, and relationship building, which is essential to all successful business models, aspiring to provide win-win services that also provide differentiation.

Real Estate

Does your company rent office space at WeWork, the shared-office-space firm, or does it rent private offices? These are two very different approaches to managing real estate, and thus two different business models.

Like Uber, Lyft, and Palantir, WeWork is losing money but steadily increasing in value as it scales its business in the expectation that more scale will eventually lead to disproportionate profits.

And speaking of real estate, what's the commercial real estate industry doing with all its empty shopping malls, the ones shutting down because so much of the economy is moving to e-commerce? Other than selling empty malls to Amazon to be torn down, they're getting into "adaptive reuse" and "mall conversion," busily converting unneeded mall space into schools, offices, and even residential space, which requires them to work out a new and different business model with different financing models and different profit profiles. In so doing, they'll rely on innovative banking for capital, and innovative insurance for the mitigation of new kinds of risks.

Entertainment

Since the majority of entertainment other than live shows and sports is now delivered in digital formats, the entire entertainment industry has been through massive upheaval in recent decades, and that will certainly continue.

Global music industry revenues plummeted following the introduction of iTunes, when you no longer had to buy the entire CD; industry revenues have never recovered, now less than half of their peak in 2000.

Netflix, which buried Blockbuster under its superior business model, then began to take on Hollywood by producing its own shows, and doing it with exceptional success. But what could have enabled them to target their shows so well? It's the data, of course, because Netflix knows

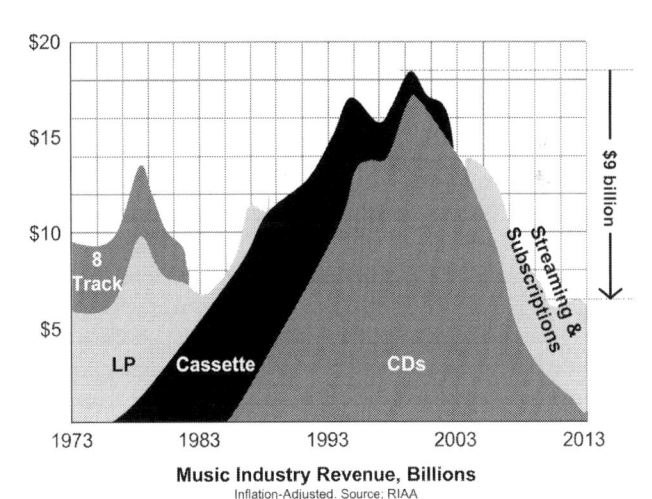

Music Industry Revenue, Billions
Inflation-Adjusted. Source: RIAA

exactly who is watching what among all 150 million of its subscribers, and can therefore target its new productions with more data than any entertainment provider has ever had about the interests and preferences of its customers.

Thus, its data provides Netflix with a significant business model advantage that no other Hollywood or Bollywood or Pariswood movie studio could ever hope to match with their by-now self-constrained business models; they, too, will have to evolve.

So who could possibly match them? Any company with a massive pool of real-time data on the interests, preferences, and habits of its customers, which includes Amazon, Apple, and Google (which, don't forget, owns YouTube), as well as Alibaba and Tencent.

Thus, following Netflix' lead, Apple will soon begin making its own feature-length films so it can enter into competition in yet another aspect of the digital entertainment marketplace, having seen from Netflix' powerful example (and from iTunes) just how valuable it is to have a captured audience of members.

Who else is coming? Who else but Walmart is coming soon, with its Vudu service, to compete with Hulu, and Sling, and Comcast, and Canal+, and the BBC, and, and, and...

Now that the design of entertainment is driven by the availability of data we are approaching the full integration of two industries, tech and entertainment converging into a new uber-industry with enough new business model niches to keep entrepreneurs busy for decades working out all the new opportunities. (This, by the way, was the original and highly astute observation behind the famous TED Conferences.)

Maybe that start-up will be funded by Softbank, Japan's giant investment firm, which recently announced that it would seek to raise more than $20 billion through the IPO of its Japanese mobile unit, and use the funds to support still more disruptive technology businesses. As Reed Hastings noted, there is no such thing as permanent success.

Energy

Energy supply is the foundation of the modern economy, for without reliable supplies in abundance the economy we know simply would not exist. As it is massive and global, it's also very diverse, with many layers of actors working from basic exploration and production through to distribution in many different core technologies and materials, from oil to solar to hydro to nuclear, while in many parts of the world foraged wood and scrub are still essential sources.

Now that civilization surrounds the entire planet in one integrated market, and given two hundred years of industrialism that has built a magnificent global economy but also brought climate change upon us, the role of the energy industry, the resources it uses, and the wastes it produces, have returned to the forefront of our attention.

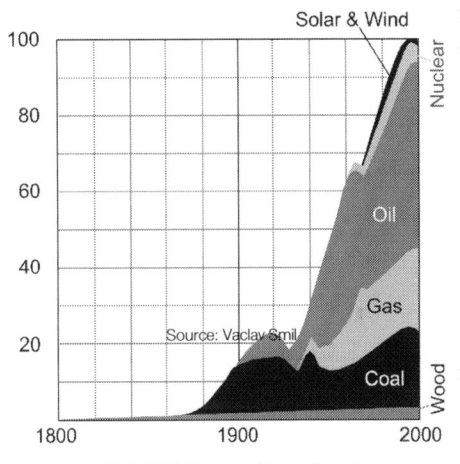

Total US Energy Use - Quads

For nearly a century the world's major oil companies have been among the most lucrative of assets, so much so that Shell Oil, for example, has not reduced its stockholder dividend for more than 70 years. As a result of this perception of stability and reliable returns, major institutional investors like insurance companies and pension funds own 27% of the shares of major oil companies.[38] But concerns about climate change have led to the introduction of hundreds of shareholder resolutions at the annual meetings of these companies in recent years, and a group of 310 institutional shareholders who together control funds totaling $32 trillion have recently formed a group called Climate Action 100+ to advocate for change.

> "Climate Action 100+ is a five-year initiative led by investors to engage systemically important greenhouse gas emitters and other companies across the global economy that have significant opportunities to drive the clean energy transition and help achieve the goals of the Paris Agreement. Investors are calling on companies to improve governance on climate change, curb emissions and strengthen climate-related financial disclosures. As institutional investors and consistent with our fiduciary duty to our beneficiaries, we will work with the companies in which we invest to ensure that they are minimising and disclosing the risks and maximizing the opportunities presented by climate change and climate policy."[39]

What does this mean for the business model of an oil company? For many firms, it means diversifying, which is why the French firm Total Oil has a broad portfolio of investments in solar, bio-fuels, and energy storage technologies, as do many of the other major oil firms.

Meanwhile, massive price volatility in the oil market is currently rattling those very same firms amid concerns about the health of the global economy, plummeting oil prices in 2018, and signs of a coming oversupply for the future. Hence, the business model of the global oil producer, which has been so steadily reliable for a century, is now coming into question, and we must expect to see some business model disruptions throughout the energy industry in coming years.

While all this is happening in the oil market, alternative energy continues to receive massive investment, and to overturn established business models. For instance, it used to cost billions to build an electrical power plant, but now home solar systems cost thousands, and the homeowner doesn't even have to buy it – you can lease space on your roof to a solar company that will sell you the power to run your house, charge up your electric car, and sell the excess into the grid. With new battery technologies this model will even be viable during nighttime.

In ten or twenty years, the power concentrated in electric cars with solar energy collectors on their roofs will perhaps be hooked up to office buildings during the day to power them, too, turning the lowly parking lot into a value-creating power plant.

This is all massively threatening to electric utility companies, which have in recent years begun to experiment with their own business models too. Instead of encouraging consumers to use more electricity to justify building more power plants, utilities like Pacific Gas & Electric in California have been paying people to conserve energy so the company *doesn't* have to build more generating capacity. Through rebates for highly efficient appliances, discounts on the cost of home insulation, and new regulations about light fixtures, their goal has been to serve California's rapidly growing population without building new energy generation capacity. It's working well, and so today Californians use about 200 million BTU per capita, ranking as the third most efficient state on the US list, and consuming just 22% of what the average resident of the most energy-inefficient state, Louisiana, at nearly 900 million BTU per person.[40]

Note also that all forms of alternative energy are high technology solutions that rely on the advanced engineering of materials, control systems, and basic generation techniques, and as technology continues to advance we will surely see new forms of energy become available, and new business models to bring them to market.

Employment

As the importance of innovation becomes more pronounced and better recognized throughout the business world, all types of organizations come to rely ever more on the creative and innovative capacity of people to recognize and solve problems, to create opportunities, and to overcome risks.

This means that while companies can buy robots to do rote work, they remain obliged to attract skilled human workers to do the essential creative work. Consequently, a company's business-model-as-employer is becoming nearly as important as the business model and value propositions it offers to potential customers. In a word, it's a war for talent.

So what does talent want? Demographic trends over the last three decades show clearly that talented young people prefer to live in cities that have vibrant and diverse social and cultural scenes. They also want to be challenged, to make a positive difference, and to be well rewarded.

Since the most skilled have choices about what company to work for, and where, this means that talent is flocking to the big cities, which is leaving rural areas with fewer and fewer workers, and fewer young people at all.[41] That is, a major trend of rural-to-urban migration is occurring worldwide.

This results in a nasty positive feedback cycle, as people leave even medium-sized cities for the biggest ones, and so the imbalance between still-growing London and still-shrinking the-rest-of-England widens, and the resentment of those left behind also increases, resentment that only heightened rural England's strong support for Brexit.

In the US, meanwhile, Google is planning to recruit thousands of employees not in Iowa City or St. Louis, but in New York City, while

Amazon chose New York and Washington DC for its two new headquarters locations largely because those two cities are attractive to workers. These two tech-era titans will also compete against one another for talent, putting even more pressure on other businesses in those cities for already-scarce talent. Salaries will rise, drawing still more talent from other towns.

But the cost of living will also rise, thus incurring the resentment of those already in New York who will see their rents and other costs rise as more highly-paid techies move to town.

Overall, it's estimated that the US will have 1.4 million new high tech jobs to fill in 2019 alone.

Silicon Valley, meanwhile, already employs millions of high tech workers, but many of them prefer to live fifty miles away in snazzy San Francisco rather than in the drab and lifeless suburbs of Mountain View (Google), Cupertino (Apple), and Menlo Park (Facebook). There are two freeways connecting the city to the high tech burbs, and both are fully jammed up all day long now that they're the main street connecting work and home. In response, all the big Silicon Valley companies offer free transportation in luxury buses, and so during the evening commutes, dozens of buses transport 50 Google employees at a time on pre-defined drop-off routes through San Francisco, the reverse of what they did in the morning. Why free bus service? Because it captures two to four productive work hours per day, which would otherwise be lost in traffic. (All the buses have free, high-speed wifi, of course.)

The profusion of buses has in turn caused massive resentment in San Francisco, where they complain that the surge in tech workers is causing accelerated gentrification and pushing out lower-paid workers who can no longer afford to live in the city (which is true), and that the private buses clog city streets and interfere with public transit (which is also true), but buses also make traffic less-worse than it otherwise would be.

Gentrification, private buses, the war for talent, locating offices in major cities (and doing so at WeWork), these are all aspects of business models that are gradually adapting the economy to its high technology orientation, and from which there is no turning back.

Speaking of competition for talent, it's happening at the senior management level, too. Apple announced in December 2018 that it recruited John Giannandrea as its senior vice president of Machine Learning and Artificial Intelligence Strategy, a new role that's just been created, and which of course reflects the growing importance of AI. Where did Giannandrea used to work? Google. (Apple did not report whether Giannandrea lives in San Francisco or in Palo Alto, but it's already well known that many of Apple's top leaders do indeed live in San Francisco.)

Apple's press release noted, "Machine learning and AI are important to Apple's future as they are fundamentally changing the way people interact with technology, and already helping our customers live better lives."[42]

Further, to sustain competitiveness in the rapidly technifying world, companies have to assure that their employees continually learn new tech skills and improve the ones they have. Hence, a recent survey by *Training* magazine showed that American companies spent more than $90 billion on staff training in 2017. A lot of that was spent by IBM, whose average employee undertook 60 hours of training; over the course of the last three years IBM employees have completed more than 650,000 courses, mostly online, meaning an investment of literally millions of hours in learning.

In Europe, meanwhile, the news on tech skills is bad just like with banking – a European Commission report found that a surprisingly high percentage of workers in Europe lack "basic digital skills," and that 88% of companies weren't doing anything about it.[43] This puts Europe dangerously on the pathway of business model implosion, exactly the place you *don't* want to be.

Education

Colleges and universities have business models, too. Northeastern University, located in Boston, recently acquired a small college in London to enhance its global presence, which underscores the growing incentives for universities to rethink their business models in an era of rising competition, shifting demographics, and increasing nationalism.

For decades, many universities in the US have depended on the high fees that international students pay to enroll in American colleges, but these enrollments declined for the second year in a row in 2018. In addition, international students serve as an important financial buffer against the falling number of U.S. high school students who graduate each year; by 2029, there will be 650,000 fewer American 18 year olds than there were in 2009 (of course we know this quite precisely because they're already born).

With operating costs rising much faster than inflation, but the supply of students diminishing, the basic university business model is under threat, and some colleges will inevitably alter their business models radically, or fail altogether.[44]

US Population of 18 Year Olds, Millions
Source: US Census Bureau

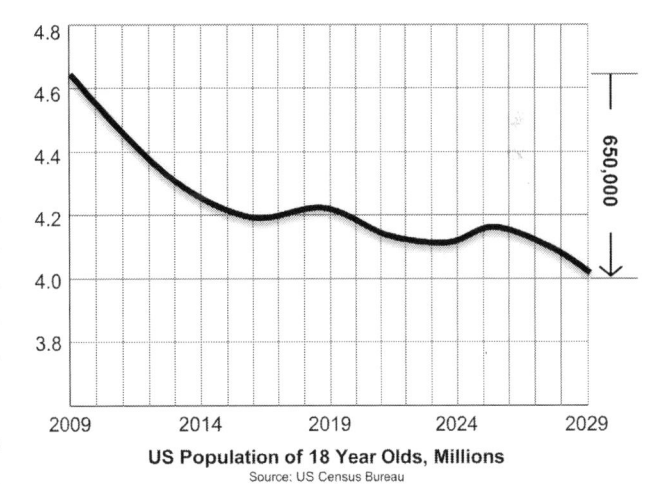

One of the new business models is of course online education, which has grown spectacularly during the last decade. Today about a third of graduate studies in the US are done online, both through established schools and also in a variety of innovative, technology-enabled startups. The University of Illinois, for example, has 99 MBA students on campus, but 1750 online.

And what are the primary advertising and recruiting tools that schools use to attract new online scholars? Google, Facebook, and LinkedIn, all of which make nice profits from their advertising fees.[45]

Privacy

We can think of "privacy" as a technology-enabled service industry that we depend upon to protect passwords and thus access to our technology-enabled private lives, our bank and credit card accounts and indeed all of our financial dealings, our online identities with the dozens of user accounts we maintain at Google and Facebook and Instagram and Twitter and LinkedIn, and on and on, and yet the arms race of technology development makes us vulnerable to thieves who steal our money or our identities and wreak havoc in our lives.

A smaller but highly lucrative segment of the privacy marketplace is the wealthy, who wish to be protected from prying eyes and government interference in their finances (i.e., taxes), and who are served by an entire industry of lawyers and accountants who set up and manage tax-protected investment accounts in locations where the prying eyes of governments are less intrusive.

The government of Australia, however, has just adopted a law that compels companies to reveal confidential information about their users to the police. For those who do not comply, the law provides for stiff penalties of up to $7 million for defiant companies, $35,000 for stubborn individuals, and those who expose cybersnooping by the police can face up to five years in prison. Yes, the Australian government really does want to know what's going on in all those millions of private accounts, but one result of the law is that technology firms are now considering that perhaps they need to relocate their Oceanic operations out of Australia to protect themselves, which demonstrates the intersection of privacy, technology, and a nation's business model.[46]

In Europe, the right to privacy has been put firmly into law through 2018's GDPR, the General Data Protection Regulation, which offers strong protections to all its citizens. In China, meanwhile, things are at the opposite extreme as citizens entirely lack protections for civil rights. The Chinese government is instituting a social scoring system that is intended to rate every Chinese citizen, and which will lead to perks for the well-behaved and punishments for the recalcitrant. It's a nationwide effort at behavior modification by carrots and sticks, in which neighbors are encouraged to report on neighbors, all with the intention to eliminate privacy altogether and assure compliance with the will of the state.

This is merely an extension of the big brother surveillance state, through which the government keeps a close eye on everyone, all the time:

> "In early 2018 a woman jaywalked on her way to work in the bustling Southern Chinese metropolis of Shenzhen, cutting across a side street to avoid a detour of hundreds of yards to a crosswalk. Two traffic policemen approached the woman and told her that she had violated the traffic regulations of the People's Republic. Eager to get to her job, the woman apologized, and pointed out that there was no fencing to block jaywalkers, and she hoped to get off with a verbal warning. The officers, however, were intent, and demanded her identity card. She said that she had not brought hers, so they asked for her ID number. She said she had not memorized it, so one officer snapped her picture with a camera phone. Seconds later he read out her name, her ID card number and date of birth. Using facial recognition technology he had identified her, and he then printed the ticket on his mobile printer, which she was obliged to pay through Tencent's messaging app, WeChat."[47]

What we have, then, is a multiple-direction dueling match, between individuals who wish to protect their privacy, companies that collect data on their users/customers to sell to advertisers, hackers and thieves who invade our privacy to steal valuable information, and government that uses technology to enforce its will, to assure compliance and detect deviation. It's a very complex landscape of conflicting goals that's changing quickly as technology evolves – facial recognition, encryption, avatars, passwords, surveillance, hacking, all are developing rapidly and thereby creating new capabilities, new risks, and enabling new business models.

Manufacturing

The development of mass-scale manufacturing created the Industrial Revolution, and is thus the basis of the modern global economy. The history of this two-hundred-year explosion of productivity is very much the story of business model competition and a very high rate of business model evolution, as companies were created, grew and prospered, but those that became complacent and failed to adapt quickly enough were cast aside.

The emergence of China as a major low-cost manufacturing center for the world has thus been just the latest chapter in a classic story of innovation and disruption, but a dramatic chapter nonetheless, as hundreds of millions of Chinese have moved from the countryside to the cities since 1990, many of them to work in the new factories that have sprung from farmland across the Chinese landscape in booming Shenzhen. Conversely, millions of manufacturing workers in others countries lost their jobs, forcing a radical restructuring of the economies and communities in Bilbao, Detroit, New York, and indeed in cities worldwide.

Part 2: Innovation Strategy

The key enablers of the Chinese boom have been the adoption of capitalism by the Chinese economy, which released the pent-up energies and talents of millions, the internet, which facilitates the instant communication between the factories and the worldwide markets they serve, and containerized shipping, which made it possible to efficiently handle the huge volume of transport required.

Containerization has thus revolutionized world trade, offering the shipping companies a much better business model by altering the entire process of moving goods in tremendous quantities. Not only ships, but trucking and warehousing are now completely different than they were 30 years ago, innovations that have in turn enabled Alibaba's and Amazon's and Ikea's business models to operate effectively.

Singapore. How many thousands of containers do you see?

Materials

As the economy evolves, the materials that society needs to assemble its good also evolve. For example, the rise in demand for modern electronics – particularly cell phones, robots, and electric cars – has led to a significant rise in the demand for rare metals such as cobalt.

But cobalt supplies are limited, and so the expectation of continued abundance is a threat to the business models of many firms who depend upon it for their products, a mismatch that will inevitably require a new wave of business model innovation.

Much of the world's cobalt comes from the Democratic Republic of the Congo, and as much as 25% of the supply is mined not by the established companies, but by people who cut through fences surrounding the industrial mines at night and work in the dark with picks and shovels, selling their output the next day to shady cobalt traders.[48]

This of course brings forth concerns about the likely emergence of "conflict cobalt," exploitation, and a highly unstable market for a strategic mineral, which is just one among dozens that are scare but essential to modern technology.

Other materials are available in abundance, but subject to trade conflict which can have a massive impact on business and on business models. As President Trump pursues a trade war with China, one of the impacts is a change in the supply of steel and aluminum, which American auto makers estimate could cost them billions as prices rise.

Aviation

When the SST aircraft made its first commercial flight in 1969, it was believed by many that supersonic aircraft would soon become common, but the technical drawbacks and the enormous costs proved to insurmountable, and an unfortunate accident in 2003 marked the end of the Concorde's business model.

While the attraction of flying the Concorde was its great speed, the actual development of the SST was also itself a business model innovation, as it was a joint effort of British Aerospace and the French Aérospatiale that foreshadowed the development of Airbus, the pan-European aerospace company which was set up as a joint British-French-German-Spanish firm to compete with Boeing in commercial aircraft, and which remains a bright spot in the otherwise rather sad

European commercial legacy.

Meanwhile, scientists, engineers, and entrepreneurs have never given up on the idea of supersonic air travel for commercial flyers, and now GE (yes, that GE) is partnering with Lockheed Martin, Honeywell, and tech startup Aerion to develop a private jet capable of reaching Mach 1.4, more than 1000 mph.

There isn't much new about this business model – it's the better mousetrap idea in ultra-high-tech, but what is particularly interesting is the joint venture organization of the effort. None of these companies could do this themselves because technology has advanced so far and so quickly that the necessary technical expertise no longer resides in any single firm. Successful joint ventures thus constitute an entire category of business models, and they will of necessity become even more common across all technology fields. The capacity to partner effectively will distinguish leading firms just as the incapacity to do so will handicap laggards.

Space

Space, outer space, is a thriving market as well, and one that supports a wide variety of fascinating business models. The value of the satellite and the launch services business is already in the hundreds of millions of dollars annually, and its growing as we find new uses for being in space. It's a technology-enabled market, of course, and the progressive improvement in computer chip power enables satellites and all space-based hardware to increase their functions while becoming smaller and much more efficient.

Thus, Rocket Lab, a startup that intends to conduct frequent, inexpensive launches of small satellites into relatively low Earth orbits, put its first commercial payload into space in 2018. Its goal is to reduce the cost to launch a satellite to hundreds or thousands of dollars for satellites weighing no more than hundreds of pounds, which compares with a price of tens of millions of dollars for satellites as large as a school bus and often weighing several tons each, and it aims to launch one rocket per week by 2020, which will significantly increase the number of satellites in orbit and greatly expand the scientific and communications possibilities that space systems offer to the Earthbound.

Rocket Lab is just one among dozens of startup companies in the growing market for space services and transportation. There are the famous rocketry companies, SpaceX, Blue Origin and Firefly, and dozens of satellite companies like Rocket Lab and also including Pumpkin Space Systems, AAC Microte, Adcole Maryland Aerospace, Compagnia Generale per lo Spazio, as well as exploration and mining companies including SpaceIL, ispace, Moon Express, and Astrobotics.

Most of these are venture-backed companies that have prepared business models which show the possibility of out-sized profits as the commercialization of space continues. But is space a new business model, or just a new venue for doing business? It's both, perhaps; it's the same as it's people using technology and trying to exploit a market, but it's possibly a setting for new business models that rely on partnerships, long term investment, continued progress in the development of new science and technology, and an entirely different type of risk profile.

Home Improvement

Back home on Earth, meanwhile, by combining nearly everything needed for residential construction, repair, and renovation in one place, Home Depot simultaneously disrupted the businesses of hardware, lumber, gardening, lighting, appliances, and home décor, changing the behavior of contractors and consumers alike. As the company grew progressively larger in scale its increasing purchasing power enabled progressively lower prices, which then enabled the company to capture further market share, creating a yet another positive spiral of business success, and leading to the closure of countless competitors.

Home Depot thus redefined the retail landscape for everything related to small scale construction and home improvement, but its successes also enabled competing firms like Ace Hardware (which is actually a co-op, and thus a different business model) to successfully position itself as the non-Home-Depot, the non-big-box, the local store where getting in and out is easy, and where you can actually find someone who may actually know the answer your questions.

What's a giant warehouse to do?

While Home Depot pioneered the home improvement super store, Lowe's plays fast follower using innovation as one of its leverage points. Lowe's "Innovation Lab" recently introduced a prototype instore "LoweBot" robot that helps out with inventory, as well as a hologram tool that enables customers to try power tools using VR headsets before they buy.[49] Using technology to augment an established business model may lead to further innovations that create new possibilities and opportunities, but Lowe's struggles in Home Depot's shadow, and as we saw above, had to close 50 of its stores in 2018. If they're going to survive, they'll have to follow faster, and innovate more.

Tourism

Space has been a tourist destination for a very few of the super rich for a few decades, but Virgin Galactic aspires to make it accessible to the merely rich with sub-orbital flights, while Bigelow Aerospace is developing an inflatable orbiting hotel, one module of which is already attached to the International Space Station for testing purposes.

Tourism on Earth is evolving, too, with new options always emerging for the ultra-luxury market for the ever-growing number of millionaires and billionaires, but also interesting innovations at the opposite end of the spectrum in the niche we might label "experiential travel."

One example is an interesting new business model located about eight hours drive from Bogota, Colombia, where you can book a room or a tent in Camp Mariana Paez, which was formerly a base of FARC guerrillas until a peace accord was reached in 2016. "Live like a guerrilla" was started by former guerrillas who found themselves without employable skills, and have started a few business ventures in hopes of improving the lives of their small community. A guest recently pointed out that the Camp, "is not the first spot you'll find on TripAdvisor,"[50] but he came away with an entirely and enriching memorable experience, which is what most adventure travelers seek.

Sports Apparel

Two significant business innovations propelled Nike to its huge success. First, the company was one of the first to exploit outsourced Asian manufacturing as its primary source of supply, thus defining itself as a design and marketing firm instead of a manufacturer. It didn't and still doesn't own factories. This was an entirely new way for a company to organize its business, which freed Nike's leadership to focus on design and marketing, and which then led them to define a different sort of relationship between the customer and their brand.

This led in turn to a significant marketing breakthrough, the discovery about how the public identifies with sports icons and how that relationship can be exploited under the premise (and promise) that wearing the same clothes as a world class athlete makes the average person feel like an athletic superstar.

The "Be Like Mike" ad campaign based on Michael Jordan earned billions for the company, and it was followed by "Just Do It," which defined the branding business model that's been followed ever since by all the firms in the market.

As they're all now operating in the same basic business model, the one that Nike invented, as all sports apparel manufacturers are engaged in a celebrity endorsement arms race focused on which is the coolest. Nike, Adidas, Under Armour, Puma, Anta, and others firms pay hundreds of millions each year to the athletes and entertainers who wear their apparel, but since the underlying business model for all of them is the same, it's obviously an industry ripe for disruption. Adidas' move toward co-creation is a small but meaningful step, but it doesn't seem to qualify as an entirely different model, just a clever and very effective extension of the old one. We will have to wait to see what's coming next ...

Health Care

Speaking of an industry that's definitely ripe for disruption, health care in the US is highly contentious, growing steadily more costly as a percent of GDP, and subject to massive upheaval by the profusion of new technologies that are coming to market on a regular basis now, from new medical devices to implants to biotech to pharma innovations. With so much money at stake the new competitors are flooding in with a variety of new business models – drug stores are becoming health

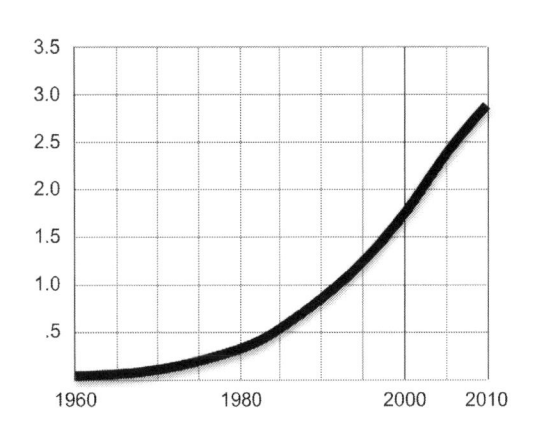

USA Health Care Expenditures – $ Trillions

clinics, drug sales proliferate on the internet, mergers and acquisitions are occurring at a rapid pace, everyone in search of a business model that's sustainable amid the tumult.

25 Business Models

These 16 industry examples offer a deep and diverse understanding of the range of "business model" possibilities, and shows how they're currently evolving as technology enables new forms of experiences and new ways to create value. We've just seen 25 different ones, and while they're not all new (actually, none of them are new), taken together they demonstrate how innovative thinking creates alternatives that offer distinct value propositions:

1. Scale (banking)
2. Displacement by technology (banking)
3. Services bundle (insurance)
4. Digitalization (entertainment)
5. Decentralization (energy)
6. Alliance (energy)
7. Paying people not to consume your product (energy)
8. Containerization (manufacturing)
9. Theft (materials)
10. Trade war (materials)
11. Market concentration (employment)
12. Training (employment)
13. Moving services online (education)
14. Shared workspace (real estate)
15. Building conversion (real estate)
16. Privacy services (privacy)
17. Privacy hack (privacy)

18. Partnership (aviation)
19. Cost reduction by 10x (space)
20. Big box retail (retail)
21. Anti-big-box/small box (retail)
22. Experience tourism (tourism)
23. Athlete branding (sports apparel)
24. Technology invasion (health care)
25. Mergers and acquisitions (health care)

How does these relate to our formula? Let's see...

As I've noted, in its simplest form, a business model tells us how a company makes money. It's a description of what the company does and why customers give it their precious money for doing it. But more importantly, a business model describes how a company creates and delivers experiences to its customers, while at the macro levels of cities, regions, and nations, how entire economies are organized to create wealth while enabling community.

How many examples can we find? There's no limit, really, and while each innovator pursues business model innovations from the unique perspective of their own background, experience, and opportunity, the successful ones converge at a common end point that enables us to identify the formula:

A vision of a better experience,
fulfilled by the means,
in a story nicely told.

Business Model Warfare

Now let's map the 25 business models listed above onto the framework of Means, Story, and Experience, to see how the various models emphasize or address different aspects of the framework.

25 business models

#	inside the MEANS	bridge the STORY	outside the EXPERIENCE
1	Scale		Scale
2	Displacement by technology		Displacement by technology
3			Services bundle
4	Digitalization		
5	Decentralization		
6	Alliance		
7			Paying people not to consume
8	Containerization		
9	Theft		
10	Trade war		
11			Market concentration
12	Training		
13	Moving services online		Moving services online
14	Shared workspace		Shared workspace
15	Building conversion		
16			Privacy services
17	Privacy hack		
18	Partnership		
19	Cost reduction by 10x		
20	Big box retail		Big box retail
21	Anti-big-box		Anti-big-box
22			Experience tourism
23		Athlete branding	Athlete branding
24	Technology invasion		Technology invasion
25	Mergers and acquisitions		

When I created the chart I simply went down one at a time and looked at where the core of each model lie, the intent being of course to show where the creators of the business model had placed their emphasis. Again, you may not agree entirely with how I've classified them, but setting that aside the chart shows that 19 of the 25 have pushed the *means* to or beyond some edge, 13 of the 19 have explicitly designed some sort of *experience* in so doing. But one, a lonely, lonely one only has focused on how it tells the story. This is what Nike pioneered for the aspirational sports apparel industry, and what Adidas has successfully copied (and actually improved upon).

My branding guru and friend Jerome (and author of two companion volumes to this one, *Soulful Branding* and *The Brand Bridge*) looked at this and said, basically, "Aha! It's just as I've been telling you! Most companies don't understand branding at all." And he continued on with a bit of a rant, but I had to agree that he was right. And then he said, "I'm going to title my next book *The Brand Bridge*," and he did.

And to be clear, I did not pick the 16 industries or the 25 business models with any kind of preplanned motive. I was just looking for a diversity of examples across a wide range of industries.

What this clearly suggests is that there is a giant gaping Grand Canyon of opportunity for those businesses that can come to grips with these higher levels principles that Jerome labeled "soulful." And certainly in addition to the ones I've examined in this chapter we would add Disney to the soulful list, and some luxury goods companies, but when you really think about there aren't that many companies that distinguish themselves because of the story they tell about the relationship between us, the customers, and them, the company. It's just not common, so as we consider the possibilities for business model innovation we have to put a giant asterisk on the guidance to...

Design a Soulful Brand

*… which is a Salient, Relevant and Resonant Brand,
a brand with a sense of humor, coolness, intelligence,
empathy, love and passion, respect,
and entertainment value.*

These are the secret attributes of soulful brands, and the opportunities doing this creates will be so spectacularly powerful. Not that it will be easy, and definitely don't try to fake it, but if you can do it well and sincerely then there are sure to be massive benefits.

SIC Codes

In the US there are about 16.3 million businesses, of which 11.2 million have 4 or fewer employees. The government classifies them all according to a four digit coding scheme called "SIC Codes," Standard Industrial Classification. By this way of thinking there are thus 9,999 different types of companies. As the economy continues to evolve, as technology continues to develop and to impact ever more deeply throughout the economy, all 9,999 will be subject to disruption, and no industry will be left behind. But which will dominate? We consider that next.

Chapter 16
BUSINESS MODEL DOMINANCE
Increasing Returns

The very first figure we saw in Chapter 1 shows the intimidating growth in the valuations of Amazon, Apple, Facebook, Google, and Microsoft compared with all the other 495 companies in the S&P 500, which also shows how dominant they are in their markets and in the minds of investors.

Interestingly, while they started in different markets, their growth paths are now intersecting, forcing them to become competitors in multiple segments.

One of these is advertising. Ads are the main source of revenue for Google and Facebook, and now Amazon is targeting a bigger share of the US digital advertising market, currently worth about $160 billion annually. Analyst forecasts suggest that Amazon's ad unit will be its most profitable as soon as 2021.[51]

The internet ad businesses of all three relies on two prominent factors, total user traffic across their web sites, the sheer number of people who

Share Price Growth, 2009 – 2019
Source: Datastream & Goldman Sachs

use their platforms, and the ever-expanding pool of data they accumulate on each user, which enables them to target ads most precisely to the interests, needs, and inquiries of their users.

The difference between the highly specific and targeted messaging that good data enables advertisers to achieve, compared with the wasteful randomness inherent in most other forms only makes these digital platforms ever more attractive to advertisers, driving the shift away from other media and making any firm that has a lot of traffic, and data about that traffic, more useful to advertisers and thus more valuable to investors.

Hence, we can easily foresee that the convergence of social media and consumerism will be a primary force shaping markets for decades to come. And interestingly, in this new competitive market, all fifteen of the largest digital companies are American and Chinese, with not a single European is among them, while only eight of the top 200 are based in Europe.[52]

European leaders are now becoming painfully aware that Europe has found itself at an extreme technological disadvantage, which bodes ill for its future as a business model innovator. "Asked whether the continent will ever produce its own Google, one European official burst out laughing" at the absurdity of the idea.

In *The Economist's* view, this is partly explained by Europe's history:

> "The 20th century also restrains Europe's technological competitiveness today. The collective experience of Nazi and Soviet surveillance and dictatorship makes many Europeans protective of their data (Germans, for example, are still reluctant to use electronic payments). Moreover, since 1945 the continent has mostly been at peace and protected by outsiders. So it has no institutions comparable to DARPA, the American military-research institution where technologies like microchips, GPS and the internet were born. Nor has it anything comparable to China's

military investments in technology today."[53]

This suggests a systemic, continent-wide European business model innovation *dis*advantage in technology, just as we saw above in banking. If the lag persists then the discrepancy between Europe and the US-China will only become greater, and Europe will fall further behind, because these are competitions subject to positive feedback, and in which those who get ahead can then pull farther ahead, while those who slip behind then lag even more.

When you've fallen behind it's nearly impossible to catch up, putting laggards in a vicious trap.

In fact, positive feedback now shows up in every aspect of technology businesses. For instance, the high stock valuations of leading firms provide them with strength during industry consolidations, as highly valued stock can be used to facilitate the acquisition of desirable young companies, whereas a weak stock has no such attractive power.

It is because of this that there's a saying in Silicon Valley that "if you're not in first place (in a given market), you might as well go home and find something else to do." Leaders capture disproportionate benefits, while non-leaders are destined to play constant catch-up, at which they rarely succeed.

> "If you're not in first place you might as well go home and **find something else to do**."

Above I mentioned the fast-follower strategy, but that only works when giant firms are chasing little ones; it does not work at all the other way around. (Note that this is true within a given industry structure; upon the occurrence of a major disruption, the mantles of leadership are entirely up for grabs, which is when the mighty fall and the youthful rise.)

Not Declining

The concepts of negative and positive spirals are essential characteristics of these high tech markets.

In contrast to high technology companies, think about firms and industries that are asset-heavy, which is a quality shared by nearly all industrial-age companies. Successful firms in mining and manufacturing accumulate massive asset bases which lock them into relatively static ways of working, and consequently the more it's necessary to invest in hard assets to compete effectively in a given business, the more difficult it is to differentiate.

Think about an auto factory, with miles of assembly lines and millions of dollars invested in heavy machinery, all of which is designed to perform repetitive functions on massive amounts of raw material. Ford's pioneering River Rouge plant in Detroit was begun in 1917 and initially made anti-submarine boats used in World War I. During the Great Depression it still employed more than 100,000 workers on 16 million square feet of floor space, and had 100 miles of interior railroad tracks. Today it's still in operation, building Ford's F-150 line of trucks, but it's not exactly a flexible or nimble asset. No matter how much money Ford would choose to invest in the plant, the value it could possibly produce is inherently limited, and thus Ford, and all companies that own similar facilities, are forced to scale back their investments.

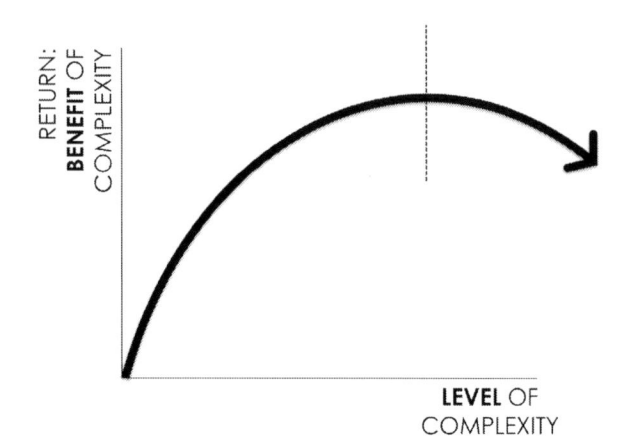

Economists refer to this as "declining marginal returns," the pattern through which investment in progressively more assets does not yield progressively greater returns. Instead, returns hit a peak due to complexity, following which further investment actually results in lower overall returns.

One of the reasons that companies employ economists is to calculate these curves, because knowledge of where the curves peak is essential to their long term survival. They have to know when to *stop* investing.

Business model innovation in technology-enabled industries, however, operates by a considerably different economic logic. Here we experience the phenomenon of *increasing returns* rather than declining returns, which is why Amazon, Google, and Facebook constantly invest to build up the size of their customer bases even when many of those investments are likely to lose money.

The underlying economics was first recognized by Brian Arthur in the late 1980s, when he described how increasing marginal returns occur.[54] The compelling business logic emerged around the same time, when electrical engineer Robert Metcalfe coined the formula that soon thereafter became known as Metcalfe's Law, which states that the value of a network increases as a square of the number of users in the network.

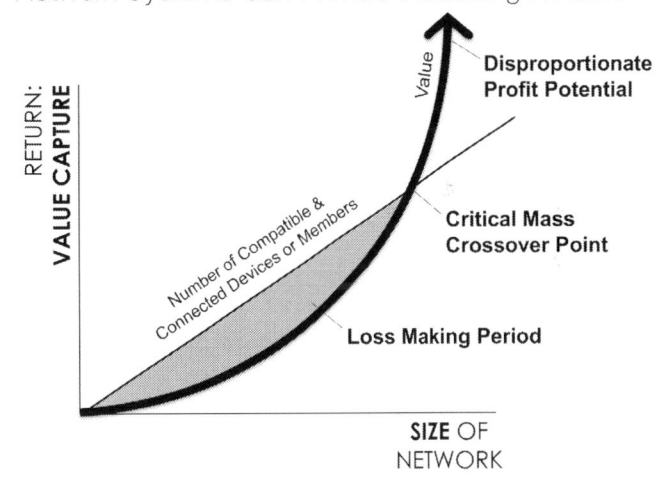

While cost increases may grow linearly with the size of the network, profit grows exponentially once the crossover point has been reached, providing an enormous and indeed disproportionate of the entire industry's profits to the firm with the largest network.

Metcalfe, who was one the geniuses at Xerox PARC and who co-invented Ethernet among many other advances made there, was thus one of the first to realize that developing a larger network of users or customers was the essential key to a successful internet-based business like Google or Amazon, and this logic is still so compelling to the Silicon Valley venture capital community that the drive to acquire users or members regardless of the operating losses that would be incurred in the process of doing so is an essential aspect of the Silicon Valley model for success. As long as a company is attracting new users at a sufficient rate it doesn't have to be profitable, because of the expectation that increasing returns will arrive sooner or later.

In the case of Google, it took the company many years to work out its business model, and in the end the successful business model was quite far in concept from where they had started. The notion of the "ad-word auction" had not even been conceived of when the firm was in its early, garage-stage of growth, and even though no one in the early days knew how Google was eventually going to make money, the fact that its user base was growing so fast meant that venture capitalists were perfectly willing to fund years of operating losses because they anticipated that sooner or later the company would devise a business model that would monetize all those web searches, which it certainly did.

Today, Uber and Lyft are in a similar situation. Venture capital investments have funded many years and billions of dollars of operating losses because investors believe that the key to ultimate success for both depends upon the sheer size of the user base. Thus, the competition between Uber, Lyft, Didi, GoGoVan, and all the other ride sharing companies is largely a battle for market share, for scale, which only works because it's a business model that relies for its viability on assets that it does not own.

If any of these companies had to own or even lease all those cars, and hire drivers as employees, it would never be any more profitable that the giant, asset-heavy car rental firms like Avis or Hertz, which are barely profitable at all.

Business leaders who are paying attention to all this have begun to bring as many attributes of asset-light digital businesses as possible into their asset-heavy business models.

For example, LCD screens are as now big as billboards, so the companies that own billboards, like Clear Channel and JC Decaux, are suddenly now digital companies that are able to sell ads in increments of one minute rather than under contracts lasting for weeks or months, because digital ads can be changed in real time.

But why would anyone want to buy billboard time for just a minute, or a few?

This is exceptionally useful only when you know exactly who's looking at the billboard, and at exactly what time they're looking at it. Somewhat disturbingly, this is exactly what's being done. (There's that privacy issue again.)

It's all enabled because of the masses of data that smart phones are creating, which tell advertisers who's nearby at any given time: "Location data are pouring off of people's smart phones. Information about their owners' whereabouts and online browsing gets aggregated and anonymized by carrier and data vendors and sold to media owners. They then use these data to work out when different demographic groups – 'business travelers,' say – walk by their ads. That knowledge is added to insights into traffic, weather, and other external data to produce highly relevant ads. Providers can deliver ads for coffee when it's cold and fizzy drinks when it's warm. Billboards can be programmed to show ads for allergy medication when the air is full of pollen."[55]

Do you want to target the 50,000 people leaving a sports stadium with an ad for souvenir merchandise or tickets to the next thrilling match? Easily done. Is it lunch time in a crowded neighborhood? Promote your restaurant between, say, 11:45 and 1:15, after which an entirely different product will be on display, maybe tickets for tonight's show.

The consequences are obvious and far-reaching.

Already high tech companies are among the top buyers of digital ads, and now they're also buying their own billboards. Netflix already owns a series of billboards along Hollywood's Sunset Strip which it uses to promote its own shows, further progressing on its quest to fully colonize the entertainment industry and capture a disproportionate share of profits.

What drives Netflix' amazing success? It's the size of its user base, of course, another example of the power of networks. Since the essence of its operating model is streaming content, the marginal cost of adding a new user (customer/member) to the Netflix network is essentially zero, thus throwing all the additional revenue straight into the profit row on its P&L.

And according to Metcalfe's Law, roughly each time Netflix doubles the size of its membership base, its value as a company should increase by a factor of four. Thus, the name of the game is grow the base, and the result of doing so successfully is "winner takes all," that is, you dominate the market, just as Amazon, Apply, Facebook, Google, and Microsoft now do. And Netflix.

Consequently, the production costs associated with creating new TV series and movies are, from a business model perspective, just a means of attracting more users onto the platform, and as they serve to attract new members and retain existing ones, they barely matter in the overall scheme of the wealth-creation machine. Since Netflix as a business

Part 2: Innovation Strategy

grows more valuable as it adds each new user, as long as the creation of great content can be correlated with increasing membership then it's like free money for Netflix.

So what is Netflix' programming department doing? They're doing massive, nonstop statistical analyses on their customer base, fervently studying who's been watching what, trying to figure out what kind of shows will most appeal to current customers and to those they can attract to become new customers. This also explains the billboards in LA, which at most will be seen by a few hundred thousand people. But which people? Netflix' success depends significantly on the positive buzz surrounding its new shows, and what better way to create buzz than to have the world's greatest concentration of pop culture media influencers talking about them. Where do those people live, and along what street do they drive almost every day? Ah, now I get it. The billboards give Netflix exposure to and thus leverage with a key influencer constituency that its business model relies upon.

Do you remember how Netflix started out? They started out sending movies on DVDs via the US mail, and their primary competitor was Blockbuster Video. Netflix won the competition between those two business models handily, seeing Blockbuster into bankruptcy in 2010 while the value of its own stock has skyrocketed.

From mailed DVDs Netflix progressed to video streaming, and as bandwidths have increased around the world this technology has come to dominate home

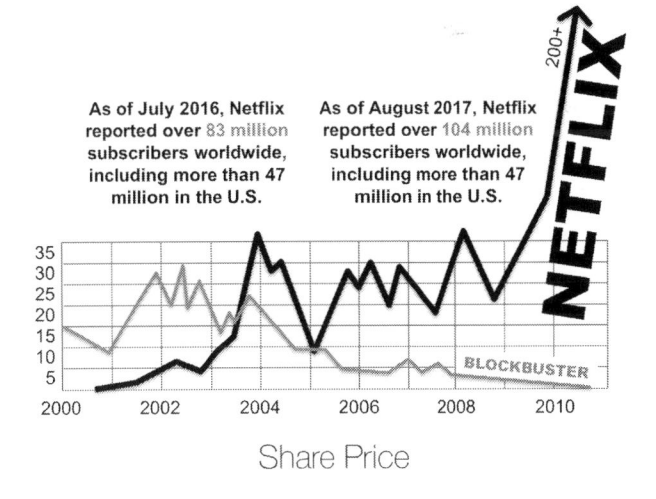

As of July 2016, Netflix reported over 83 million subscribers worldwide, including more than 47 million in the U.S.

As of August 2017, Netflix reported over 104 million subscribers worldwide, including more than 47 million in the U.S.

Share Price

entertainment. But the underlying business model is the same – it's all about the number of members.

Google's success likewise depends on how many people visit its primary asset, its search engine. Amazon's success requires constant web traffic too, and the same is true for Facebook.

Apple, in contrast, was a struggling maker of computer hardware that had about 5% share of the PC market, but then rose to business model dominance largely because it created iTunes and then the App Store, both of which enabled and promoted network effects, and which around it developed thriving communities or ecosystems of complementary businesses. That is, Apple turned itself into a digital-asset-platform company, and by the time the iPhone arrived they had fully worked out the economies of platform scale and they knew exactly how to optimize it.

The clear message from all of this is that an asset-heavy business model is almost never as profitable as a network-based business model, and that the pathway to market success and even market dominance is to transform a user base into a network:

How can you do this in your own business?

Chapter 17
BUSINESS MODEL PLATFORMS
Extensible Leverage and Super-Networks

A business platform is a foundational element around or upon which an entire set, suite, or ecosystem of complementary products or services is organized or delivered. The platform model exploits the benefits of network dynamics by incorporating other organizations and by implication their networks, into your own. It provides massive leverage. In this way, iTunes and the App Store are networks of networks, and because of their huge reach are capable of generating huge value multipliers.

There are thousands of apps in the App Store that were created by independent third party software firms, just as there are hundreds of third party programs on Salesforce, millions of sellers on eBay and Craigslist, and similarly millions of independent companies that sell through Amazon and Alibaba as their affiliates.

Platforms expand networks and amplify network effects, and the most successful aggregate networks into super-networks, and enable firms to aggregate tremendous value. The concept of the "platform" has thus become a central theme that most digital and many clever non-digital firms pursue to improve their business models.

Who wants to do this? In truth, who doesn't? Alibaba, Android, Apple,

Craiglist, eBay, Etsy, Facebook, Google, Netflix, Spotify, even Charles Schwab does it through its mutual fund marketplace.

The competitive opportunity is therefore to create the most usable and extensive platforms upon which the most useful and interesting services can be delivered. From the consumer side, engagement with these platforms is now a central part of the digital consumption experience, and is thus one of the major and most immediate impacts that digital technology is having is on our social and consumer behavior, affecting how we think about ourselves, the world, and everything else.

Almost universally, the consumer's involvement with all these platforms isn't described as a "customer" relationship, it's a membership, a careful choice of words precisely because the type of relationship that membership connotes.

When you join a group, club, or association, it's implied that you're no longer separate, you're now an insider, perhaps even part of the family. That's why Facebook, LinkedIn, and Netflix don't have customers or users, they have members. So do the American and United Airlines rewards programs, and in fact all travel rewards programs, as well Costco and Sam's Club. Membership implies a different relationship, which is why American Express also calls its customers "members." They're better, because they're insiders.

This semantic shift is an act of seduction, an attempt to reframe a commercial relationship as something more. And it can be more when services are provided to members that others cannot access, when members receive inside information, and when they participate as co-creation partners. We will return to these themes later on.

Digital Mash-Up

A digital billboard business is a mash-up, the clever combination of two quite different digital elements. It's the giant LCD screen that was installed in a prominent location, which required purchasing the right to install the screen there, the labor and materials that get it there, the power that illuminates it, the digital content that is displayed upon it, and the high bandwidth connectivity that connects it in real time to servers from which the ads are sent.

The other part of the business model is the data collection and analysis that enables advertisers to decide that they want to display image x in location y at time z because target group g is most likely to see it. It's a triangular business model, which is how nearly all advertising works.

The data that makes this work aren't useful in and of themselves, they're useful because of what they enable the business to do, which is to identify, to target, to persuade, to sell. That is, the data have to be mashed-up with the message and with the display platform to create value for the advertiser.

The same thing happens in the transportation business when Ford realizes that data from urban bicycles and scooters are valuable because they help the company understand how people move through the city.

The progressively digitalized world facilitates all this collection and connectivity in ever new and ever more precise ways, and under the influence of this precisely-targeted, mashed-up digital barrage, the poor consumer cannot evade the constant messages.

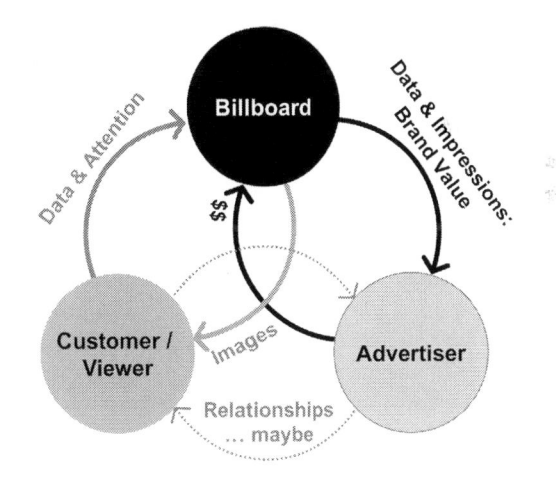

And of course the mash-ups will only improve, not only in advertising, but in every other aspect of our progressively more digitally-enabled lives; digitalization touches everything.

So it may surprise you to learn that farming is also a highly digitalized profession too. For a mere $500,000 the John Deere company would be very happy to sell you a brand new digitalized combine tractor with which to harvest your massive Nebraska corn crop. Equipped with a GPS device accurate to within one inch (2.5 cm), it will steer itself along in perfectly straight rows. In the cab of the harvester you'll view seven digital screens, each displaying a different type of information, all with the intent to help you become a more efficient farmer.

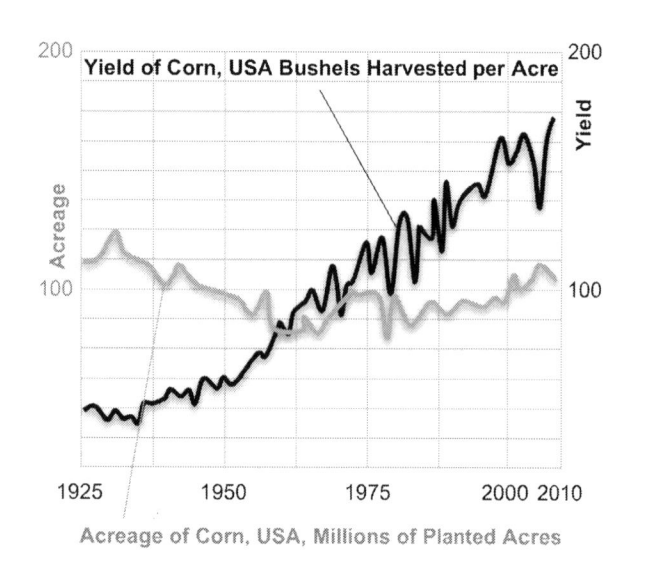

Corn farming in the US Midwest has become a high tech profession, now known as 'agri-tech' or 'precision agriculture.' The result shows in the graph as a boom in the productivity of corn farms in the US, a three-fold improvement in productive yield over the last century.

What the graph doesn't show is the drastic decline in the number of people. In fact, today there are far more cows than people in Nebraska, as the number of farmers needed to tend the state's 10 million acres of corn fields has been declining while productive yields have been increasing. Today three people can effectively manage a vast corn production as large as 2000 acres, as they are invisibly supported by software engineers, satellite services providers, GPS signals, high tech sensors, real-time analytics, etc., etc.

1200 miles to the west in California's strawberry fields, the nasty lygus bug turns lovely red fruits into misshapen lumps, and to remove them farmers now use a relative lo-tech but giant 'bug vacuum,' a clever form of pest removal that reduces the need for chemicals. In nearby strawberry-growing greenhouses, meanwhile, instead of soil the growing medium is ground coconut husks, an innovation that doesn't require fumigants, and which requires about one-tenth the amount water needed for growing strawberries in the ground. Further south in California, lettuce is grown in giant greenhouses and protected from bugs by garlic sprayed by robots that roam the aisles, taking care of the job that humans once considered the most unpleasant task in the greenhouse.

> In the words of strawberry farmer Steven Newell, 'We're almost more of a technology company than a farm or produce company.'
>
> Adds Nebraska corn farmer Scott Wagner, 'We are better environmentalists because of technology.'
>
> Hana Medina
> *Costco Connection*
> April 2018

All this reminds us of what Daniel Webster noted a century ago, that 'When tillage begins other arts follow. The farmers therefore are the founders of human civilization.' This accurately describes how industrialism got its start as an offshoot of farming, and still describes how many innovations find their way into cities. Self-driving vehicles, robots, water conservation, reduced chemical usage, drones, these and many more are being pioneered on farms.

The digitalization of farming, whether you call it precision agriculture or agri-tech or robo-farming, involves satellite technology and digital market-making, software analysis and robotic workers, plant genetics, and alternatives to pesticides, and it's a global phenomenon that has impacts throughout the entire farming cycle, from selecting crops to grow, planting, growing and harvesting, bringing to market, and caring for the land.

Far away from the massive corn farms of the Midwestern USA, farmers in Zambia in Southern Africa generate about 20 percent of the country's overall economic production, about $4 billion, but employ 75 percent of the country's 17 million people. The Zambia Agricultural Research Institute also uses advanced technology, applying genetic engineering to cultivate new plant variations. It also encourages farmers to plant a wider variety of crops to help diversify local diets and improve nutrition and health, and its method is to issue electronic vouchers that farmers can use to buy seeds and supplies. Yes, technology is infiltrating everywhere.

Industrialized agriculture mechanized the manual process and replaced animal labor, while digitalized agriculture is the application of even more advanced technologies to make farming even more productive – digital machines, digital genetics, digital soil and water management, digital vouchers, satellites, etc., etc., and all replacing human labor. It's still farming, but as we see, even the life of the soil is transformed by the power of technology. Yes, you still need the land, the sun, the water, the seeds, and all that equipment, but many of the decisions that farmers make about all these factors are heavily influenced by digital technology, and much work is done by digitalized equipment.

Today's tractor takes soil samples as it plows and harvests, assessing 22 (or more) chemical and mineral factors in near-real time, so as farmer drives, the tractor builds and then revises the digital map of the field.

And what about those seeds? The digital manipulation of plant genetics brings us to the controversial world of GMO and non-GMO, gene editing and CRISPR and genetic engineering. Are GMO seeds safe? Are they ethical? Will they lead to catastrophically unintended outcomes? Or will they enable farmers to feed all those billions of hungry people?

In the context of our focus in this book, business model innovations, the principles of platforms and network effects, of digitization and digital mash-ups show us how pervasive digital technology has become already, and prod us to consider how much more pervasive it will be five or ten years in the future, and the massive impact that it's inevitably going to have. Digitalization is indeed one of the global economy's central patterns of change.

Chapter 18
THE PATTERNS OF CHANGE
Digitalization: Technology Drives Us Now

Only a few macro factors are the most significant drivers of change throughout the global economy, and technology is unquestionably one of them.

Modern technology begins with computer chips, and due to progressive improvements made during the last half-century, chips are cheaper and more powerful each year, and as a result they can do more useful work, so of course people are finding scads of useful work for them to do. Smart phones and digital billboards, self-driving cars, robots, ATM machines, and every other app and device are all based on computer chips that are now immensely powerful and astonishingly inexpensive.

When computer chips were invented in the 1960s they began to influence all aspects of society. The digital revolution was on, and today chips are everywhere, in everything, and they're disrupting existing business patterns, geopolitics, and human relationships worldwide.

Chips get faster, more powerful, and amazingly, less expensive with each succeeding product generation, and since there is so much money to be made with the next better chip, chip makers have relentless incentive to continue their remarkable streak of progress.

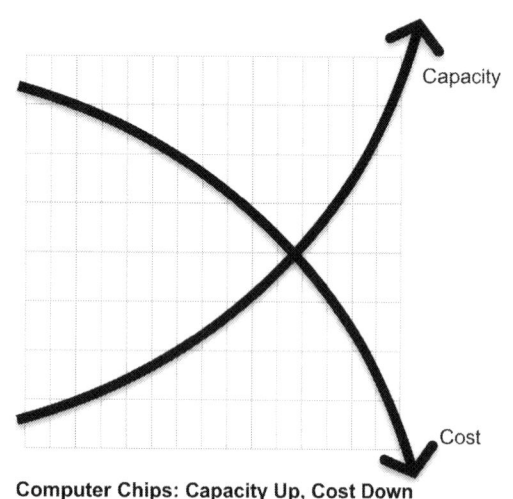

Gordon Moore noticed this in 1965, and his observation soon became known as *Moore's Law,* describing the fact that computer chip capacities and speeds double about every two years even as cost declines along the reciprocal curve. This amazing rate of progress has been sustained for the last half century, and now the global economy, including farming, is entirely reliant upon chips and the digital infrastructure of the internet that enables instantaneous flow of information from anywhere to everywhere. With each technical advance the capacity of machines to make useful calculations improves significantly, thereby increasing their utility and our dependence.

Computer Chips: Capacity Up, Cost Down
The Capacity Curve is also known as *Moore's Law.*

For a glimpse at how digital technology has advanced, consider that the $500 iPhone of 2007 was about 1000 times *more* powerful than the $9 million Cray computer of 1977. Please take a moment to reread that stunning sentence. It's an impressive *18 million-fold* improvement. Yikes!

Scientific advances have taken silicon to the very limits of its physical properties, beyond which silicon chips may not be able to be improved at all, which is why researchers are experimenting with many alternatives. One possibility is carbon nanotubes, which could offer a 50-fold improvement in speed and energy efficiency. The US government's DARPA R&D agency is supporting research at many universities including MIT, Stanford, and Arizona State that are working to develop new computing technologies for the future, always faster and more powerful, and able to do still more useful work.[56]

"The Pentium IIs we used in the first year of Google (1997) performed about 100 million floating point operations per second.

The GPUs we use today (2017) perform about 20 trillion such operations — a factor of about 200,000 difference — and our very own TPUs (special chips for AI applications) are now capable of 180 *trillion* (180,000,000,000,000) floating point operations per second."

Sergey Brin
Co-founder, Google
2017 Founders' Letter

Highly capable robots are soon to be a major part of the story, and if robots fulfill even a modest portion of their potential then the next phases of digitalization will be even more impactful and thus more disruptive, possibly wiping out millions of jobs.

Industry forecasts project that the total number of chips in use will increase roughly by a factor of 10 during the coming few years, spreading technology further across all phases of commerce, culture, and life.

The global market for computer chips was about $410 billion in 2017, leaping up 21% from about $325 billion in 2016 (although the numbers vary considerably depending on the source). Each year the number increases as the power of chips also increases, but the number of firms making chips decreases. In 2001 about 30 companies operated at the leading edge of technology, but now as design and manufacturing costs have risen sharply, there are only five firms left[57] (and none are European).

2020 – 2030:

Digital Explosion & Digital Danger Zone

Number of Computer Chips in Use

As chips become better every year, both more powerful and cheaper, they'll take over still more and more functions. Which functions? As we saw above, health care is shifting to be digital, finance is already entirely digital, entertainment, information, news, advertising, communications, publishing, buying and selling, nearly all are fully digitalized now, all enabled by computer chips. Consequently, today the world's biggest ad agency isn't an ad agency, it's Google; the biggest retailers aren't just traditional retailers, Amazon.com and Alibaba are dominant and feared; and the most significant phone maker used to be a computer company, Apple.

Industrialism remains at the heart of this because industry enabled the scientific and technological advances that make it possible for computer chips to impact all facets of economic activity. Thus, industry created computer chips and now computer chips are transforming industry.

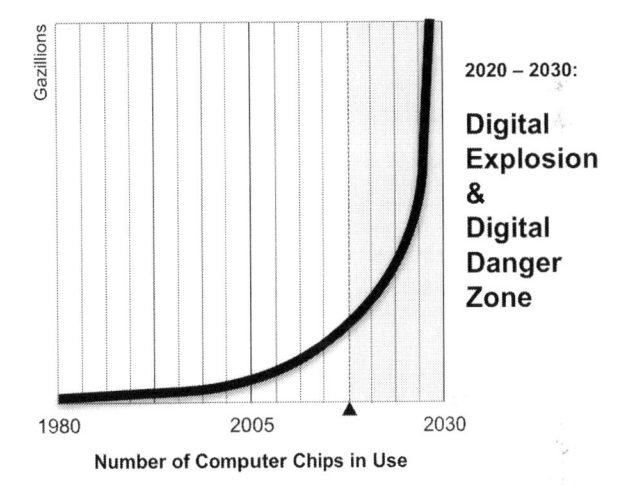

Looking ahead, the combined impact of all the new digital capabilities will inevitably result in the continuing transformation of the economy, and the replacement of industrialism with its sequel. There will still be industrial activities, of course, and we'll still depend on them. But as they're becoming ever more automated and require less and less human involvement, the way we think about, manage, and act in the economy is already changing. It's the digitalization shift.

As more and more products and services become based on digital technology, more and more of the world's economic activity is channeled through the technology companies, another instance of positive feedback. I've mentioned dozens of them already, but there are dozens of others that you probably haven't heard of. Do you know Palantir?

It's a software company whose core tool analyzes massive data files to find patterns. It's used by agencies in the Department of Defense to hunt through the internet for terrorists. This wasn't relevant or even possible three decades ago, but now it's a big concern.

Palantir is both evidence of fundamental change, and also a driver of still more change, the classic positive feedback loop we saw before, a change process that comes into existence because of some sort of change, and which then causes still more change to occur.

Palantir also embodies another new business model dimension in its core functionality. All law enforcement and military organizations are now largely structured and managed with extensive guidance from Palantir and programs like it, which shows how society has shifted key thinking and pattern recognition tasks to computers. Why do this?

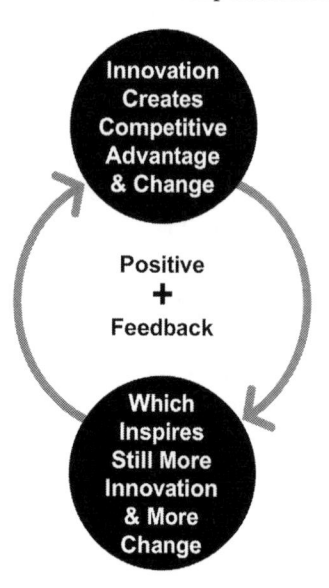

Because computers can scan through massive databases so much faster and more effectively than people can.

What we're experiencing today is just the beginning of a phenomenon that will now endure indefinitely and spread throughout every nook and cranny of civilization. Yes, it's largely about technology, but even more importantly, it's about what you can do with technology, how you can apply and deploy it to serve and to differentiate, how it shapes your business model. It's all about the knowledge, understanding, and wisdom that you can extract from the data and information.

Palantir is just one example among hundreds, a new technology that's only been available recently because it's only been technically possible recently. Like many technologies, its use drives the need for, use of, and further development of more new technologies, which then drive more change. You can easily see where this is headed – an endless cascade of new stuff, new capabilities, new behaviors, and so new business opportunities and threats.

Palantir is also notable because it's another one of those highly valued startup companies that have never been profitable. Today, growth without profit actually is a viable business model, although it's a quality that investors in previous eras would not have tolerated. It's the network effect, and the potential of a large network to eventually generate out-sized returns.

And when we consider that technology firms become massive profit machines when they pass the increasing returns crossover point, this has forced them to also become investors at the scale of hundreds of billions of dollars each year. We begin to see the cascading effect, whereby their success at

> We have begun to see a **cascading effect**, whereby success at creating profit gives successful technology companies the power to dominate through investment of their excess capital, which only **increases their domination**.

creating cash gives them power to expand, which if done even only moderately well will only increase their market power.

We thus see scale having the same effects in banking, farming, and in technology-based networks, and all of this leads us to some key questions that all business model designers should ask themselves:

How can we generate these network effects in our business model?
How can we establish a platform presence?
How can we induce a positive feedback cycle?

Concentration

It took a couple decades for the leaders of companies in the industrial economy to understand that their asset-heavy industries are typically characterized by the economics of declining marginal returns, whereas digital firms that they once eyed with such suspicion and often contempt operate according to increasing marginal returns. Do you remember when Warren Buffet said he would never invest in technology because he didn't understand it? Of course the gloating over the internet bust of 2000 didn't help them to grasp that a fundamental shift was happening, but once Amazon and Google began to grow rapidly, their awareness shifted, and the iPhone-induced transformation has made the point definitively. Understanding change has required a new mental model, while those who still cling to the old ways will undoubtedly suffer because of it. They'll be the ones ignoring the actual rate of change, and sitting on the going-out-of-business curve.

The 'Going Out of Business' Line
Source: Gyr and Freidman

There's no doubt that digitalization is now driving a compelling process of wealth creation, and there's also no doubt that new technologies which have not yet arrived will compound and accelerate this process.

This shift to digitalization is also driving an unprecedented concentration of economic power in the hands of a very few companies that have grasped leadership in important markets. This isn't new, as the same thing happened repeatedly throughout the history of the modern era going back to 1800, and even earlier than that; all that has changed is that the types of companies have changed as the economy has evolved, and now it's the digital leaders that have the mojo.

The first companies to figure out steam power and large scale manufacturing dominated in the early 1800s; in the late 1800s it was the steel companies, railroads and oil firms that earned their founders the uncomfortable title of "robber barons" as they came to dominate. In early 1900s it was autos and mass production, Fordism and the assembly line, and the creation of the first mass markets. Mid-century saw the growth of consumerism, shopping malls, suburbia, and by the 1980s it was financial services that led.

And now we have shifted into the era of technology dominance.

Manufacturing, autos, railroads, steel, oil, and consumer goods are all still essential parts of the economy, but as they've matured they're no longer able to generate disproportionate profits. Decades of competition have eroded the differentiation between the various competitors in most industries, and while the best still outperform the others, the gaps have mostly narrowed.

Let's take the airlines as an example. In the 1960s the airline industry in the US was highly regulated, which left air fares relatively high, and the airlines operated with a comfortable sense of entitlement that bred arrogance. Regulations protected them from change, and also prevented them from innovating.

Entrepreneurs attempted with little success to penetrate the market, until a tiny start-up in Texas developed an entirely different business model. Instead of trying to push its fares higher, it worked to push them lower, considering its competition to be not so much the other airlines, but cars and buses (yes, in those days there was a not-quite thriving but solid business to be done with inter-city bus transportation).

To make its innovative business model work, the company, Southwest Airlines, had to rethink its entire approach to operations, which led to the creation of a wide range of innovations. For instance, it normally required an hour from when a plane landed to when it could take off again, the time to taxi, unload, reload, and get back to the runway. But operating under extreme constraints, this startup couldn't afford an hour; by thinking it through anew they got it down to ten minutes.

The ten-minute-turn was an innovation created in a crisis, and of course crisis is a common situation for any startup. The back story is that by the time Southwest had fought through all the legal and regulatory barriers that the competing airlines had thrown up, a process that took years, nearly all its cash was gone. It owned three aircraft, and it flew just three routes on a loop, Dallas to San Antonio, San Antonio to Houston, and Houston back to Dallas.

Business was looking promising and brand recognition was growing, but to make payroll early on the company was forced to sell one of its aircraft. The challenge, then, was to run the same route schedule with two planes that they had previously been flying with three.

Over a pressure-packed weekend, "an innovation SWAT team" of leaders and managers from all aspects of operations invented the ten-minute-turn, and in so doing they saved Southwest, and also developed renewed confidence in their own ability to innovate. It was a skill that they exploited to great advantage over the following decades, as Southwest built a national business and a very loyal customer following by finding innovation after innovation to grow its business.[58]

But why, you might ask, was it necessary to fly the same schedule with two aircraft as they had flown with three? Why not just cut back on the number flights? Their concern, certainly a correct one, was that cutting back on flights would signal to customers that the company was in trouble, which might quickly lead to a loss of confidence and a collapse of the business. The last thing a startup can sustain is a loss of confidence in its brand, so the company absolutely had to project confidence and strength even if behind the scenes it was taking constant innovation, heroic effort, duct tape, and rubber bands to keep the thing running.

In the end as you know it worked brilliantly, and within a decade Southwest had transformed the American air travel industry. While most other airlines struggled to sustain profitability and the big ones went through one or even two rounds of bankruptcy, Southwest thrived and grew. By the 1990s the market capitalization of Southwest was equivalent to the next five airlines combined, even through the others were all much larger by revenue and by passenger-miles flown. The difference, of course, was that Southwest was much more profitable, having mastered its business model and simultaneously redefined the basic structure of competition across the entire industry.

Alas, if you look at the market cap of the largest airlines today, Southwest no longer stands out.

What happened?

First, the other airlines went through their own gut-wrenching reinventions, changing the own business models in response to the many layers of innovation that first Southwest and then all the airlines got engaged in implementing. For example, American Airlines pioneered the frequent flyer program, AAdvantage, and got so good at creating value through loyalty that for a while the market value of AAdvantage was higher than the that of the parent company. While the airline was struggling financially and making heavy losses, AAdvantage was making handsome profits. Some stock market investors clamored for American to sell off AAdvantage as a separate company, which it wisely did not do.

Through rounds of consolidating mergers and excruciating labor negotiations, through bankruptcies that enabled them to shed massive pension obligations but left tenured employees with a fraction of their promised pension benefits, through reinventions and de-reinventions of service, by cramming seats closer together and optimizing route structures, Southwest's competitors returned to profitability by imitating as much of Southwest's innovative business model as they could.

Southwest also spawned lots of imitators that adopted its entire business model, including EasyJet, RyanAir, and WOW in Europe, Jet Blue and Virgin America in the US, and AirAsia and Dragon Air in Asia. In effect, the entire air travel industry business model was reinvented to look just like Southwest's.

The other things that happened to Southwest also happened to all of the US airlines, the macro events of 9/11/2001, 2008, and 2014. The attacks of 9/11 sank all airline stocks because it exposed a new form of vulnerability not just to their business models, but to the business of air travel itself. Terrorism, the business model of fear, hit all the airlines hard. Southwest was hit perhaps worst of all, and it was hit again by the global financial crisis of 2008.

Part 2: Innovation Strategy

Things turned around significantly in 2014 when oil prices dropped by two-thirds, which of course had a major impact on the profitability of all airlines. All their stocks gained significantly.

Since then, however, Southwest hasn't introduced any transformative innovations, and so the magnificent business model innovations that brilliantly differentiated Southwest for its first three decades ran their course, and in statistical terms we would say that Southwest has regressed to the mean of its peers. The forces of competition combined with geopolitics and macroeconomics pulled Southwest and the other airlines into relative parity.

And this is the story of just about every industry, going back thousands of years – eventually the innovators run out of transformative ideas, and competition evens things out.

Is anything different today? Today, the "eventually" part of the equation can be lightning quick, largely because the rate of innovation in technology is so fast. Technology innovations are driving business model innovations, enabling new products, services, and relationships to evolve very quickly, a process we must to continue at its breakneck pace for at least the coming few decades; this is the relentless pattern of constant reinvention.

Look at your smart phone, and count the apps that you use regularly, none of which existed fifteen years ago. Most of them didn't even exist five years ago. The things that you do with your phone today used to require a whole set of different devices. A camera for pictures, a video camera for movies, a music player like a Walkman, a TV, a cinema, a pager, a watch, a calculator, a compass, a map book (printed), an alarm clock, a Gameboy, and we read the news on something you don't see much

Delta	$34.2
Southwest	$26.1
United	$22.8
American	$14.8
Lufthansa	$10.7
China Southern	$10.7
Air France	$4.6

Market Cap
Selected Airlines
Jan 1, 2019

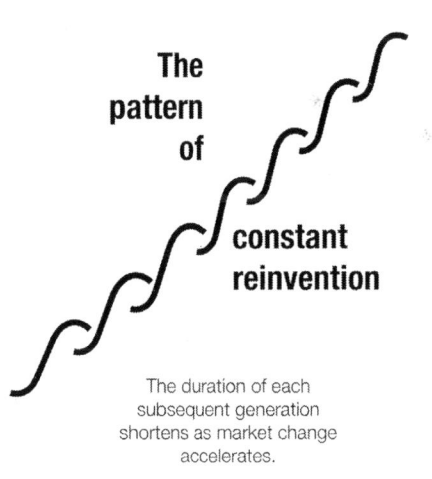

The pattern of constant reinvention

The duration of each subsequent generation shortens as market change accelerates.

anymore, a "news-paper."

Now we get all that and much more on our phones.

Successfully transformative technologies are not common, but when they arrive create their own demand, and they feed this change cycle. They become platforms upon which entire ecosystems of other products, services, and companies operate in their sub-niches.

Think about the apps that you'll rely on five or ten years in the future. Do you have any idea what they'll be? It's a difficult question, and we really can only guess; foresight fails us here because we're dangerously likely to merely extrapolate current experiences, when what's more likely are radical leaps. Why leaps? Because the rate of improvement of technology is accelerating and will enable functions tomorrow that we have difficulty even conceiving of today.

What we should expect is that they'll be even more central to our lives than the apps we already rely so much upon today.

But there's a dangerous assumption embedded in the question – did you notice it? The framing of the question assumes that we'll use "apps" on "phones." How likely is that?

It's much more probable that within a decade, apps and phones as we know them today will be entirely outmoded, gone, obsolete relics, replaced instead by better ways to organize and access information and tools.

After all, won't our clothes be our computing devices? Won't chips be embedded under our skin? Or worn like bandaids, or like tiny fake moles or beauty marks?

Well, that's not the future we're talking about because it's already happening. Chips are already under our skin, at least they can be if you're Swedish. 3000 Swedes have tiny chips implanted in their hands in a technology trial, through which they buy access to public transit by merely walking onto the train, the tiny chip communicating via RFID.[59] All it takes a special needle to inject the chip, which is the size of a grain of rice. This a technology that obviously soon will find lots of uses (many of which are already or soon will be illegal).

And chips are already in clothing, too – Tommy Hilfiger sells shirts with its own embedded version of *Pokemon Go* sewn into the fabric, and NBA souvenir jerseys have RFID chips embedded in them that communicate with your phone, only two examples among hundreds (thousands?).

An interesting and thought-provoking variation on this is Zozo, which makes a full body suit covered with 350 position markers. Put the suit on, take photos with your phone, send them to Zozo, and they'll happily make custom-fit clothing just for you.[60] This business model combines the physical and the online, applying technology in clever ways, and while it may or may not succeed, what matters is how it inspires us to consider the potential impact of a clever business model innovation focused on 100% customization at scale, and to think about the cleverness of our own that it might inspire.

Business models are in flux today because we live in a rapidly-changing society with a rapidly developing technological foundation that's busily rendering many business models entirely obsolete, while it's simultaneously enabling new business models to come into existence. The pace of innovation is accelerating, putting increasing pressure on all companies, and driving many of them out of existence. No matter what your organization does, there's no question that technology is absolutely central to the future of your market, and to your organization's business model.

Companies are being driven to death **by the rate of** innovation

Let's take a deeper look at what's coming.

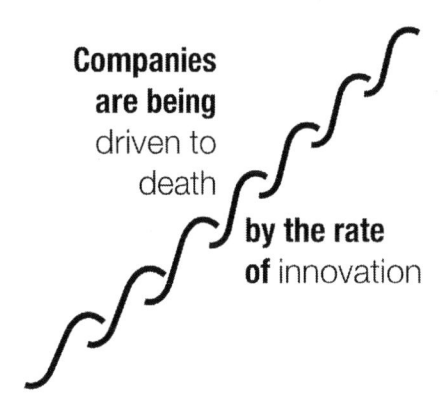

Chapter 19
IT'S THE TECHNOLOGY …
But It's Not Stupid

Numeracy is the ability to count and calculate with numbers. It originated unknown thousands of years ago as a learned, cultural skill, but then about five thousand years ago with the invention and spread of money, the ability to count became an essential survival skill and it spread quickly throughout civilization.

A computer chip is, at root, just a fancy and speedy device for counting, and as Charles Babbage and Ada Lovelace understood nearly 200 years ago, when you can count you can do much more than just count, you can organize, design, decide, and act. Today, as a result, even a basic auto has 30 to 50 computer chips that are busily counting to control nearly everything from acceleration to braking to gear shifting, along with all the various motors that operate windows and wipers and fans and lights. Chips are also essential to the many sensors that monitor the car's functioning, its position, and its surroundings. A luxury car with even more gizmos and gadgets may have 100 chips, along with as many as 100 to 200 *million* lines of computer code that tell the chips what to do and process the data they collect.

This partly explains why hardly anyone can fix their own cars any more. Digital diagnostics are essential, and so while Tesla cars perform

Part 2: Innovation Strategy

software-driven self-diagnostics continuously, without the million-dollar diagnostics machines the do-it-yourselfer is just out of luck. When necessary, Teslas can be reprogrammed from the central factory location because they're connected wirelessly to the internet. So, too, by the way, are the jet engines your airline uses to fly you around the world, monitored remotely and constantly so no one has to look inside to know how the engine is performing.

This conquest of society by the computer chip suggests that a car is no longer a car as we have previously thought of it, it's really just a computer with wheels. A road, the one covered with sensors, is a computer for driving the other computers upon, a house is a computer for living within, an office one for working in, and clothing is soon to be computers for wearing.

Where this logic takes us is to the recognition that fairly soon we'll stop thinking about computers as separate things, because computing capabilities will be embedded everywhere. The term 'computer' will likely disappear from common usage, or maybe it will switch back to what it used to mean, referring to a person with advanced math skills as it did half a century ago before the PC and the internet came along.

Knowing, then, that computer chips are the small (and getting smaller), inexpensive (and getting cheaper), and hidden enablers of the digital economy that are tucked away inside every device, and knowing that chips are continuing to get more powerful and less expensive, we also gain insight into why robots are now becoming common: the very powerful chips and sophisticated computer code they required now exists, and can perform the massive volume of information processing that's necessary for robots to do useful work.

At the current rate of improvement, in ten year's time a generic computer chip will be about thirty times more powerful than today's comparably generic chip. Imagine, then, what a magnificent

The conquest of society by the computer chip means that a car is no longer a car, **it's a computer with wheels.**

Roads are covered with sensors so they're **computers for driving the other computers upon.**

A house is **a computer for living within**, an office one for working in, and clothing is soon to be computers for living in.

metallic/silicon thinking beast you'll be able to create then, and then consider what the economic impact is likely to be. The likelihood of another wave in the digital revolution takes hold in your mind, and as robots get better, human workers will become even more expendable.

The robots are coming ...

Here Come the Bots

No, they're here. A fast food restaurant named Spyce recently opened in Boston, and its kitchen operates almost entirely with robots; it will be no surprise that the prototype was developed in the basement of an MIT frat house.

By the time you read this, Spyce may already be a distant memory, but then again perhaps it will have become the next McDonald's, operating in hundreds of locations where it will utilize thousands of robots. And whether Spyce succeeds or fails, it's surely a sign of things to come, or more accurately, of robots to come.

Seven hardy robots busily at work cooking lunches at Spyce Restaurant, Boston.
One of them made my lunch.

Robots have been living in our imaginations for centuries, where we have seen them laboring for us to improve our lives and eliminate the drudgery of menial and heavy tasks. Greek myths described machines that moved on their own many centuries before Mary Shelly's story of Dr. Frankenstein, and it will not surprise you that Leonardo da Vinci sketched designs for a mechanical military knight that we would today think of as a robot. In our own time, these myths along with countless science fiction stories are quickly becoming science and social facts.

Part 2: Innovation Strategy

The first crude and very experimental robots were built in labs in the 1970s, and now as we approach their half-century, robots are commonplace and highly productive laborers.

Of course we find more uses for them now that their capabilities are increasing so fast, which is a result of the increasing power of their computer chips and the increasing skill of programmers who write the necessary computer code.

How many are there? Amazon.com reportedly uses more than 100,000 warehouse robots, up from the mere 25,000 that the company used just 2 years ago. We might call them 'digital laborers,' but the idea that machines replace humans is not a new story. In fact, it is the essential story of industrialization.

The mechanization of agriculture and manufacturing during the 1800s enabled the transformation of the economy and society in every respect, so what we're experiencing is perhaps just the next steps in this process.

What today's robots all have in common is that they perceive their environments through arrays of sensors, process the collected data to determine patterns and decide actions, and act in their environments to produce outcomes. That is, they accomplish work.

As nearly all of this was formerly done by people, we fear that robots may displace human workers on such a large scale as to cause massive unemployment, and thus massive social disruption. When robots run the farms and the factories and drive the vehicles and cook the meals you begin to wonder if people will have any work to do at all.

Will they replace your job? Will they replace your company's business model?

Some of today's most useful robots are simple devices only by today's high standards. Amazon robots organize stacks of bins so humans can pick the items you ordered, small robots vacuum your carpets, security robots roam parking garages, while gigantic mining trucks go up and down the mine roads without human drivers.

'CIMON' is NASA's AI robot on the International Space Station, Baxter a delivery robot in hospitals, and countless companies and universities are working on new ones with the intention of creating new products, or as learning tools to train the next generations of highly advanced robot designers and engineers.

Yes, we do have to ask if they'll cause mass unemployment, or conversely if they'll enable mass creativity and mass leisure. If we follow the economic logic of industrialism in which all factors of production are made into commodities, then unemployment is probably the outcome, but the social costs of this will be so enormous that we may indeed choose a different way. This, too, implies a different economic logic, not industrialism but something else.

Prudential Billboard

And yes, there are already sex robots (sexbots), as many companies anticipate a huge market and are already quite far along in their development; entrepreneurs are even now planning to open sexbot brothels.[61]

This trend is already so advanced that the term 'bot' is universally understood to mean something that does something with a computer, or as a computer: sexbots, chatbots, warbots, kitchenbots, twitterbots, and more taskbots are arriving daily to tackle more jobs.

Another intriguing and also intimidating prospect is that robots will eventually design, build, and then quickly improve themselves and other robots at a pace so fast that humans are left behind entirely. This scary possibility even has a name: it's called the 'singularity.'

The Singularity

The terms 'artificial intelligence' and 'machine learning' describe the capacity of machines to gather information, make interpretations, and initiate actions to achieve desired outcomes, all with little or no human participation. When we peer a bit further into the future we wonder what might happen when the power of a computer approaches the processing power of a human brain. Would that computer be as 'smart' as a human? And how long would it take for that computer to design and build a family of still better computers, thereby rapidly accelerating their own development and leaving humans a distant second in brainpower, relegated to an entirely dystopian or even post-human landscape?

The possibility that computers will equal and then exceed human intelligence, and then through a spiraling process of self-improvement far surpass humanity, has been given the name 'singularly.' The technical meaning of singularity, a term borrowed from physics, is the point in time and space at which the known rules break down into something quite else, quite unknown, and presently unrecognizable. A black hole is a singularity described by physics, and so is the super-smart, uber-brained robot a potential singularly due it's possible impact human society.

By charting the historical development of computing power and projecting it into the future, computer scientist Ray Kurzweil has forecast that by the 2040s the computation power of chips will reach and then surpass that of humans. According to Kurzweil's calculation, computers capable of simulating human brains will exist by 2025, and by 2045 nonbiological intelligence will be one billion times *more* powerful than all human intelligence was in 2005. This is the point at which humans become evolutionarily obsolete,

"The Singularity is a future period during which the pace of technological change will be so rapid, its impact so deep, that human life will be irreversibly transformed.

"Within several decades, information-based technologies will encompass all human knowledge and proficiency.

"By the end of the 21st century, the nonbiological portion of our intelligence will be trillions of trillions of times more powerful than unaided human intelligence.

We are now in the early stages of this transition."

Ray Kurzweil
The Singularity is Near

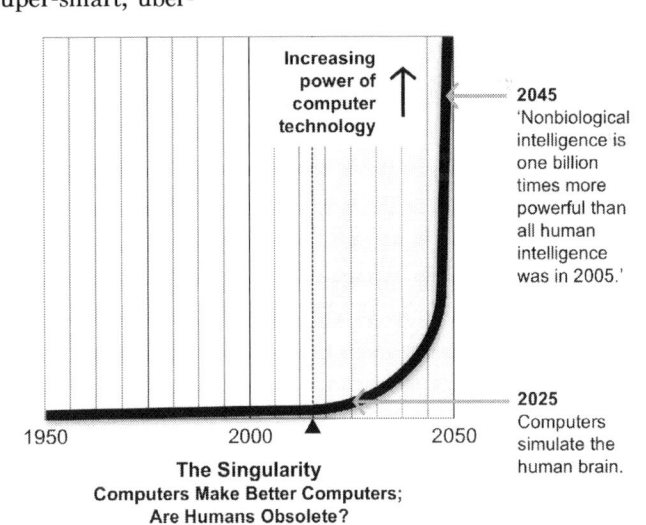

2045
'Nonbiological intelligence is one billion times more powerful than all human intelligence was in 2005.'

2025
Computers simulate the human brain.

The Singularity
Computers Make Better Computers;
Are Humans Obsolete?

surpassed by our digital creations. What this will mean for the digital economy is impossible to predict, but fascinating to consider.

Kurzweil makes a strong argument in his fascinating 600 page book *The Singularity is Near*,[62] but he could just as easily be completely wrong. Perhaps computers will never become *that* powerful; perhaps essential qualities of thought and intelligence actually *cannot* be replicated in computer code; perhaps the economy will falter and economic progress will stop before the singularity arrives; perhaps human-level robotic intelligence will be outlawed. But if Kurzweil is right, and his forecast does indeed come to pass, what then? Then, everything changes...

This discussion about computer chips, robots, the singularity, and the emerging digital economy could go on for hundreds of fascinating and frightening pages. Clearly it's all about disruption, and obviously it's pretty much all disruption all the time from now until forever.

And it's not just about robots, as there are plenty of other disruptive technologies heading our way. Such as ...

Facial Recognition

While the Chinese use facial recognition for everyday police work, *Rolling Stone* has reported that pop musician Taylor Swift, who has hundreds of stalkers, is also using facial recognition software at her concerts to scan the crowd, hoping to identify them:

> "Fans of the pop star were unknowingly monitored by facial-recognition technology at Swift's May 2018 performance at the Rose Bowl in Los Angeles. The system, built into a kiosk showcasing rehearsal footage for Swift's Reputation tour, was intended to weed out people who threaten the pop star. Images taken at Swift's performance, were sent to a command post in Nashville to be cross-referenced against a database that included

hundreds of people who had stalked the singer in the past."[63]

Reminds you a bit of some recent science fiction, except it's not fiction. The emergence of widespread public surveillance is also not fiction, and not only in China.

If you walk around New York City and look carefully you'll notice police cameras mounted throughout the city, usually with a sign nearby advising us that we're under video surveillance. New York has invested heavily, with 2000 cameras on city streets, 7000 in public housing, and 4000 more in the subway system. The police can also tap into 4000 private cameras, for a total of 17,000 opportunities to track you and the other millions people also moving throughout the city. 17,000 cameras operating 24 hours a day creates data at the rate of thousands of petabytes, but the camera count is probably already out of date and the data rate is rising, as more are being added all the time.

exabyte: 1 quintillion bytes

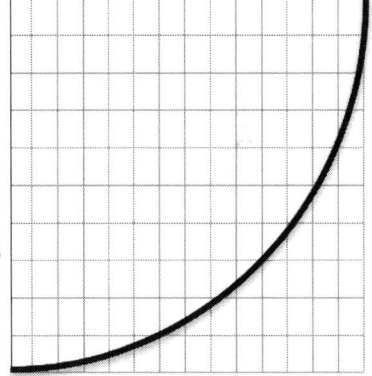

petabyte: 1 quadrillion bytes
terabyte: 1 trillion bytes
gigabyte: 1 billion bytes
megabyte: 1 million bytes

Bytes

But wait – who's looking at all those video feeds? It would take thousands of people to look at these street scene videos all day and all night, which would defeat the purpose of replacing people with technology. Instead, software analyzes the files, looking for suspicious behaviors that AI-trained software can now indeed identify. And, as Taylor Swift's security team has done, to apply facial recognition to identify exactly who you are.

There's sound recognition, too. For example, strategically placed acoustic sensors that detect gunshots revealed that the extent of firearms activity (i.e., gunshots) in some U.S. neighborhoods was much higher than most people, including the police, had realized. Police departments used to believe that citizens would call 911 about 80 percent of the time after shots were fired in their neighborhoods, only to find that it actually can be as low as 20 percent. This surprising discovery led to many quite useful changes in how police monitor neighborhoods and assign patrols. Now, instead of (mistaken) assumptions about where guns are being used and how frequently the public calls in to report them, sensors provide accurate data upon which to make decisions.

IoT and the Surveillance State

This is the essence of the IoT (internet of things) phenomenon – collecting data where such data never existed before, and using those data to make better decisions, and thus shifting from a reactive to a proactive stance.

Shanghai

IoT implementations enable police departments to collect many new forms of data on urban crime, which has many implications, not all of which seem so positive. For example, I recently took a taxi from my hotel in the center of Shanghai to the Pudong airport, and during the 30 minute ride I counted about 20 times that the taxi's license plate was scanned or photographed via a fixed monitor that was quite visibly mounted on a giant beam that spanned across the freeway. (I probably missed some of them, too.) This implies that the Shanghai city government knows where nearly all the city's 2.5 million cars are at all times, (assuming, that is, that their software is good enough to sort that out, which is a reasonably safe assumption). In authoritarian states this is now the disturbing, big-brother norm.

Deepfakes

The flip side of accurate facial recognition is the fake face, or "deepfake," which is a computer generated image or video that depicts not real events, but made up ones. This can make for interesting entertainment, but also for frighteningly effective propaganda.

Imagine the intense and violent reaction that would occur if a video clip went live on Facebook showing a Western government official planning a covert operation for political assassination in China, or a video depicting a political leader burning a Koran. Recent advances in artificial intelligence technology has led to the creation of "deepfakes," fakes so convincing that they are *impossible to distinguish from the real thing.*

Deepfakes are produced by artificial intelligence systems that learn through neural networks in which pairs of algorithms are pitted against one another, one to generate content, and the other to assess it. By working together at very high speeds, the two create a positive-feedback learning system that quickly results in realistic, but fake, content.[64] In the hands of terrorists or other provocateurs the consequences could be disastrous, instantly fabricated riots, and even wars. Deepfakes are already common in pornography, and in our era of "fake news" and rampant disinformation, the line between real and fake, genuine and made up, is dissolving before our eyes.

> By working together at very high speeds, two computers create a **positive-feedback learning system.**

The cinema version of this is special effects, which are already so good that, "We can put any digitalized animal next to a real one and not be able to tell the difference," according to Disney's Richard Stammers.[65]

Ray Kurzweil's expectation for the arrival of the singularity is based on the idea that computers will soon be able to learn, and that their pace of learning will vastly surpass that of humans. It appears that this is no longer just a theoretical possibility.

Biotech

Just as the boom in computer chip technology is leading to new threats and possibilities across the spectrum of all high technology and communications industries, so chip technology has enabled breakthroughs in the life sciences as well.

In a bit of scientific-historical shorthand, observers have noted that the 19th century was the century of chemistry (such as the Periodic Table, steel, pharmaceuticals, and fertilizers), the 20th the century of physics (weapons, power systems, aerodynamics, space travel), and now in the 21st it's the century of biology, the design of alterations to the codes of life.

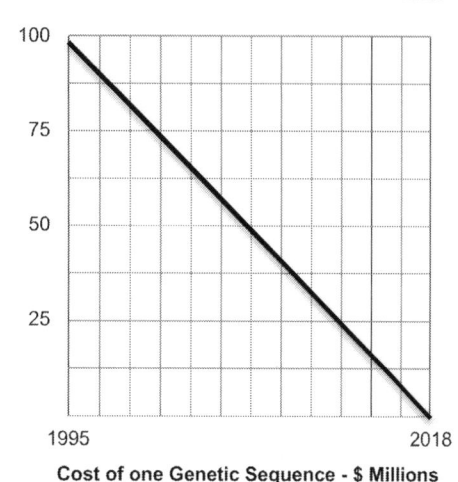

Hence, a very real technology that was once a matter of speculation but is now a daily occurrence in the lab offers the means to alter our DNA. That is, biologists and geneticists now have the tools that enable them to create clones, to alter individual genes through CRISPR, to select in or out preferred or unwanted qualities and characteristics, all of which are capabilities that also depend on progressively cheaper digital genetic sequencing technology, and all of which are altering the global gene pool day by day.

This naturally raises many concerns, including some expressed by scientists themselves. The three presidents of the US National Academy of Medicine, the US National Academy

Cost of one Genetic Sequence - $ Millions

of Sciences, and the Chinese Academy of Sciences recently co-authored an editorial in Science magazine in which they stated, "The ability to use CRISPR-Cas9 to edit the human genome has outpaced nascent efforts by the scientific and medical communities to confront the complex ethical and governance issues that they raise."[66] Science, in other words, has outpaced society, and is now capable of introducing change that society does not fully understand, and which it cannot control. So it's no longer *risk* we're talking about it's *RISK* at the macro level of all human society.

Meanwhile, the marriage of biology and technology is yielding many breakthroughs in health care. For example, a hybrid of biology and computer science is the nanogenerator-powered-electric-bandage, more mundane the gene editing, but nevertheless with significant consequences:

> "Researchers in the US and China recently developed self-powered electric bandages that promise to be as easy to wear as ordinary dressings. They include tiny electrodes powered by nanogenerators wrapped around your torso, and all you have to do is breathe – the movement of your ribcage activates the nanogenerators, sending low-intensity pulses to the wound area. While it's not fully clear how the pulses help, scientists noted that they increase the viability of fibroblasts (a kind of skin cell) and encourage them to line up, which is key to the healing process. The results in lab tests were dramatic. Wounds on rodents that took almost two weeks to heal the normal way only required three days with the electric bandage."[67]

It's all quite fascinating, the compelling and exponential growth of knowledge and the explosion of technology, and the tremendous range of these examples makes it quite obvious that no part of our lives, and no aspect of society or the economy will be untouched by these revolutions.

Blockchain

Suppose that there was a form of money, useful money that people would happily accept in trade, but it wasn't issued by any government, it was instead was created by anyone who wanted to. What then?

This is what the Bitcoin experiment is intended to find out. It's a new form of capital, digital money, (also called cybercurrency or cryptocurrency), intended to replace paper money.

Why would anyone want to do that? Because nations have the unfortunate tendency to print too much money, thereby making their currencies less valuable, which of course is bad for everyone who holds that currency. Do you remember the tragic photos of the 1920s when appalling inflation meant that people needed a wheelbarrow full of money to buy a loaf of bread? Runaway inflation happens when the government creates oversupply in order to buy more of whatever it wants, whether that's guns and aircraft carriers, jobs and urban infrastructure, or foreign exchange.

The dream of a digital currency as the remedy to inflation has existed for a long time, but it wasn't until a long list of conceptual and technical barriers were solved that it recently became possible. The blockchain is thus a set of techniques used to represent information in computer code using nearly immutable records, significant not only as a technical platform on which Bitcoin operates, but also for many other uses. It thus it appears that this technology is likely to become just as disruptive as the internet itself has proven to be.

For instance, since blockchain records are nearly immutable, they're ideal for storing public records, because immutability prevents fraud, theft, and corruption. Hence, property ownership records stored on blockchains in corruption-prone cities would significantly improve

Part 2: Innovation Strategy

protection for owners, preventing illegal land seizures that are today common across many parts of the world. Blockchains also make complex business transactions easier to accomplish, and they therefore facilitate trade.

They also authenticate identity, ownership, and even represent abstract qualities including 'trust,' 'reliability,' and 'reputation' in digital form. The United Nations, for example, is developing blockchain-based identity records for stateless inhabitants of its many refugee camps, which will enable people who would otherwise be trapped to emigrate, get jobs, and rebuild their lives.

Blockchain-based 'tokens' are evolving into a new form of securities, smart securities in which the rules for ownership and transfer are written into the design of the token itself, thereby preventing fraud while promoting transparency and compliance.

What blockchain technology lacks at present is a friendly and easy-to-understand public face, and so most explanations of what blockchains are and could become are expressed with mountains of unrecognizable and unhelpful jargon, but that's only temporary, because it's an entirely new technical language, one that's still being invented to describe an entirely new capability whose implications are still being discovered.

But then it wasn't so long ago that we didn't know what 'TCP-IP' was, or the 'world wide web,' a 'browser,' a 'Boolean search,' a 'search engine,' 'wifi,' 'bluetooth,' 'emoji,' or 'app store.' Now they're all common knowledge and part of everyday life, and when blockchains fulfill their potential then today's obscure and unrecognizable language will mature and be simplified to become just as familiar.

•••

All this technology – AI, IoT, Deepfakes, precision agriculture, electric

> According to the World Economic Forum, the cost of processing trade documents is as much as a fifth the cost of transport. Removing administrative blockages in supply chains could do more to boost international trade than eliminating tariffs.
>
> According to the United Nations, full digitalization of trade paperwork could raise exports from Asia-Pacific countries alone by $250 billion per year.
>
> *The Economist*
> March 24, 2018

bandages, kitchen robots, sexbots, facial recognition, pervasive surveillance, the singularity, blockchain, and biotech doesn't just have enormous potential for disruption, it's *already* profoundly disrupting the market, society, and the economy. New companies, new strategies, and new business models are cropping up everywhere, which should lead you pretty quickly to raise the question,

What does all this mean for my business model?

And you're exactly right to ask that.

Because the consequences for your business model are likely going to be decisive, even overwhelming. These forces will impact you no matter what your industry, and you're going to have to change; the sooner you get started the better off you will be.

How to begin? What questions should we ask? This is not only a question of intellectual curiosity and strategic anticipation, it's also very much a question of leadership, your leadership, which we consider next.

Part 3
INNOVATION LEADERSHIP

Innovation is one of the most important achievements that any organization can attain, as it's though innovation that they create their futures, and thus prolong their viability.

And we know from all the literature and from every study and every one of the bazillions of books on the subject that leadership is absolutely essential to success at innovation. This is not because the leaders are the innovators themselves, but because they put into place the policies and programs and funding that makes innovation possible, and because they align innovation efforts with organizational strategy.

Conversely, leaders can also kill innovation, squash it flat. They do this either by neglecting it or by subverting it. Hence, leadership is essential to innovation, and as innovation is essential to future survival, developing the skills necessary to effectively lead innovation is no longer optional. These skills are the subject here in Part 3.

Chapter 20
GROWTH AND MATURITY
Sustaining Success or Losing the Mojo

In 2017 a new CEO was appointed to lead struggling General Electric because his predecessor had made a series of costly strategic blunders. In 2018 the new guy was fired.

GE's drama is a fascinating example of the immense challenges facing those who lead giant global corporations in these times of accelerating change, and it's interesting not only for the story itself, but also as a harbinger of the broader shift across the entire manufacturing sector.

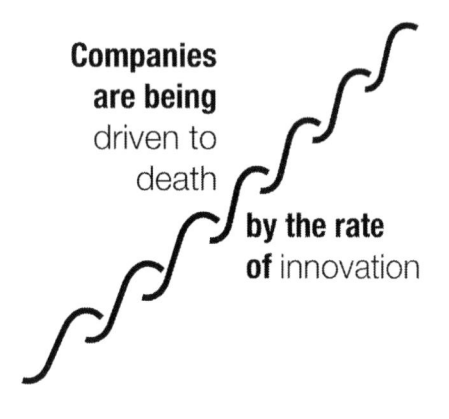

Companies are being driven to death **by the rate of** innovation

Here's what *The Economist* wrote about the fired CEO, John Flannery, in October 2018: "He may have been pointing GE in the right direction but he was not moving fast enough, perhaps because he was too much of an insider to make cuts of the necessary severity and speed."[68]

Here again are themes we've already been discussing repeatedly – too much attachment to the old ways, moving too slowly, not adequately recognizing or acknowledging change, and being driven to death by change, by innovation. During the course of Mr. Flannery's one short year as GE's CEO, the firm dropped a stunning $100 billion in market value, showing that the stock market had also little confidence in his leadership.

A follow up story four weeks later noted that in GE's power division alone, a manufacturer of huge turbines, the company was obliged to write down a catastrophic $22 billion of "good will" from its balance sheet. The term "good will" is a vague, catch-all category, but the write-down suggests that even the company's accountants knew that there had been a significant deterioration in the company's standing in the market.

Dropping that much value off the balance sheet will mean, among other consequences, that GE will face higher costs to borrow working capital, and this higher operating costs, thereby compounding the miseries that the new CEO Larry Culp will have to cope with.

In response to this and other difficulties, Culp was immediately obliged to reduce GE's quarterly stock dividend by 92%, which put it down at the very lowest it could possibly be above zero, as it now sits at one miniscule penny per share.

> "When the rate of change in the marketplace exceeds the rate of change in the organization, **the end is in sight.**"
>
> Jack Welch
> Former CEO of GE, accurately prophesying the challenges facing his successors

Another American industrial giant, IBM, has also been suffering from revenue declines for 22 straight quarters from 2013 onward, more than five years, suggesting that it, too, is trapped in a mindset problem as well as a market problem. But is it fair to call IBM an "industrial" company? After all, it famously transformed its business model back in 1992 from genuinely being a manufacturing company – a manufacturer of mainframe computers – to being primarily a software and services company.

That transformation was led by Louis Gerstner, and it marked perhaps the unofficial start of the shift to a software-driven world economy, coinciding as it did with the early days of the internet and prefiguring all the changes the internet has subsequently wrought.

In operations and mindset IBM does seem to be slow-to-change, and thus IBM's current CEO Ginni Rometty has presided over the five year slide while trying so far unsuccessfully to transform the company's business model again, now from software and services to cloud computing. But IBM realized the need for this shift later than its more nimble competitors like Salesforce, and it hasn't been able to catch up.

This trap is perhaps the most common one that successful firms fall into, as once a company gets its products, services, operations, and supply chain all functioning decently well, all the "means" fully aligned, and it has customers willing to pay, it's only common sense to pour intense effort into sustaining the momentum of this super-complex system to extract every last centime of value from the massive investment.

But then, sooner or later, a competitor comes along with a different and possibly better business model, and then what? Then the game changes, and the company has to respond, or face the consequences in lost market share. Slip too far and you become like IBM, with revenue declines each quarter; keep slipping and you're like Sears, first walking dead, and then just plain dead.

Highly preferable to waiting for the competitors to disrupt your business model with a better one is to come up with the better one of *your* own. That doesn't happen nearly as often as it should, primarily for reasons of leadership and mindset, and so the lesson is clear enough:

In today's world your choices are to disrupt, or wait and be disrupted.

But why is it so common for established firms to wait too long to change?

Part of the challenge that gigantic companies face is that they have many different types of competitors that can pick off finely targeted pieces from the giant's market share, leaving the giants in the vulnerable position of suffering a painful death-by-a-thousand cuts experience. They suffer further because their most senior and in some cases also most talented and experienced executives aren't actually running businesses and interacting with customers directly, they're running conglomerates of businesses.

Thus, a bit of black humor often expressed at GE was that GE's business unit leaders had their "faces toward corporate headquarters and their rear ends toward the customer."[69] (But they didn't say "rear ends.") This wasn't just a saying, it was the day-to-day experience of even the most senior business unit leaders. Even those in charge of $5, $10 or $20 billion P&Ls still had to answer to corporate and pay taxes to corporate. This can only be a hindrance to the quickness and agility that these times of rapid change require, and one of the reasons to anticipate the full demise of the industrial conglomerate model. And since most don't control their own R&D budgets, they can't invest in the future even when they know what to invest in.

GE is already spinning off its health care subsidiary into a separate company via an IPO, and Pfizer and GlaxoSmithKline (GSK) recently announced a deal that will split GSK into two separate companies, one of which will merge with a Pfizer unit to create a global behemoth. Said GSK's CEO Emma Walmsley, "Ultimately, our goal is to create two exceptional, UK-based global companies, with appropriate capital structures, that are each well positioned to deliver improving returns to shareholders and significant benefits to patients and consumers."[70] Apparently that's better done as two companies rather than one.

Thus, all the huge industrial conglomerates face a possible future in which they're broken up and sold off in pieces, the conglomerate model itself a victim of accelerating change because it's just too slow to change, and the expected advantages of scale do not materialize across disparate business units, but only in a unified business model. GE faces this possible fate right now, and IBM will face it within the next couple years, as may others including Tata in India, Siemens, and 3M.

Asset-Light Business Models

Here's another piece of data that sheds light on the demise of the industrial conglomerate. *The Economist* reported in July 2018 that as of the end of 2017, China's internet giant Alibaba had a total market value roughly comparable to the 700 largest Chinese industrial firms combined, which in and of itself is astonishing, and yet in total it owned but 12% of their combined assets, another astonishment.[71]

Naturally, if "technology" is capable of yielding comparable or even superior value with substantially less capital investment than "industry," then surely there are economic consequences. Hence, we see the shift of investment to high tech companies, and the growth in their stock prices even as the old firms languish.

Indeed, another key observation in the article was that the world's biggest tech firms, predominantly American and Chinese, have accumulated such massive amounts of cash that they are now of necessity becoming gigantic investors themselves. They're spreading it into everything from acquisitions (like IBM's 2018 purchase of Red Hat for $34 billion, and Microsoft's purchase of LinkedIn for $24 billion in 2016), to facilities (like Apple's $5 billion headquarters UFO in Cupertino and its $1 billion campus in Austin, and Amazon Web Services $9 billion investment in data center server farms), to R&D (Facebook spends $14 billion each year, up from $3 billion only five years ago).

This only reaffirms the ever-more predominant role that technology is going to continue to play in the economy, not only as a force for what it does, but as a force for where it channels the money – primarily to other technology firms. Still, R&D spending is will not be a panacea for Facebook. Just ask Nokia. At its peak, Nokia was one of the world's biggest R&D spenders, but massive R&D spending does not a successful company make when your core product is suddenly the distant second choice. As noted above, it's the process rather than the dollar amount that matters, but alas, Nokia's senior management just loved their core product so much that they couldn't see the iPhone as a credible competitor.

And that's exactly the challenge that business leaders face, they tend to get so deeply attached to their existing business models, and they protect them so diligently and for far too long, trying to keep the old mojo going long past its viability. The s-curve model shows this quite clearly.

The Danger Zone
The downturn is coming.
Do we foresee it in time?

New technologies, new attitudes and expectations and behaviors, new advances by competitors, all of these factors change the market. If we learn one thing from GE, IBM, and Nokia, this is it.

Still, it's perfectly well within the reach of established companies to be the innovators and come up with the new ways themselves, and by rights they are often in a better position to do it successfully. They have staff, market share, market knowledge, and cash flow, but they are so often trapped in a backwards-looking mindset that they fail to innovate, leaving open opportunities that younger, nimbler competing firms are hungry to exploit.

So when established companies *don't* change, then they leave openings the size of the Grand Canyon for competitors to step in and demonstrate a better way, and of course this is nothing new, as it describes the history of business competition since commerce began thousands of years ago.

Part 3 is entitled "Leadership" because the lack of innovation really is a leadership problem.

From Challenger to Leader

But what happens when the upstart becomes the incumbent? What happens when it's no longer Apple vs. Nokia, but Apple has the target on its back and it's everyone vs. Apple? What happens when Blockbuster is long gone and now Netflix is the incumbent giant?

When Netflix has completely monopolized and saturated its market (if that ever happens) then the nature of its business will change fundamentally, from acquiring new members for growth, to sustaining current members and avoiding shrinkage. And who wants to make that harder? All the companies that want to take market share and members away from Netflix, as now that Netflix has locked in the successful business model it's become the target that Disney, Apple, Amazon, and soon Walmart will focus on.

And thus a fundamental problem that all mature businesses face is that managing during growth is fundamentally different from managing when growth slows or stops. Often it's even difficult to know exactly where you are on the curve.

Sears, for example, was enjoying the view from Sears Tower and apparently didn't even know it had peaked when it negligently left a void in the market that allowed Walmart to establish itself and grow. What was the void? Walmart stores were located in smaller rural markets that Sears had assumed to be nonviable. Sam Walton knew differently, because it was his home turf. He knew first hand that the interstate highway system had changed behaviors all across rural America, where it was now just no big deal to drive 30 or 40 miles to do some shopping.

Walmart smartly added many stores without going head to head with

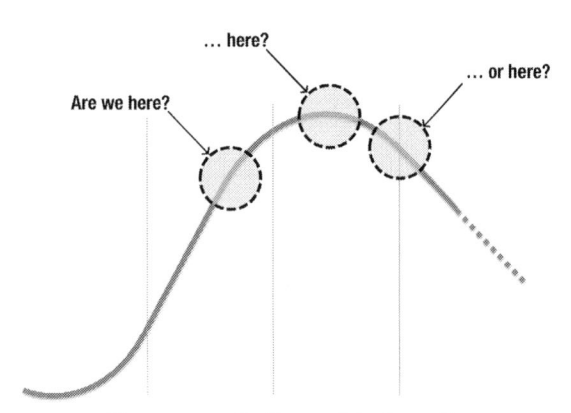

Where are we on the S-curve of development?
Sometimes it is not easy to know.

Sears, keeping a low profile as it gained scale. It then applied innovation processes throughout its growing supply chain to significantly lower its overall operating costs, at which point it was strong enough to compete directly with Sears, K-Mart, and Target in their urban markets. Sears became a second-tier player almost before it realized what had happened, while K-Mart soon found itself in bankruptcy. (And then, strangely, Sears CEO Edward Lampert decided that a merger of the two failed companies was the solution for both.) Target tried to find its own mojo through a strategy of clever product design, and it has fared better.

The underlying point worth emphasizing is that Walmart's success has been based not on the products in its store (every store carries the same stuff now), but primarily on how it managed its supply chain to optimize efficiency, which enabled the company to lower its prices and establish a brand promise that resonated throughout its market, and was captured in the slogan that the company still uses, "Always Lower Prices." Sears never even imagined making a claim like that, much less that such a claim that could be kept. Walmart grew while Sears contracted.

A side note, but a relevant one, is that Walmart's booming growth coincides exactly with the boom in Chinese manufacturing and the shift of massive volumes of production from the US to China. These two booms are not a coincidence, they're connected in cause and effect. Although American by brand identity, Walmart's dominance has come through its skill at utilizing offshore manufacturing, and thus at the expense of American manufacturing jobs. Walmart's "always lower prices" have thus come at a high cost for rural American manufacturers, a bitter irony to the very Walmart customers who've been laid off.

Just as Sears overlooked Walmart, American auto makers focused on annual style changes in their competition with one another, but pretty much ignored the importance of underlying quality improvements until quality suddenly became an important attribute for American buyers in the 1970s, and the quality-conscious the Japanese manufacturers began taking significant market share. Before 1980, GM simply hadn't taken the Japanese seriously as competitors, and it didn't take the issue of quality seriously either. Today GM is still struggling to catch up to Japanese quality standards, and as a result GM's share of the American car market declined from 50% in the 1970s to less than 35% between 1980 and 2000, and further down to about 17% today.

During his rather unsuccessful 10 years as CEO of GM between 1998 and 2008, Rick Wagoner saw the company's market valuation drop by 90%, and the company's accumulated losses totaled more than $80 billion. This, together with the story of Nokia, shows just how bad things can get when a company loses its fit with the market, and competitor innovations take hold in the market. What must it have been like to be Waggoner, and to see the once-great company melting away beneath you? (And what could GM's board of directors have been thinking in allowing this to happen?)

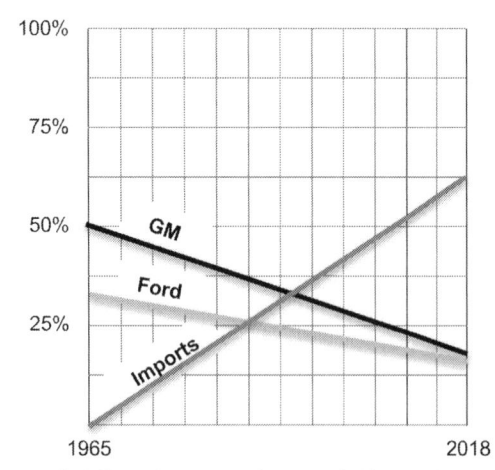

GM, Ford, Imports – Shares of US Auto Market

Defending the Lead

It takes exceptional discipline and clarity of vision to defend a competitive advantage and carry it through to a next generation of innovative offerings.

The challenge, particularly for board of directors of companies slipping into trouble, is to know who *is* the right person for the job, because the CEO must look after both the current business and also the future, and these two dimensions require quite different expertise and perspectives. Past success enables present growth, and as a company increases in size and scope, the nature of management's challenges shift considerably. Managing Xerox, Google, Apple, or Walmart during its start-up stage is an entirely different problem than steering a global colossus.

When a company is small, even its top managers are usually in direct contact with customers as a regular part of their role in the company. But as they deal with the complexities inherent in ever-larger enterprises and have to cope with multiplying layers of organization, they often become further and further removed from direct experience of the market. Lacking direct contact and current interactions, they are intuitively forced to rely on past experiences, and they have a progressively more difficult time hearing the voice of a changing market that's different than the one they remember from back when they talked to customers themselves.

Technology has brought such massive shifts in consumer expectations, attitudes, and behaviors that leaders who rely on what it was like "back then" when they were coming up in the business decades ago are often badly misled. Things have changed, but they fail to appreciate how significant the changes are.

Meanwhile, the need for intense focus on administration distracts management from innovation, and at the same time, dysfunctional and bureaucratic behaviors grow endemic inside of large organizations. Where GE's leaders face could be equally attributed to any number of large companies, and they commonly result in huge distortions to the flow of critical information about the changing external market. Corporate politics gets more and more attention, and emphasis shifts to internal events, while key external factors become obscured from view. Meanwhile, change waits for no organization, and innovations from competitors are introduced without adequate responses.

Hence, it's one thing to be an innovator in a small market, and quite a different matter to bring creative drive to a large operation. As a company grows and the stakes become higher, the risks that the small company has taken as a matter of course are now subjected to a lot more scrutiny, and reaction times slow. Sometimes they slow disastrously. More levels of management have a stake in major decisions; time lags in decision making are longer. It's not uncommon for "analysis paralysis" to set in, and even when leaders admit that this is happening they still can't get past it.

Smaller, more nimble competitors have more to lose, fewer people to convince, and often a sense of desperation that sharpens top management's perception of market needs. They pay attention better. In fact, the well-tuned senses of entrepreneurial top managers become magnets for capital – small, new companies are founded specifically to attack new market niches that only their entrepreneurs and the capitalists that back them even recognize. This is the death-by-a-thousand-cuts danger.

The Next Generation Arrives

The result of this complex process is a pattern that nevertheless repeats with amazing regularity. As formerly innovative companies grow, they tend to become followers rather than leaders. Despite these vulnerabilities, however, their sheer size, combined with control of distribution channels, often makes them formidable competitors even when their subsequent innovations are really copies. They can coast for some time because of their sheer enormity, as Wagoner's tenure at GM shows, but sooner or later the acceleration of their decline becomes terminal, and they die or are fundamentally re-invented while meanwhile the next generation arrives with its new business model.

Economist Joseph Schumpeter referred to this process of economic change as "creative destruction," and he was right. Innovation creates new ways, and simultaneously destroys the old ones. It's up to the leaders to anticipate the future, or else to get out of the way of those who can.

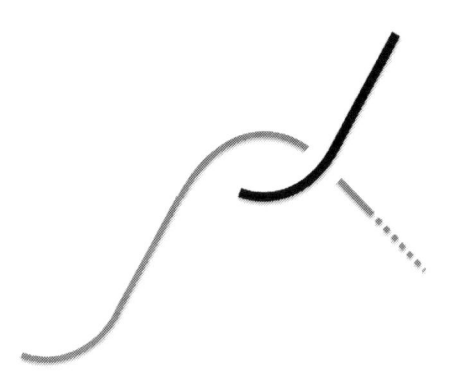

Chapter 21
CREATIVE DESTRUCTION
Coping with Accelerating Change

While the sense of crisis and the time compression caused by accelerating change is certainly real, the underlying dynamics of the competitive marketplace are not new. It was in the 1940s that Schumpeter came up with the concept "creative destruction," and he pointed out that the natural behavior of capitalist systems brings revolution not as the result of vague external factors, but from within. *Change, Schumpeter observed, is the common condition of capitalism, not stability.* And in an utterly prescient comment about prevalent management practices at the time (and still today), he wrote,

> "The problem that is usually being visualized
> is how capitalism administers existing structures,
> whereas the relevant problem
> is how it creates and destroys them."[72]

The significance of this comment is nearly impossible to overstate. While so many observers and leaders focus their attention on how businesses perform in today's markets, Schumpeter points out that it's inherent in the very nature of market evolution to weaken some companies while creating enticing opportunities for others. Therefore, just as important as today's market structures, or today's technologies, or today's competitive advantage, is how the forces of change will affect a firm tomorrow and the day after.

But unfortunately, the instinctive habit of management is to look forward at a 90 day sales forecast and the next quarterly report, or backwards to the past quarter, to guide a course into the future. Neither approach is adequate to the challenge.

We call this short-term mentality the "logic of operations," and it's characterized by a pattern of behavior whose goal is to create a stable, scalable enterprise that returns strong, steady profits to its stakeholders. The qualities that are important from this perspective include predictability, the capacity to forecast near-term growth, revenues, and profits, and as a result tremendous emphasis is placed on management of today's business. Standardization, policy, procedure, organization structure, and short-term decision making are tuned and fine tuned.

The problem, of course, is that the obsession with predictable scalability ignores the realities of external change, and in an era characterized by the nasty change conspiracy, the obsession with the short term cannot and does not succeed.

To take Nokia as a poignant example, it does no good to be far and away the globe's leading cell phone maker, the firm with 9 of the top 10 selling phones worldwide, as Nokia was in 2007, when the iPhone comes along and you have no credible response. Nokia doesn't even make phones now, it's retreated back to its infrastructure business.

If you go back and look, you'll see that Nokia's 2007 Annual Report was written in glowing language that was highly optimistic. It's rather humbling, actually, now that in hindsight we know how fast the company collapsed.

the four driving forces of market dynamics: Increasing Competition, Increasing Complexity, New Technology, Acceleration of Change

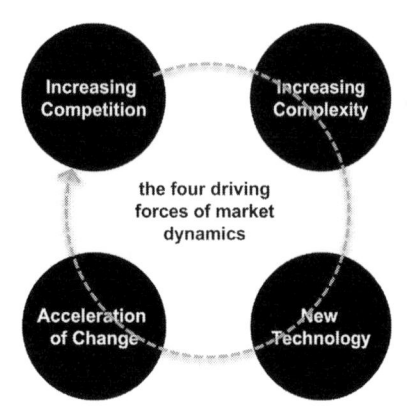

The "Change Conspiracy"

Military leaders are familiar with this problem, which they refer to as "preparing to fight the last war." Such preparations, even fully implemented with rigor and discipline, consistently fail when the character of warfare has in the interim changed. Whether it's armored knights slaughtered by the long bow, France's Maginot Line (the 20th century's iconic monument to backward thinking), the Polish horse cavalry that rode out to face Hitler's blitzkrieg, the American army confounded by Viet Cong guerrilla fighters, civilian aircraft hijacked and turned into guided terrorist missiles, or a new class of weapon based on the cell phone, the "IED," "improvised explosive device," the history of warfare is the history of innovations that render past strategies ineffective. This is also the story of business, past and future.

Hence, the relevant and poignant questions are,

Are you leading?
And what's your strategy for dealing with accelerating change?

Part of the challenge in thinking about strategy and change is that a misplaced focus is usually evident only in hindsight, when wars, market share, jobs, or stock value have already been lost. Commentators (and authors) have a pretty easy time picking apart a failed company strategy five or ten years after the fact; the challenge is doing it before the fact.

And this is why I keep repeating the expectation that another wave of disruptive technologies is about to arrive, and warning that you'd better get ready. To do so, you'll have to find a different way of thinking, as well as a different way of working.

In fact, it's a new kind of radar that you need, along with a different approach to making decisions. For business leaders as for military generals, hindsight does not provide sufficient preparation, and it's therefore essential to have an effective way not only to look toward the future, but even better, to create it. This is the imperative of innovation.

The term "creative destruction" thus gives us a warning, a name, and a general explanation for the waves of change that flow continually through the marketplace, and "fighting the last war" warns us as well that we have to both *think* and *do* differently if we're going to survive and thrive. Both help us direct our attention toward understanding the forces of change rather than supporting the illusion of stability, and they also remind us that the waves of competition and change are themselves created not by mysterious forces but as a result of purposeful innovation in the competitive arena of the market.

Another factor heavily influencing market evolution is that at any given time in any given market, only a few critical value dimensions yield the key combination that proves most attractive to customers. Whichever company happens to have just the right mix gains a temporary advantage, but the emphasis remains on "temporary" because the market's need change, and very few companies sustain leadership over a long period of time; change never stops.

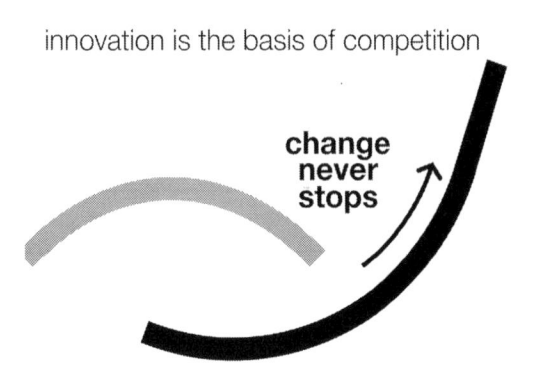

innovation is the basis of competition

change never stops

Thus, we find countless examples of companies that distinguished themselves by focusing on one or another of the many dimensions of innovation, but then faded into obscurity when the dimension in which they were particularly strong became a secondary or tertiary concern, or a non-concern, of customers.

From a manager's perspective, however, the many dimensions of innovation presents a daunting challenge. For old school giants such as GE, GM, or IBM just as for new school leaders such as Apple, Google, or Cisco, there are too many opportunities for innovation to address at once, which brings up a critical dilemma that confronts managers every day: How to choose?

That is, in what aspects of a business should efforts at innovation be focused? Should a company apply itself to innovation in its products and services, or its brand, or its organization, its leadership team, its technology, its capital structure, or any of the others among the possible targets.

Or should it choose any of them?

Individual situations and circumstances may explain the success achieved by this or that company in this or that market, but it's obvious that while any of the areas *may* be important, no one of them consistently explains emerging success and failure. Wouldn't it be far more useful to have a robust explanation of the emergent successes as well as the astonishing failures, and thereby a better way to both examine the competition and to direct innovation efforts? Of course it would.

In search of such an explanation we could ask, What makes Apple, Apple? What makes Fedex, Fedex? Or, What makes Amazon, Amazon? Or, What makes Home Depot, Southwest Airlines, or any flourishing company successful? Is there a way to accurately describe success and to explain how success emerges?

If we take this question seriously, what we're really looking for is more than innovation localized to a particular dimension, but rather a comprehensive innovation framework. And yes, that's the business model. Coping successfully with this requires careful targeting, and a solid appreciation for any business as an integrated, whole system.

Chapter 22
INNOVATING THE WHOLE SYSTEM
Thinking About Your Business Model

When you think about all the different ways that a company can innovate you realize that there are literally dozens of aspects of a business where innovation efforts *could* be focused. We already found 50 of them in our list of "means." They all have interesting potential, but it's insufficient because it's a fragmented world view.

products & services	technology applied	supply chain	organization & operations

We know that products and services need constant innovation to remain relevant, but so does the organization itself, across all its many dimensions. The supply chain has to remain current and efficient, for as we learn from Amazon and Walmart, there are high costs to be slashed and great value to be extracted from thoughtful design and redesign.

And across all dimensions of innovation, new technology is now arriving regularly that will require a fundamental rethinking of just about every facet of the business.

Viewed as a list of possibilities, each may seem separate, interesting perhaps, but apart. This way of looking at it is necessary and useful when you need to inventory what could be done, but it's also a quite distorted view, because looking at an inventory parts will never give you an appreciation for the whole, and in the end it's the whole that matters.

> **So if you could look at the problem of innovation as one process, what would you see?**

You would probably see this: Yesterday a whole range of clever and determined competitors were creating new products, services, distribution systems, brands, and infrastructures that are bringing change to the market. Recognizing the imminence of the creative destruction that results from this, we have to accept the absolute imperative of innovation, and take action accordingly.

Which means we are then confronted with the following question:

> **How do we innovate with a clear focus not on the parts of the system, but the system as a whole?**

This is of course a perspective most accessible to senior managers, that is, "understanding a business as a system" is a task for its leadership.

A Business as a System

To accomplish *this* we first have to understand what the "whole system" is. It's not a particular department, a product, a service, or a brand. It's the entire organization together as one thing, working as a unit, as a system, to create and deliver value. For this new integrated whole to be a useful managerial concept we also need to give it a name, and design a process to help us manage the enterprise more effectively.

And we already have it, because this whole is the business model.

The business model is a comprehensive description of business as an integrated system, functioning in an intimate relationship with its broader market ecosystem.

As I've by now mentioned multiple times, the business model is how you make money, which is a function of experiences you deliver to customers, and which you accomplish by applying the means of organization and operations to create products and services using supply chains and applying technology both in the process and in the product/service itself, and then you tell the story to brand it.

What matters most to the success of the whole *is the way all the elements work together* to enable the organization to create value and deliver it to customers.

A business model therefore describes a whole system as the integrated methods of delivering products, services, and experiences to the market in a particular way, or ways, supported by an organization, positioned according to a particular branding concept that, most importantly, provides positive experiences to customers that yield a particular set of strong relationships with them.

Further, a business model describes how the processes of creating and delivering experiences and value may evolve along with the changing needs and preferences of customers, and in conjunction with evolving technologies. That is, the future view.

To make this all useful we now need to understand some critical characteristics of the whole. To begin, we need to know how this whole is different from the parts that comprise it.

Defining a "System"

A key insight for this discussion is that the distinguishing characteristic of any system is that its outputs emerge not as a result of the action of any single part, but as a result of the way the parts are *connected together.*

An excellent example of the meaning of connectedness is the Boeing 787 airplane, all 2.3 million parts of it. Each of the airplane's components and all its major sub-assemblies has the absolute tendency to fall towards the ground. Take them up to 5 feet, or 5,000, or 35,000 feet and let go, and they invariably tumble straight down. Thud.

It is only – only, only, only! – when all the parts are assembled just right, and working together properly, that the system we call the airplane manifests "airplaneness," and actually flies.[73] Without the connections it is *only* parts; it is the connections that make airplaneness, and which overcomes the inherent tendency of each of the parts to behave in exactly the opposite manner as the plane is intended to behave.

Similarly, the system we call "a company" consists of many different parts – departments, divisions, work groups, teams, individuals – which, if left alone and taken only unto themselves, have the absolute tendency to behave in random and generally unhelpful ways. Imagine what chaos would result if the people in an organization couldn't communicate with one another; it would devolve very quickly into a hopeless mess. Thud.

The ability to communicate is a minimum requirement for any organization to be viable, but of course it takes a lot more than communication to attain success. It takes purpose, process, and products and services delivered to customers.

If you take a part of any company – say the accounting department – and put it into a market by itself, what you have is approximately ... nothing (unless you want to run an accounting services company). The accounting department has no relevance outside of the larger company because accounting is only meaningful when there are transactions that have to be accounted for.

Similarly, manufactured outputs require a sales force, distribution, and customers, or there's just no point. Marketing has no purpose independent of a company's identity, its products and services, and the perceptions of outsiders.

This is basic, obvious stuff, and the only reason that it's worth even mentioning is that this extremely fragmented approach describes exactly how most companies approach the problem of innovation. Rather than looking holistically and systemically, they come at it astonishingly randomly. So how can they reasonably expect anything other than disappointment in the results?

The simple reason that there aren't many companies as good as Apple, Amazon, Google, or Toyota, is because most companies just don't manage their innovation processes very well.

There's another aspect of the airplane analogy that may also help explain this, which has to do with the process of optimization. Let's say we have a nicely functioning airplane and we cleverly want to improve it. We want to make the engines more powerful so the plane can go faster. But doing so might put too much stress on the airframe, or the wings, or it might change the control properties of the plane, and so render it unflyable. Indeed, any variable that we want to adjust in a system engineered to attain performance depends on the other parts of the system to function properly. Success is entirely dependent on the mutual fitness of the parts, and no part can possibly be optimized except in the context of all the rest. Therefore, we must direct our efforts toward optimizing the system as a whole; we have to approach innovation systematically.

The product that cannot reach the customer provides no value; the service that cannot be delivered serves no one; distribution systems lacking effective products provide no value.

Indeed, Coca Cola discovered this a decade ago, when the world's most proficient marketing machine lost half of its market valuation because ... the market for Coca Cola stopped growing. This misfit between product and market slashed the company's stock price. Largely because of its obsession with its past, the company's leadership had failed to notice what was happening, an oversight that enabled Pepsi to shoot ahead in terms of market capitalization, and it also cost the CEO of Coke his job. It took the next CEO of Coke many years to get the system working properly again.

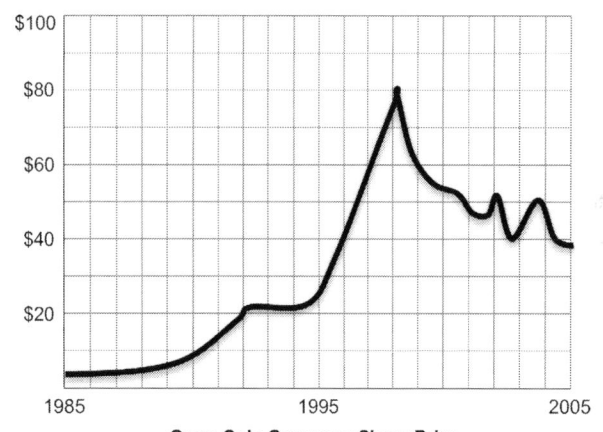

And of course all this is made exceptionally more complex because of competition – organizations participate in bigger systems we call "markets," which in turn are part of the still larger system we call "the economy."

Certainly the optimal approach to marketing depends on the actual products that you're manufacturing and the customers for whom they're intended. Product design, manufacturing, marketing, and sales all have to fit together, and the definition of this fitness *is* the business model.

Consider another example of what happens when the parts don't fit together well. Suppose there's a company that through brilliant engineering and unparalleled customer insights creates an amazing breakthrough technology, a stunningly transformative device, but that company's sales force is incapable of selling it, and senior management is largely indifferent to prospective buyers because they don't understand what the product is, does, or could be. Actually, that's not so difficult to imagine; Xerox had exactly this experience.

Xerox, you may know, is the company that literally invented the personal computer, which occurred at PARC back in the early 1970s. (Bob Metcalfe was part of the team.) Naturally, Xerox wanted to make money from this profound invention, but because Xerox management didn't understand who would use the product, or what for, they pushed it through an entirely unsuited distribution channel, to a market that was neither prepared for it nor able to understand it. It went nowhere.

Well, it went nowhere for Xerox. But other companies made excellent use of Xerox insights and technologies, and in subsequent years they have made billions – hundreds of billions – by applying Xerox inventions to their own products and services. In particular, Apple and Microsoft were big beneficiaries of Xerox's remarkable insights. Apple borrowed from PARC the concept of the graphical user interface, which has become essential to its success and its identity ever since, and Microsoft then borrowed it from Apple to create Windows.

There is a lovely but also painful book about this fiasco with the entirely appropriate title *Fumbling the Future*,[74] and that's exactly what Xerox did. They had the future in their hands, and through incomprehension and negligence they fumbled it away.

Now imagine a company with a brilliant sales force that is also adept at bringing back news from the marketplace, but the company ignores the warnings? This is what happened to IBM in the 1980s when it overlooked (i.e., ignored) the emerging computer workstation market, a device occupying a market niche between the PC and the mainframe, and allowed Sun to become the market leader when IBM failed to even make an attempt to address the new client-server IT paradigm. Louis Gerstner then had to rescue IBM by inventing for it an entirely new business model. (It should be noted that Sun's business model also subsequently faltered, and it was acquired by Oracle in its own fire sale.)

Or let's look at cars. GM has a vast dealer network that is deeply embedded in the commercial fabric throughout North America and in fact the entire world, but the company somehow couldn't manage to produce an Oldsmobile-branded car that enough people actually wanted to buy, so although its headquarters was packed with thousands of very bright minds, GM was compelled by a persistent lack of innovation and a chronically worsening shortage of capital to shut down the Olds line. And then it did the same with Saturn. And then with Pontiac. And then with Hummer. The execution of these brands was yet another aspect of Rick Wagoner's painful legacy.

Do you remember the story at the beginning of this book about Jim Farley, and his highly memorable advice that if you're not scared, you're not paying attention? The specific situation that Farley described when he shared that advice was the demise of Oldsmobile. Toyota's Japanese leadership was stunned that a revered American auto brand, one that was nearly a century old, could be turned so quickly to nothingness. This caused them to think deeply about how change was affecting *them*, and how it would affect them in the future. In Tokyo, Farley mentioned, they were "scared to death" by the Oldsmobile experience, and appropriately so.

Much of the work that Farley led at Toyota USA was specifically intended to address the issues underlying these fears, and it turned out that he was very good at it, so good that Ford hired him away. When I found out that Farley had left Toyota, I asked someone there how that news had gone over, and from the frosty response to my question it was very apparent that Toyota was quite upset about losing his talent.

What Farley clearly understood very well was the full scope of what a business model can be. It's not just a quick line you toss off that says, "Oh, people pay us because of blah blah blah," a complete business model description encompasses the structure of the *entire* marketplace. It thus explains the relationship of a company to its very broad commercial environment. It's a precise definition of who customers are, and how and what a company does today and intends tomorrow to satisfy their needs.

> **A business model expresses a specific assessment of today's competitors and tomorrow's too, and considers the technologies that are today and will tomorrow be embedded in various competing versions of products and services.**

So if Xerox had been thinking about its newly invented personal computer technology in terms of its business model, perhaps the results would have been better. If IBM had understood that workstation computing was a new and important business model, perhaps Sun would never have attained prominence. If GM had considered the business model underlying its Oldsmobile line earlier, before the brand was lying moribund on hospice, then perhaps it would still be viable.

While in each of these examples it's impossible to know the exact root causes of the problems without knowing the actual people involved and what they were thinking and doing at the time, the sad outcomes strongly suggest that top management was probably not asking the right questions, and they were probably not having the right kind of conversations about the future and how to adapt to it.

This all goes to the very heart of "creative destruction," a brilliant concept that explains the macroeconomic perspective and raises tough microeconomic questions about change and change management in individual firms. It's why Toyota's leaders, who certainly are paying close attention, openly admit that they live in chronic fear.

It also brings focus to how leaders and managers handle change, and it highlights the necessity of constant regeneration of the business from within through the R&D process and other creative and *innovation-seeking* endeavors, that is, on activities that are directly and intentionally creating innovations.

Leaders must look holistically at marketplace change, competitive dynamics, consumer tastes, new technologies, new communications techniques, new branding approaches to take a broad stance in scope – both in time and space, opening up the new ideas funnel for business model regeneration.

Over the past twenty years many super useful new tools have been introduced within thought-leading companies, including design retreats, strategic planning retreats, marketing concept generation workshops, brand development ideation workshops, R&D portfolio management, consumer pre-search, exploratory research, category context analysis, competitive brand position analysis, the art of using projection techniques to image better results, trend forecasting and tracking, advanced materials and technology integration planning, etc. Gasp. Lots of tools!

And while leaders of successful companies show a knack for reinventing their organizations using these and other clever techniques to help them, among the failures we see repeatedly the consequences of not understanding or following Schumpeter's advice. Too many managers assume that change is the aberration, and they behave as if the market is stable. Perhaps the business school curriculum is partly at fault, for the very notion of a Masters in Business Administration assumes that the critical competence is *administration*, implying that continuing and well-controlled operation under managerial control is the focus, intent, and purpose of management. It is not so.

For most managers to succeed, however, the ability to *create* is far more important to their companies than skills related to administrating and controlling. Furthermore, as the deep-thinking business theorist Russ Ackoff once pointed out, a serious flaw in the traditional MBA curriculum is that in the real world, managers are not presented with tidy and objective "cases" to solve[75] – they must first *figure out* what the problem is, which can itself require a great deal of insight and creativity.

Foresight

In today's markets change is the norm and stability is an aberration. Leaders grapple with the disruptive forces of change and they figure out for themselves what lessons and challenges are present in the current situation, and what responses will be most effective in harnessing change so that their organizations can survive. Somewhere in the competitive environment it's likely that a new innovation is about to appear that will dramatically impact on the current structures that your business depends on.

And yet the relentless day to day demands on every manager's time immerses them in a flood of pressing issues, and many simply fail to recognize important underlying factors that portend significant disruption. It's not that they're not interested, or that they don't realize the trap that they're in – most will tell you that they deeply regret not spending more time on strategy and innovation, but somehow the urgent but unimportant stuff just takes over their lives.

Consequently, they tend not to account adequately for systemic change, and they are then surprised and unprepared when they should not be.

> Did personal computers and networked workstations surprise the computer industry? Absolutely.
>
> Did the lifestyle performance sport shoe surprise the shoemakers when Nike invented the category? Yes, they did.
>
> Why did Apple create the iPod instead of Sony? Because while Sony had all the component technologies, they did not understand the tacit dimensions of the user experience, which is exactly what Apple did understand.
>
> Why didn't Nokia see the iPhone coming?
>
> Did efficient and high quality Japanese cars surprise the Detroit automakers?
>
> Why did Walmart have to buy jet.com for $3 billion when Amazon was crushing its online business?
>
> Why did Blockbuster turn down the opportunity to buy Netflix when they had the chance? (Yes, they really did have the chance, and they really did pass it up.)
>
> **The answer to all of these questions, of course, is "because they didn't see what was coming."**

We don't want to arrogantly pretend that predicting the future is easy as we sit here with the benefit of hindsight and look at how things unfolded, and yet still it's also obvious that too many leaders are themselves looking in the rear view mirror, gazing backwards at what they have accomplished, instead of forward at what must be accomplished. We and they have to anticipate change.

During his tenure as CEO of IBM, when he turned the company around from its path of disastrous decline, Lou Gerstner commented that, "Many successful companies that fall on hard times – IBM, Sears, GM, Kodak, Xerox – saw clearly the changes in the environment. But they were unable to change highly structured organizational cultures that had been born in a different world."[76]

Here he acknowledges that it can be intellectually as well as psychologically difficult to shift the focus from the operations mentality and actually confront the need to do things in a very different way.

So the claim that there's too much to do today is just an excuse, and a weak one. Try to be the loyal customer of a fading or failing business and you have to wonder, "What could they possibly be thinking?"

And as Mr. Gerstner also pointed out in his book, a primary reason seems to be that some leaders actually make the choice for their enterprise to fail, to die, rather than confronting the need to change and adapt, that is, to innovate.

In this regard, it's very interesting to note how Mr. Gerstner got the job as CEO of IBM in the first place. The story as it was mostly reported in the media at the time was that Gerstner's predecessor John Akers was fired by IBM's board of directors. But in his book, Gerstner reveals that actually Akers himself realized that he wasn't the right person to design and lead IBM's turnaround, and he went to the board and insisted that it was time for a change. While it's also true that Akers probably waited too long to admit it, at least he had the honesty to recognize what was needed, and the courage to admit it, and to realize that to survive and to win, IBM required a completely different approach.

Chapter 23
WINNING AND LOSING AT BUSINESS MODEL WARFARE
Technology Applied in a Business Process

The concept of business model warfare explains a lot about how the ebb and flow of winners and losers in the marketplace reflects the creatively destructive marketplace, and it also enables us to define a set of principles and skills to enable leaders to be effective at this critical game.

It's not a new game, but it seems that each generation of leaders has to relearn the dangers of standing pat when the whole outside environment is changing in such a whirl. As I mentioned, in addition to erroneous assumptions about stability, managers also fall into the trap of focusing far too much of their attention on what's happening inside their own organizations, a particular danger facing middle managers who are under pressure from upper levels in the hierarchy. Their quite logical sense of self-protection forces them to pay great attention to the behaviors and desires of senior management, but far too little attention is often paid to customers or to the future.

As I also mentioned, this is even more true in the conglomerate business, where senior leaders have to report to even more senior leaders who don't have any customers. Vast amounts of time get sucked into the game of corporate politics, all of which is detrimental to the real mission, understanding customers, understanding change, understanding technology, and designing the next steps in the evolution of the business model.

To engage successfully in business model warfare, managers cannot be internally focused on products, or on services, or on administration, and forget that

what actually matters are the critical relationships between these elements, and the even more crucial interactions between the company and its customers.

Don't forget the metaphor of the airplane, and the essential role that the connections between the parts play in its capacity to fly; the parts are just expensive garbage, *unless* they're connected together in just the one and only correct way.

Similarly, thinking about innovation in the business model as a matter of the *overall* relationship between the company and its customers, rather than innovation isolated in this or that aspect, will yield greater insight and better management performance. So it's not a coincidence that the winners in business model warfare are those who manage their customer relationships in the most effective ways possible, by creating compelling experiences across every possible dimension.

Relationships

Facebook's 2 billion users spend a total of about 900 million hours per day posting and looking at pictures of themselves and their friends, which each one apparently does on average 8 times per day.[77]

Every minute there are 400 new Facebook users, 54,000 new shared links, 147,000 new photos uploaded, and 317,000 status updates, which speaks to the profound depth of attachment that our progressively deepening engagement with technology has awakened. It appears to be a new form of addiction.[78]

While Facebook is only on our devices (at the moment), Apple and Android have successfully insinuated themselves into our entire lives. According to Deloitte, Americans between age 18 and 24 look at their phones an average of 74 times each day,[79] and across all age groups the average is 52 times per day. As I mentioned above, we're now so fully addicted to our phones that the Cambridge Dictionary's 2018 Word of the Year is the newly invented "nomophobia," the intense fear of being without your mobile phone. How many times a day do you check yours?

Scientists have discovered that when we use social media our brains often respond by releasing oxytocin. Oxytocin invokes feelings of love, trust, empathy, and generosity, and it lowers stress, which means that social media like Facebook really are addictive.

Oxytocin invokes feelings of love, trust, empathy, and generosity, and it lowers stress, which means that social media like Facebook really are addictive.

These usage patterns reflect preferences, dependences, and affinity, and one of the earliest and still most successful marketing organizations to nurture its image toward these very high levels of attachment was Nike.

During the 1970s Nike redefined the nature of competition in the sports shoe and sports apparel business by transforming star athletes into social icons, first with runner Steve Prefontaine and later with Michael Jordan. In so doing, Nike created new markets for its shoes and clothing, and quickly surpassed Adidas to become the global leader in a market that Nike ruptured by introducing a new way of marketing. Nike's core business model innovation was thus its ability to transform its brand into a key element in the self-identity of its customers. Customers came to see that their Nike shoes and clothing defined themselves, and made them the Michael Jordan of their household, their neighborhood, their school.

Nike elevated the practice of brand management to such deep alignment that the company could then open its brilliantly successful Nike Town stores, another pioneering innovation for a clothing maker, and one that contributed enormously to the company's image and brand value. The first Nike Town in Portland was intended as an experiment, but it quickly became so successful that it was soon followed by other locations. The second Nike Town was located in Chicago and was for many years that city's number one tourist attraction.[80]

Toyota's innovations in alternative fuels with the hybrid Prius came far in advance of American manufacturers, and won it added market share as buyers develop a preference for fuels other than oil. The Prius was the best selling car in California from 2011 to 2013, but then lost its mojo as the cars that looked cool in 2010 looked stale in 2014. The spirit of risk-taking that created the Prius was lost, and the company lapsed into a risk-aversion stance that turned out to be riskier.

In Europe, retailing giants Auchan and Carrefour redefined the French grocery business in the 1960s by applying new cash register technology to create the hypermarket, and at about the same time Novotel introduced a new kind of hotel that was designed for business travelers. All three firms are now global giants.

American Express once dominated the credit card industry by carefully cultivating an image of prestige and exclusivity. Visa entered into competition by offering credit cards to just about anyone, and by creating a global network that was far more fluid, flexible, and low cost, rendering American Express nearly irrelevant.

Dell created a commercial powerhouse by completely re-inventing the manufacturing and distribution process and built PCs to order rather than to inventory, an entirely new business model in the personal computer industry. Mass customization at a competitive price defined a new kind of customer relationship in the PC industry. But in a dramatic display of changing market structures, the company's unique business model lost its charm. What caused the change? Why did Dell's model, once so successful, implode?

Commoditization came, and by the early 2000s there was nothing distinctive about a Dell machine, and made-to-order offered no cost advantage. So founder Michael Dell took the company private in 2013 in his attempt to recreate the magic of its past, and the company increased its share of the global market, from 12% in 2011 to 15% in 2017, and also shifted its business to address other parts of the computer industry, developing a robust business in servers.

IBM came to exactly the same conclusion in 2005, that the commoditized PC business had no charm and not much profit potential, and sold its entire PC division to Chinese manufacturer Lenovo, openly admitting that it had no interest in, and no skill in running a commodity business. That just wasn't its business model, but it fit very well with Lenovo's ability to utilize inexpensive Chinese manufacturing, and for the next 10 years Lenovo was the world's number one or two seller of PCs, alternating with HP for leadership. In 2017, HP and Lenovo had about the same share of the PC market, about 21% each.

As I mentioned above, Southwest Airlines developed a highly differentiated approach by commoditizing the entire airline industry, a business model that was quite unlike any of the other airlines at the time. It kept its edge until 9/11, when the entire industry slumped due to the fear of terrorism, sadly demonstrating that terrorism is in some cases a quite effective model of social disruption.

Nevertheless, one of the most interesting things about Southwest's business model is that there isn't much technology evident in the business at all. What's clear is that the leaders of Southwest thought through air travel in a comprehensive way, and avoided falling into high-cost traps that hurt the others. The company wasn't burdened by restrictive labor agreements that weighed so heavily on its competitors. It focused on keeping operating costs low by standardizing on only one type of aircraft to minimize maintenance costs, and by design it initially avoided airports that charged high landing and gate fees. It still doesn't participate in centralized reservations systems. Southwest has not attempted to be something that it is not, a mighty global airline, but has instead focused on understanding its mostly short-haul market niche and serving it profitably.

Like the many innovations that made Southwest's business model so effective, the distinguishing characteristic of Fedex is not the pioneering idea of overnight delivery, nor its innovative use of information technology to track packages, nor its reputation as a reliable, courteous, and service-oriented alternative to the post office. No, it is all of these factors integrated together into a seamless whole, as a coherent system. The fusion of these elements into an effective organization that is precisely what we mean by the business model.

But now Fedex does have a worthy competitor: Amazon is creating its own delivery network, and already owns 40 airplanes.

What's in the future for all the delivery companies? Well, a big disruption that's no longer on the horizon are drones. They're coming – oh, no, wait, they're already here. China's second largest ecommerce firm JD.com, has implemented a drone delivery network in 100 rural Chinese villages that is already providing same day delivery at a cost of about 80% less than using a truck and driver.[81]

Home Depot also demonstrates how the successful integration of numerous factors creates a business that's so appealing to customers and so devastating to competitors. Impressive scale on two dimensions –

gigantic stores and a huge number of them – leads to high sales volume that enables the company to pay lower prices to its supplies, and charge the lowest prices to its customers. The local hardware store or lumber yard can't compete unless it, too, undertakes its own business model innovation and positions itself as something that Home Depot cannot be. Which is highly personalized service, fast transactions, proximity, better selection, different products .... and so as I noted above, Ace has recognized that this is exactly its niche, the anti-Home-Depot.

Indeed, when you want to get in and out quickly then Home Depot, Walmart, and Target aren't attractive, so what are the giant retailers doing? They're also opening small format, urban stores. Yes, they're innovating their own business models, by going small. Walmart, Target, Ikea, even Nordstrom are experimenting, trying to find the right small-store formula to enhance their brands, a new venture and new business model innovation combined.

Amazon's experimenting too, opening its own retail stores and buying Whole Foods to give it a footprint in hundreds of malls.

This demonstrates how the evolution of a successful business model creates new niche opportunities for competing concepts. Thus, at a retail clothing conference in the early 1990s, a speaker was openly critical of the Gap, claiming that he could easily start a competing business (model) and undercut Gap's prices simply by buying lower quality goods from China. Donald Fisher, then the Gap's CEO, happened to be in the audience, and he realized that this was quite true. In 1994 the Gap opened its Old Navy subsidiary, which is now significantly outperforming the parent.

What we see consistently across all these examples, and with widespread consistency across the entire history of business, is the following:

> **It's rarely, if ever, a single innovation
> that propels a business to success.
> It is instead, a suite of innovations
> that complement one another
> and work together
> to provide a novel or distinctive
> value proposition that underlies success.**

The key is not necessarily the product or service itself – which could be highly innovative or even just acceptable – but something brought to market in an innovative way, supported in an innovative way, branded in an innovative way, and in the end provides an experience that builds enduring relationships between the company and its customers.

This tells us that while pushing some elements of the means to the edge of possibility and beyond may be important and necessary, more is needed in addition. In fact, it's an entire integrated suite.

The Ratings Game

How does Netflix decide what new shows to produce? It's got the data.

Jeff Bezos, too, recognized that perfect information would change the structure of the market, about which he was entirely correct, and as his comment implies, it's not only perfect *pricing* information, but also (nearly) perfect information about countless other factors including quality, reliability, design, usability, and durability. And preferences, especially preferences.

Welcome to the essential new universe of user ratings, which are now a compelling part of the business landscape (as compared with the past when it was expert ratings from organizations like Consumer Reports and the Insurance Institute that mattered).

Indeed, because viewer recommendations are so important to its business success, in 2009 Netflix ran a contest for programmers to improve the accuracy of its viewer recommendation algorithms. The prize was $1 million, a clever PR trick with meaningful business impact that enabled Netflix to move up on its market map, toward still better customization.

Now it seems everyone's into it. TripAdvisor users rate all kinds of travel experiences, hotels, airlines, ships, etc., to help fellow journeyers to make more informed choices.

Rate-My-Professors.com helps students select classes based on how previous students felt about their classes, and Angie's List uses customer recommendations to rank contractors and other service providers. Seat Guru can help you identify which seat on an airplane you prefer, all part of an entire sub-genre of product and service evaluations and recommendations that provide consumers with much better information than they ever had before.

It also provides some recourse. Post a negative review on TripAdvisor, and it's quite possible that you'll hear back from the property manager with an apology (as I did), and maybe an offer of compensation or a future discount (I didn't).

Ratings enable a transformative change in the relationship between a company and its customers, as customers not only inform one another, they have newfound leverage through rating and through social media.

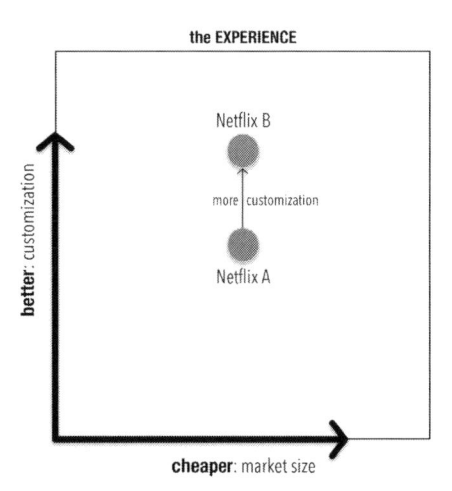

In fact, social media matters so much to the reputation of every company that all the big ones and many of the mid-sized ones have set up "social media listening labs" and command posts where staff monitor social media networks for mentions about their own firms and their industries. Wells Fargo, for example, has two labs, one on each coast of the US for coverage 24 hours a day, which scan and analyze millions of messages flowing through all the major and minor social media networks.

Of course this is a huge boon for software makers, who also provide monitoring as a service for all those firms that don't have their own labs. One of them, talkwalker, tracks 187 languages, 150 million websites, 30,000+ brand logos, and discussions on 10 social networks. Of course this requires artificial intelligence, which brings us back to Palantir, the software company funded by the US government to develop intelligent anti-terrorist scanning and pattern recognition tools, which is essentially the industrial-strength, military version of the same thing.

Why this matters is of course that what people say about your company or your brand or your products matters so much now that sentiment on social media can balloon into a public relations nightmare in minutes; proactive trend spotting and in many cases intervention is the only course of action that makes sense for a consumer brand (and for an authoritarian government).

For proactive brands, it's not only a matter of monitoring social media, it also presents an opportunity to use social media to promote, advocate, and educate.

Technology Applied

As we examine industry after industry, we see that wherever there is an exemplar, a company that distinguishes itself above others, that company is almost always a business model innovator that applies creativity across many different dimensions of the customer experience to become that market leader.

This does not, however, mean that every business model innovator is also a market leader, for innovation always involves risk. Many new business models fail, just as old ones do.

It's also important to reiterate a point I made earlier, that the core of an innovation value proposition need not be built around a technology per se. In many the examples mentioned above – Amazon, Apple, Toyota, Honda, Nike, Visa, Fedex, Home Depot, and Southwest Airlines – proprietary technologies may play a part in the company's success, but there are always many more layers:

> **The key to success**
> **is to focus not only on technology itself,**
> **but technology applied in a business process**
> **to optimize the relationship**
> **between the company and its customers.**

In today's environment, nearly any technology can be, has been, or will be copied, so the important competitive advantage is knowing how to *use* the technology in a way that adds the greatest value for customers.

With all of this in mind, we now have a better way to characterize marketplace competition, creative destruction, and innovation.

> **We thus see that effective innovation**
> **is not a matter of exploiting individual technologies,**
> **nor of exceptional performance in any individual element of a business,**
> **but rather a matter of connecting the elements of the business model**
> **into effective and responsive wholes.**

What this means is that the winners at business model warfare have to apply innovation to create competitive advantages by building stronger relationships with customers, which they do by developing business models that fit ever more closely with customer needs and preferences across multiple dimensions.

Winners who have figured out these principles then seek to sustain and extend their advantages through further business model innovations that defend newly-won territory, and that venture into new domains. It is therefore the business model itself that must be the focus of innovation, and innovation in any or all the possible dimensions must be undertaken in service to a larger framework that is defined by the business model.

Chapter 24
INSIDER AND OUTSIDER
The Thoughtful Mash-Up

One of the significant challenges we all face in coming up with business model innovations is that's when you've been working in a given field or industry for a long time, you get used to it and become blind to its deficiencies and weak points. When you hear the phrase, "This is how we do things here," you know it's being spoken by someone who's deeply enmeshed in what's now an accepted way of thinking.

That's not the way of thinking that leads to innovation.

Thus, when we look at business model innovators from the recent past, it's no surprise that many of them weren't insiders, who had the ingrained insider perspective. Instead, they were definitely outsiders, but who somehow managed to know enough about the inside that their ideas were relevant, and not just wildly unrealistic fantasies.

Here are some examples:

Southwest Airlines was started by Herb Kelleher, an attorney, who know the problems of the Texas airline industry as a customer, not as an airline executive. His insider-partner was Rollin King, who owned an air charter company and thus knew the industry from the inside.

The turnaround of IBM was led by Louis Gerstner, who had been CEO of the food manufacturer RJR Nabisco, a large IBM customer. He knew IBM well, but as an outsider, because Nabisco signed multi-million dollar checks to IBM each year for hardware and services. And before he was CEO of RJR he had been a senior executive of American Express, which was also a major IBM customer.

What did Jeff Bezos know about selling books before he started Amazon? He had bought a lot of them ...

Friends Travis Kalanick and Garrett Camp had both already built and sold high tech startups when they were attending the *LeWeb* conference together in Paris in 2008. Unable to get a cab on a winter night, the idea for Uber was born in frustration.

Howard Schultz worked in New York selling coffee makers in the wholesale market, and one his customers in Seattle was buying and reselling a whole bunch of them. To find out why he went to visit, and inspired by what Starbucks was doing, he persuaded the founders to hire him as marketing director. Eventually he bought the company from them, and turned it into the Starbucks we find on every street corner.

Phil Knight was a runner. His coach Bob Bowerman experimented with shoe designs. Together they created Nike.

What these and dozens of other examples have in common is the marriage, or mash-up, of insider knowledge and outside knowledge.

Insiders know how a company or an industry operates, which can be both good and bad. It's good because this deep insider knowledge is essential when you're innovating operationally, but bad when it prevents you from even noticing what's awful, or even merely mediocre. Insiders often don't realize when things aren't working because the way it's going seems so normal to them.

How else can you explain how the post office works, or insurance claims, or the Motor Vehicle Department? These horrible experiences persist because the insiders have grown accustomed to the bad service, bad experiences, and bad attitudes, and because they're protected by monopoly or quasi-monopoly status from competition, (and thus temporarily insulated from innovation and change).

Outsiders, on the other hand, know how customers feel and what they want, frequently because they are themselves customers and they themselves have experienced the frustration and disappointment.

By combining these two perspectives, new business model insights often arise quite readily, but it takes clear intention to make it happen.

But suppose you're an insider, and while you'd like to innovate your business model, you're not sure where to find the outsider perspective. For this, another simple thinking tool is quite useful, which is the distinction between the insider perspective at the core, and the outsider perspective at the edge.

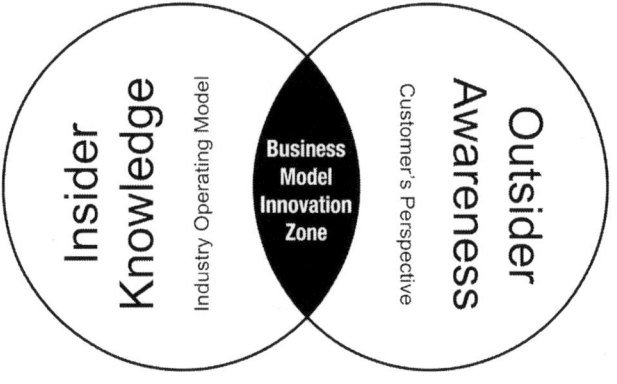

Chapter 25
CORE AND EDGE
Where to Find Innovations

A useful way to think about any market is by drawing a classic bell curve, and labeling the heart of the curve as the core market, and little tails on either side are the edges where customers are not.

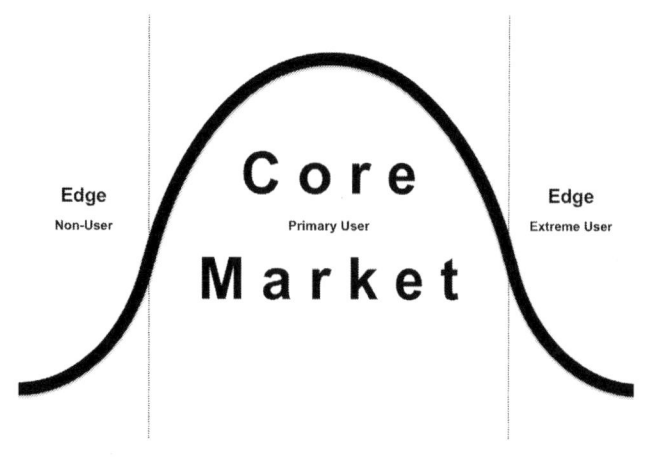

Edge
Non-User

Core Market
Primary User

Edge
Extreme User

Who's in the core? These are the insiders, the mainstream customers. Your marketing department knows these people intimately, and they're the immediate place to go when doing a focus group on a new product concept, or a customer service survey. This is where your organization targets its advertising, because these are the people you have to please to sustain your business.

The people on either edge, however, don't usually get much attention at all. Maybe none. Because they're not customers, they're non-customers. Or, alternatively, they're such extreme customers that no one inside your company can even vaguely relate to them. Maybe they buy your product, but not for any purpose you had in mind. What they do with it is their problem.

Of course I'm overstating this difference to make the point, and hopefully you do get the point – it's on the edges where your future customers are likely to be found. But if you keep looking only in the core, then guess what? You'll never find them. (But your competitors will.) Opportunities on the edge are usually shrouded, hidden, and you lack the knowledge to recognize them; it's the tacit knowledge problem again.

Some examples may be useful.

Remember Oldsmobile and Toyota, and the fear that Toyota's leaders felt (and probably still feel) that what happened to Oldsmobile could also happen to them? Oldsmobile's core market was upper-middle class Americans, who had worked their way up from basic Chevrolet models to higher-class Buicks, and from there to Olds. Owning an Olds was for many an expression of accomplishment, a social statement of success. So the brand's marketing was naturally targeted at this upward-striving, aspirational core market.

This brilliant business model segmentation was invented by GM's Alfred Sloan in the 1920s, but by the 1980s, the model of Chevy>Buick>Olds>Cadillac was clearly breaking down as new auto makers came into the US market from Europe and Japan, and all the old categories were thrown askew. Olds, however, didn't change its approach, and as its fifty year old customers turned sixty, and then seventy, they were buying fewer and fewer cars, and soon the brand was so deeply stagnant that it died. In fact, it followed its core market customers right into their graves.

Toyota leaders recognized that their core American customers were Baby Boomers, and they, too were aging. How could Toyota attract their children and grandchildren? It was based on this insight that the Scion brand was conceived, a Toyota sub-brand targeted specifically at America's Gen X.

Jim Farley led the team that created Scion, and he reported that the key insights about the brand's positioning came from extensive interviews with young people who would have never considered themselves to be Toyota buyers. So from Toyota's perspective *they* were the edge, and what the Scion team did was ethnographic research to understand the cultural values and expectations of its target market. To appeal to them, Toyota then had to create an edge brand, which is exactly how Scion was positioned in the market.

Scion thrived until the 2008 financial crisis, by which time Jim Farley was at Ford, and facing the collapse of the low end of the car market, Toyota ended the Scion experiment. Had Farley still been there it's likely that they might have chosen to keep the brand going, but lacking his leadership insights they reverted to "core market thinking," having learned a great deal about market segmentation and brand positioning along the way.

While Toyota is a core brand that experiments at the edge, Amazon's entire business model was originally targeted exclusively at the edge, at the very tiny proportion of people who bought products online, based on the expectation, now proven, that future core customers would adopt the behaviors of then-current edge customers. *Which is exactly what happened.* Amazon has grown with that market as its business model has come to be exactly at the core, and has thus switched places with Toys R Us, for example, which stayed in its core, and died there.

Following Nike, Adidas became adept at

profiling, segmentation and targeting inner city, ethnic/urban, creative/artist, not just athletes, but rappers, musicians, fine artists, movie and video makers, and even counter-culture figures.

It's "Calling All Creators" campaign co-opted Nike's elite athlete vibe with a new urban consumer culture focus. This new target for Adidas *is* the edge, played to a rap soundtrack with a fashion sensibility that's becoming the new core.

Walmart, meanwhile, is working to evolve its business model from retail stores to online sales, reflecting its awareness that in fact the entire market is evolving, and now there's a new core where the edge used to be.

Uber, Southwest, Nike, they were also edge brands that captured the market and made their business models into the core from the edges where they started, displacing the others to become the core.

In 1990 Netflix was a startup brand on the edge when its founders went to meet with the leaders of Blockbuster Video to propose a merger: Blockbuster would buy Netflix to create a multi-channel brand. The Blockbuster team couldn't understand why that might be the least bit desirable. According to Netflix CFO Barry McCarthy, "They just about laughed us out of their office." This was also a classic insider-outsider problem (for Blockbuster), as having the dominant business model (at the time) made any alternative completely inconceivable. You know the result.

> "They just about **laughed** us out of their office."
> — Barry McCarthy

These transitions from core to edge begin to be obvious when you start to see the structure of the market through the lens of these concepts, and thus it can be exceptionally useful to undertake your own explorations –

What is core, and what is edge for your industry?

From a macro perspective, the evolution of the broader market suggests that there is now a structural change occurring that reflects the explosive adoption of technology throughout society, and the impact this is having on our experiences and attitudes. What was once edge is now becoming core not only with respect to specific business models like Amazon and Nike, but also as it pertains to a subtle transition that's now occurring across the entire economy. This is the shift that sometimes referred to as the emergence of the creative economy. It, too, may have significant implications for your business model.

Chapter 26
CREATIVE ECONOMY BUSINESS MODELS
From Mass to Custom

The 20th century was undoubtedly an era when the concept of the mass market was born, and then it was relentlessly perfected. Mass merchandising, mass media, and mass entertainment all came into dominance, all targeted at the booming mass of the middle class. The post-war period at mid-century was a time, most of all, of mass consumption in the developed world, and all the tools of mass consumerism were developed and refined upon the retail order that was established to manufacture and distribute goods to everyone.

But as that old consumer-culture world retail order has been shaken to its economic foundations by the internet/mobile apocalypse, the world of mass-consumerism, which sits squarely in the core of the market, is no longer the only viable path to market. What's emerging instead is a new creative economy, one in which more people are taking part, and which is becoming more significant and more influential each year.[82] As noted above, Adidas has fully embraced this new ethos, and in so doing has surpassed Nike not in total sales, but in brand cool and cultural relevance.

Many of the factors that Jeff Bezos discussed in his talk at Legg Mason evoke this new pattern, which is in fact a new type of relationship between companies and customers, a partnership of co-creation rather a one-way provider-to-consumer path. These are the new creative economy business models that have quite different characteristics.

In the new models, the customer is the partner not only in the design of the product or service, but in its conception and creation. This is of course an aspect of customization, which has always been a characteristic of the top of the business model map, but now that capability is in fact accessible to everyone.

Additive manufacturing, the 3D printing Maker Bot movement, is just the beginning of what will soon be common. Earlier I mentioned Zozo, which already makes custom clothing according to your exact measurements, as determined by its body suit with 350 position markers. With 3D printing, any store can become a factory where customers will design and make it themselves. Which brings up the next logical question, why do we need a store at all? When PCs were first available but they were too expensive to buy one of your own, there were service bureaus like Kinko's where you could rent their PCs by the minute, or do your printing because printers, especially color ones, were too expensive for most people to own. That's all different now, and 3D printing will likely traverse the same progression, which will only put more pressure on companies to offer something special.

Of course it's not only goods, as, for example, custom-designed medicines will be common as well, since pharma companies will soon be able to craft a formulation and dosage to your exact metabolic and genetic requirements. Perhaps you'll only buy the formula, though, and then "print" your medicine at home.

Speaking of your home, you can now print one of those, too. In about 20 hours a gigantic 3D printer can print the exact one for you, designed by you.

Are you ready to be the architect? Why not? You already design your Facebook page to express the uniqueness of who you are, and possibly your web page as well.

And it's not as though this is so leading edge that there's just one firm in the home-printing business. *3D Natives*, the web community of 3D printing, recently identified 11 firms in the market already, coming from Russia, France, Holland, Italy, China, and the US, using a wide variety of technical approaches and business models.[83] While they probably won't all succeed, they show clearly that even in the ancient art of construction there are abundant opportunities for innovation, and new business model opportunities as well.

This is exactly what we mean by co-creation and what the creative economy is all about. Creative economy business models transform customers into partners and into co-creators, thus transforming the relationship away from passive consumption, and showing that value is in what you create *together*. To succeed, companies must therefore enable and empower customer creativity.

The Adidas "Calling all creators" ad campaign that I mentioned in the previous chapter is a rich and evocative series of ads in which athletes and artists talk about the profound power of the act of creation in art, sport, and life, and invite customers to become co-creators with them. This of course transforms the idol, removing him or her from the pedestal to become instead a peer.

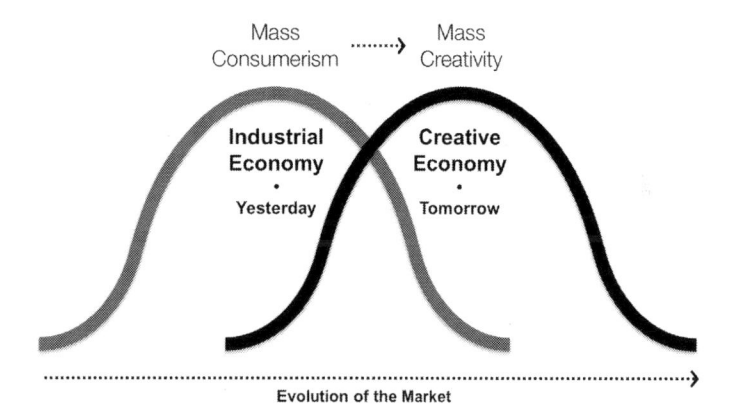

Consequently, it may not be you wearing Michael Jordan's signature shoes, maybe it will be him wearing *your* creations. Indeed, at the Fashion Institute in New York, students are working with IBM's Watson to design custom fabrics. Explains Michael Ferraro, executive director of FIT's Infor Design and Tech Lab:

> "The machine learning analysis gave us insights about the Tommy Hilfiger colors, silhouettes and prints that we couldn't begin to consume or understand with the human mind. This enabled the FIT Fashion Design students to take their inspiration from Americana or popular fashion trends and marry that with the 'DNA', if you will, of the Tommy Hilfiger brand across those dimensions to create wholly new design concepts."[84]

Co-creation thus transforms edge consumers into the very core of focus, and turns outsiders into insiders, which also means that co-creation will be a tremendously powerful source of innovative ideas.

Attributes of Creative Economy
Business Models

1. Customer is the **Partner**
2. Customer is the **Co-Creator**
3. Value is Created by what you do **Together**
4. Growth of the **Relationship** is Constant
5. Each Relationship is **Unique**

To succeed in this transformation requires that the company must genuinely respect its customers, as condescension and hollow promises will be exposed immediately, at an immense cost in lost credibility.

This also means that each relationship will be unique. As Jeff Bezos understood, power in the new marketplace is emphatically and inexorably shifting to the consumer, who is becoming co-designer as well.

What, then, does the creative economy mean for your business?

And how will you transform your business model?

Business Model Warfare

Part 4
STEP INTO THE RIVER

While Austrian economist Joseph Schumpeter recognized that the capitalist economy simultaneously experiences and embraces the forces of creativity and destructiveness, the Chinese philosopher Lao Tzu pointed out that we cannot step into the same river twice, by which he meant nearly the same thing.

With each passing moment the river may look to be the same, but its flow is constant and the water that envelopes your foot as you step in this morning is different from yesterday's water, as it will also be different tomorrow. You will also be different, and so will the entire world.

We have no choice but accept the inevitability of change, and to align our expectations and organize our actions accordingly. You cannot just watch the river flow past, you have to step in and do something.

Here in Part 4 we consider tools that will help you to design and organize your business model innovation actions, and so to prepare for whatever tomorrow's river brings.

Chapter 27
TOOL #1: INSIGHT

As I write this, GE's new CEO Larry Culp has been on the job for a couple months now. What's he been up to, besides slashing the company's stock dividend to a penny? He's working very hard, no doubt, to turn the gigantic enterprise around, but to what extent does he also have to reinvent it? For that he requires insight into the past, present, and future of the company's many markets in both consumer and industrial settings.

The challenge he faces is the same as the one that faced Louis Gerstner once he got the job at IBM, Ginni Rometty at IBM today, and even Mark Zuckerberg at Facebook and Jeff Bezos at Amazon, and indeed it's the challenge facing every business leader: while they have to keep the organization moving in the right direction from day to day, it's imperative to also assure that their organizations are continually engaged in the process of innovation for the longer term, of which insight is the essential driver. How, that is, do you decide on the right targets?

Start by learning what's most valuable to your customers.

This immediately takes you into the tacit dimension of experience, and requires that you engage in deep study to identify the important hidden factors that underlie their preferences and decisions.

As we have discussed, for consumer markets this quest often takes the form of ethnographic or tacit knowledge research, through which we expect to gain a deep understanding of subtle attitudes, behaviors, and expectations that will shape future choices.

In B2B or industrial settings, however, the necessary approach may be somewhat different, as here it's possible to partner with your customers to jointly discover the future. This is often referred to as "Fourth Generation R&D," a set of principles devised by William Miller and described in the book that he and I wrote, which focuses on developing shared learning agendas and pursuing joint research between partner firms to understand how emerging technologies are impacting on emerging markets.[85] This complex domain of double emergence requires the useful fusion of market knowledge and technical knowledge, and thus not only technical collaboration, but also the engagement of marketing and production.

Tacit knowledge capture through tools like ethnographic research and joint research through fourth generation techniques are both essential methods for gaining a deep understanding of the evolving character of the evolving marketplace. Together they also offer a foundation upon which to map your equally profound understanding of emerging external trends and macro factors that are shaping the economy and society, the subject of which is foresight.

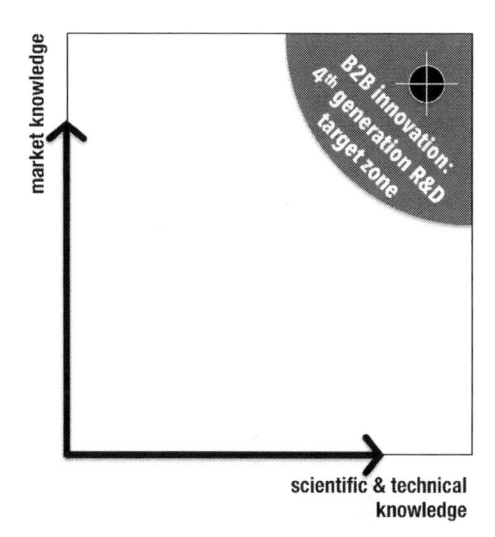

4th Generation R&D
Learning with customers

Changing From Inside

But before we shift the discussion from insight to foresight, consider also that to lead successful change in your own organization you require insight about its culture, about internal politics and which way people are facing – are they facing headquarters, or towards customers? About bureaucratic obstacles and funding balances or imbalances, about how your R&D and marketing and branding teams are working, and what it's likely to mean to them to consider and then implement deep and meaningful change. In other words, is your organization ready for innovation at its core? (And this is critical regardless of your stance regarding business model innovation, of course.)

Politics and power are constant factors in all organizations, and there is a status quo reinforcement system built into every organization too, and the people responsible for maintaining the status quo will always be anxious about their jobs when a new order of things is proposed. And by definition, innovation requires a new order, which implies either conflict (which could take place primarily below the surface, where it will be harder to detect, and harder to counter as well), or very thoughtful anticipatory management.

This tells us that change mastery on the human level is essential to accomplish change mastery on the systems and business model levels. This also means that it may be necessary to do tacit knowledge research on your own organization:

Continue by learning what's most valuable to your own organization.

Find out where things presently stand, who the supporters of change are, and devise the strategies and tactics that will be most effective in generating the culture of receptivity and enthusiasm for change, and the knowledge and skills to pinpoint where business model change (and all types of innovation) should be targeted.

Furthermore, since authenticity is essential to the success of brands with soul, and companies and their brands are increasingly transparent in this era of social media and instant communication, developing and implementing the right new business model just won't be successful as a purely intellectual exercise, a predatory power grab, or a copycat promotion. It must be sourced from the genuine commitments of genuine sentiments, and to both tap into the organization's current sentiments and through leadership to evoke a spirit of aspiration and engagement, you've got to know where you are, and then work diligently to craft a culture that is in alignment with the soulful qualities that will succeed in the marketplace.

Thus, as you see, developing insight is a multi-dimensional exercise in both learning and in creating. Its scope encompasses customers in both consumer (B2C) and industrial (B2B) market, the organization itself (B2Me), and its output is clarity about who they are, who we are, and how we can best serve them.

On that basis you can then turn your attention to the broader outside world, the exponentially-change maelstrom of competition and technology and macro factors that will also have fundamental influence on the future of your organization. In particular, you're interested in what's ahead, in *foresight*.

Chapter 28
TOOL #2: FORESIGHT

The original Ford cars of the early 1900s beginning with the Model T were brilliant and innovative examples of automotive imagination and engineering, but as important to the company's success was the innovative production process (the first vertically integrated assembly line), the national and then global distribution system (the dealer network), and the company's pricing model, affordability. All these innovations enabled Ford to create an enduring relationship with American car-buyers that literally transformed lives in cities, towns, and also the countryside.

By the 1920s, however, GM had copied and caught up with Ford's innovations, and began introducing its own. A minor GM innovation with major impact was the availability of cars in colors other than black.[86] Ford suffered steady decline thereafter, and was rescued from what would probably have been fatal demise only by the enormous demand for military vehicles caused by World War II.

After the war the company was soon staggering, and it was nearly bankrupt again by the late 1950s.

The Ford story illustrates two important aspects of competition in nearly every market. First, each industry has its own rhythm of technical innovation, driven largely by advances in materials and methods. These advances often lead to cycles of changing market dominance. In the auto industry, Ford was supplanted by GM, and more recently GM by Toyota and Honda. Today, we wonder if Tesla will be the future automotive giant. And what new car company that we haven't heard of yet will be the leader in 2025, or 2035?

The second aspect, however, is what seriously complicates the focus on technology. Ford's choice of black paint was an economic one, part of a relentless strategy of minimizing costs which had direct benefits to customers. From 1903 through World War I this strategy was a significant contributor to the company's growth. But by the 1920s, the nature of the market itself was changing, and Ford's success as a cost-cutting pioneer did not serve so well when market dynamics began to favor factors related to comfort and style.

The point is that within the framework of any given market cycle, a company can grasp and sustain leadership. But the greater challenge is managing what happens when a new cycle begins amid the relentless pattern of constant reinvention.

This is what has caused the recurring crises at GE, GM, and IBM, and what creates fear at Toyota and paranoia at Intel and Netflix. Very few companies sustain leadership beyond a single cycle because they don't foresee the impact of change.

And this is what made the work of Gerstner so impressive at IBM. In the face of a major shift in the market the company had the choice to

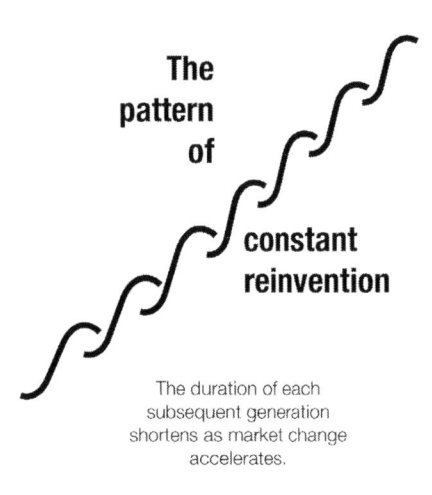

The pattern of constant reinvention

The duration of each subsequent generation shortens as market change accelerates.

Can you manage this?

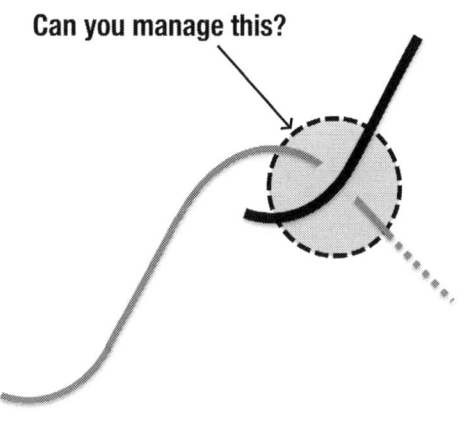

reinvent itself or collapse, and Gerstner led the process of reinvention with great success. Now Ginni Rometty is confronted with the same challenge, and as John Akers waited too long to face the reality of the collapsing mainframe market in the late 1980s, Rometty was also slow to shift.

How common is this?

- **Xerox led the copier market, but has nearly collapsed when the age of the PDF arrived to make life for document users much easier.**
- **Kodak was the world's number one manufacturer of film, but collapsed when digital cameras displaced film cameras.**
- **Nokia led the cell phone market, but was not prepared for the smart phones that customers overwhelmingly prefer.**
- **Sears led American retail for decades, but lost out to Walmart when discounting and supply chain management became the key differentiators that enabled continual price cutting.**
- **Between 1995 and 2004 Coca-Cola dropped 50% of its share price when customers switched their preferences to healthier beverages (but it has since recovered).**
- **We used to take taxis.**
- **Yahoo used to be a great search engine, once.**
- **Oldsmobile was once a successful brand, and so was Scion.**
- **Amex dominated, until it became irrelevant.**
- **There were many happy, charming, and entirely beloved bookstores all over America until Amazon.com undercut their prices by 20 or 30%.**
- **Etc. ad nauseum.**

So the point ought to be clear – just because the current structure of the market favors your solution absolutely today, does not mean that the structure of the market will also favor you tomorrow. Preferences and needs change, and when they do a set of products and services that was exceptionally well-suited to the market at a particular point in time no longer meets expectations.

It's surprisingly rare for a company to successfully adapt its products and services to changing market conditions quickly enough to sustain its leadership position, but only because leaders lose sight of their inherent vulnerability to change.

If there is one key message from these last few pages it's that nothing can possibly substitute for foresight, and those who neglect to look into the future unnecessarily compound their risks. This doesn't mean that you have make all correct predictions about what's coming, because we all know that's impossible.

What's necessary, instead, are ...

- **A leadership mindset which anticipates that change is coming, and embraces it,**
- **Constant alertness to the arrival and meaning of new technologies, trends, and patterns,**
- **Foresight-generating thinking tools like scenario planning to explore possible futures and challenge old mindsets, and a**
- **Commitment to invest proactively in preparing for change.**

And in the spirit of preparing for change, what follows is a very concise discussion of just a few of the key macro forces over which you have little to no control, but which may have significant impact on your business and its business model, which is the essence of foresight.

Business Model Warfare

The Macro Forces

The following sections have been adapted from our recent books Foresight and Extreme Creativity, The Big Shift, *and* Blockchain City.

While you may have some control over your own business model, as we saw with Southwest, which was buffeted by 9/11, 2008, and oil prices, there are countless outside forces and events over which you have no control whatsoever, but they may nevertheless turn out to be the decisive factors that your business depends upon for success. (Conversely, Coca-Cola's abrupt demise from 2000 – 2004 was entirely self-inflicted.) Thus, it's necessary to be constantly alert to the major and minor disruptive forces waiting to pounce, and to think strategically about what it might mean when they indeed leap upon you. Here are a few thought starters to mull over as you prepare your own disruption plans.

Climate Change

If your key facilities are located on a coastline or in a low lying area, climate change may present a fundamental threat. The Coast Guard, for example, has begun to think about what will happen to all the port traffic that the economy depends on if the oceans levels were to rise so quickly as to make port operations dangerous or impossible in places like Houston, LA, and Jacksonville, where the ports are not only essential hubs for the local economy, but essential to the nation. Shanghai, Rotterdam, Dubai, and Singapore will be massively impacted as well.

Any business that has anything to do with food is certainly at risk from climate-caused disruptions, and so are tourism, insurance, and real estate.[87] What happens, for example, if Miami's prestigious South Beach neighborhood get submerged under 20 feet of water?

Energy

When we think about the potential impact of climate change we also immediately think about fossil fuels, and the likelihood that the entire energy infrastructure of human civilization will transition away from fossil sources to solar, wind, hydrogen, and perhaps nuclear, and that at best this is going to be a huge, expensive, and contentious process. Since there's little likelihood that we'll get even close to "best," we can be sure that major energy-related disruptions are in our future.

Blockchains

Do you understand the blockchain, and what it might do to, or for, your business? If blockchain usage expands as some predict that it will, it could be a great boon to your firm, or a major hindrance.

Walmart, for example, is starting to require its food suppliers to certify the quality and provenance of their products using blockchains, which enables Walmart and its customers to trace the entire supply chain backwards to the very beginning, to pinpoint the farm and even the field where their produce was grown, the chemicals used in the process, and the trucks, trains, and ships that were used to transport it.

Walmart is just one company, and food is just one example. If blockchains really do become pervasive, and that is a still a pretty big if, then they'll have huge impact throughout every corner of the economy.

Robotics

We've already discussed the immanent arrival of robots and the startling forecast that by mid-century, computer technology will have advanced so far that it will provoke a singularity, a total transformation in human culture because machine intelligence will be so incredibly capable, far surpassing human intelligence. Long before that happens, if it does, robots are already having massive impact on the way we work and on who works.

Demographics

You may not realize it, but the population explosion of the 20th century is rapidly coming to an end. The population growth rate has already slowed throughout most of the world, and in only a few parts of Asia and Africa are birth rates still high. This is already having massive effects throughout Europe, for example, where entire countries are shrinking, and in Japan, where there are so few babies being born that within a few decades the aged will outnumber the workers. This has the potential to be a budgetary calamity for Japan, because there will be so few workers for each retiree that the nation's fiscal health is already in doubt. In Brazil there were eight workers for each retiree in 2000, but by 2060 there will only be two workers, creating a massive fiscal imbalance that has overwhelming consequences for all of Brazilian society.

A New Economy

Occurring separately, climate change, the transition to a new structure of energy supply, blockchains, robots, or changing demographics would each cause major social and economic change. But they won't occur separately, they're all occurring now, at the same time, and they are resolutely and absolutely forcing the global economy toward an entirely new set of structures. What will emerge from this tumultuous period is unknown, but we can be sure that the core functioning model of economic growth cannot be sustained as it has been sustained for the last 150 years.

•••

This has only been a short summary for recap purposes, but nevertheless what does it tell you? What actions does this call for?

It means that you have to pay much more attention to the macro processes of change than ever before, because their impacts are likely to arrive much more quickly than ever before.

Model what's coming through techniques like scenario planning, and then prepare your organization to pivot to a new business model when the threats arrive, and when the opportunities arrive as well. Get ahead of the s-curve.

Chapter 29
TOOL #3:
THE BUSINESS MODEL MAP

One of the confounding problems you face when thinking about business models is that they can be pretty abstract. It would be very helpful if we could visualize them in some useful way, which is exactly what the business model map enables us to do. As we've seen, it's both an analytical tool that helps us to understand many of the trends that are occurring, and a predictive tool that helps us to anticipate trends that may occur.

The map presents a market space on which we label the horizontal axis "market size," and the vertical axis "customization" or "differentiation." This is of course a simplistic way to think about the market, but in this case simplicity is our friend because the map helps us to addresses these three essential questions:

- Where are we today, where are our competitors, and in which directions will we find our best future?
- What business models will be most successful in the future?
- In which directions should we target our innovation efforts?

The far left side of the map denotes the highest prices, with the far right is lowest; moving toward the right means reaching a larger market and thus more customers, and the lower right hand corner thus designates the largest mass market, the one with the lowest prices and cheapest manufacturing. The American company called "Dollar Tree" occupies that spot, along with garage sales and thrift stores.

Hence, the business model intent of both Walmart and Ikea is to move progressively to the right without falling into a quality abyss. "Lower prices every day" is not just a Walmart advertising slogan, it's the central element of the company's value proposition.

In the lower left, conversely, you would find the nonsensical combination of highly priced mass goods, definitely the worst place to be, and fully meriting the name "death zone." No business would consciously choose to occupy this spot because it is a hopeless place without a future, the end point for bankruptcy. This is where you go to die.

The upper left corner, meanwhile, is where you find exclusive products that only the richest can buy, private yachts and jets, Picasso and Van Gogh paintings, mountain-top estates and private islands.

Simple as it is, the map enables us to locate our relative place in the market, to consider the behavior of our competition, and then to us think about our preferred course for the future.

As an example, let's take the example of Sears, at one time the dominant American retailer and an innovative company that grew to enormous size and great influence. Sears did this by offering great value, and it was very specifically targeted at the core of the market. Both as a matter of its business model design and its marketing, it strived to be the iconic American retailer. Headquartered in the heartland of the country in Chicago, the company expressed self-confidence and reliably produced handsome profits for many years.

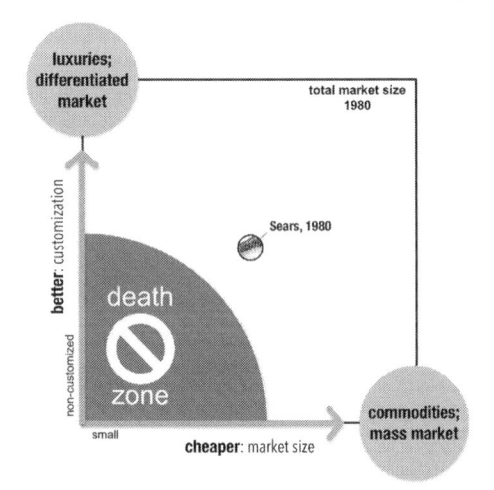

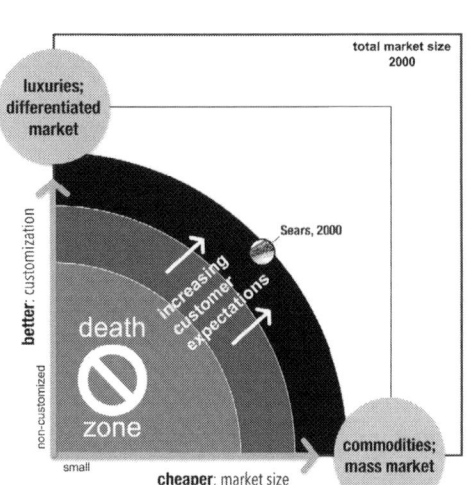

Here is Sears sitting happily at very center of the market map in 1980. Its prices were neither lowest nor highest; its brand positioning screamed "middle market" in every respect.

However, by 1980 Sears had a young rival, and within 20 years the rival had far surpassed it. Walmart out-innovated Sears, and while Sears suffered on its way to total collapse, Walmart grew both in the US and then throughout the world, and now employs millions in its thousands of stores.

Our market map of 2000 shows that the overall size of the market has grown significantly, reflecting the impact of economic progress, and the map also mentions a key factor, which is that overall customer expectations changed from 1980, and parts of the market that were viable in 1980 have been overtaken by the expanding death zone of 2000. The death zone grew because the retail value proposition of 1980 was no longer viable by 2000 – *customer expectations had changed.*

Sears management did not grasp this change, and kept the business locked resolutely where it had been for decades. If you went into a Sears in 2000, and used a time machine to venture back to 1975, the store would seem unchanged; the encroaching death zone was already swallowing it up.

There was simply not enough innovation, and its management seemed to be stubbornly ignorant; the market changed

Part 4: Step into the River

while Sears stayed the same.

The management teams of Walmart, Target, and Amazon were certainly grateful that Sears seemed so oblivious to the changing times. By developing new innovations throughout their supply chains, in product designs, and in fact across the entire scope of their business models, all three companies succeeded in moving their business models both upward, by steadily improving the quality of their products, and to the right, with progressively lower prices. (Note, however, that they all also adopted predatory employment practices.[88])

Walmart and all successful mass market business model innovators, like Target, Amazon, and Ikea, aspire to continue moving both up, toward more quality and customization, and to the right, toward ever lower prices and larger addressable markets.

Soon Sears will be only a memory, while Walmart will continue to move up and to the right, even as it chases Amazon and the death zone chases both of them up and outward. Hence, the Walmart of 2025 cannot possibly be the same as the Walmart of even 2020, as creative destruction, and a very competitive marketplace, push and pull it ever forward.

Innovators in both organizations will ask how they can further customize the experience of shopping, and they will look to new technology for some of the answers. Will Amazon and Walmart warehouses use drones to get packages to you within an hour or two? Will they use quantum computers to devise irresistible purchasing recommendations? Will they use AI to predict future fashion trends, or 3D printers to create customized products that the drones deliver? All these seem likely.

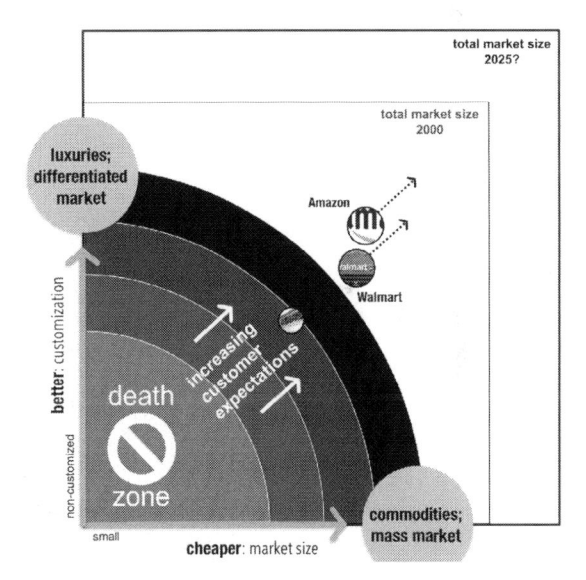

237

Business Model Warfare

the MEANS:
50 opportunities to improve your business model

products & services	technology applied	supply chain	organization & operations
product / service design user interface functionality product offering product family product life cycle product platforms product availability packaging segmenting sales model R&D innovation process sustainability warranty after-sale service	technology (hidden or embedded) technology (evident) materials connectivity interfaces platforms api apps	sourcing provenance manufacturing distribution system communication automation partners inventory distribution	business structure type capital formation governance IT infrastructure employee / contractor mix insourcing / outsourcing employee experience decision making processes strategy formation process to improve processes administration information flow automation in operations partnering alliances facilities infrastructure facilities effectiveness

Now look again at the full list of 50 internal innovation opportunities, and notice how many of them would provide operating efficiencies to support further price reductions. This is the field of play.

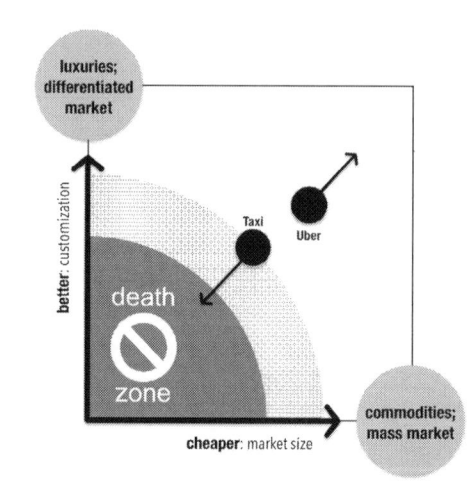

Another simple but illuminating example compares taxis and Uber. Here we see clearly that Uber (and all its ride sharing competitors) offer a better quality of service at a lower price, which completely marginalizes taxis and leaves them languishing in a newly expanding death zone (shown by the cross-hatching).

As another example, let's look at Mercedes and Lexus. Earlier I mentioned that a $45,000 Lexus once competed successfully with a $75,000 Mercedes, while the $20,000 Chevrolet and Toyota are intentionally positioned in the center of the market, similar in brand identity and corporate culture to Sears.

For decades the center was a profitable spot to occupy, but now it's high risk. So as Sears was swallowed up by growing customer expectations, the failure of Chevrolet to innovate was a big part of the problem that Rick Wagoner was unable to fix, and a significant contributor to the drastic decline of GM. Now GM is going even further in admitting its lack of innovativeness and cutting production of all its four-door sedan models, shifting entirely to trucks and SUVs, and abandoning the classic sedan auto market to its competitors Honda and Toyota. They are very happy to have one less rival in a market that they continue to find very profitable.

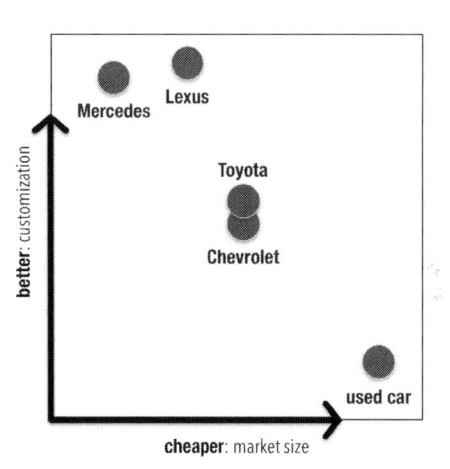

Map Your Business

The point of this is obviously that you can use this framework to think about the aspects or dimensions of your business where customization can be offered, and where it can be improved by lowering prices, thereby moving your entire business model continually upward and to the right. Use the map to help you think about the future of your business, and to compare your company's ambitions and performance to your competitors, as we have compared Sears and Walmart, Uber and taxi, and autos.

The Sweet Spot

As with the taxi industry, improvement may not be optional, and indeed when we look at the companies that have failed we see many examples in which competitors offered lower prices or more customized solutions, or both at the same time.

You may remember, for example, that in the early days of the internet there were many search engine companies, but over time they've all fallen away. We know why – the search results that Google provided using its proprietary algorithms were simply better. What made them better? Customization. Google search results were and remain more customized to the specific requirements of searchers.

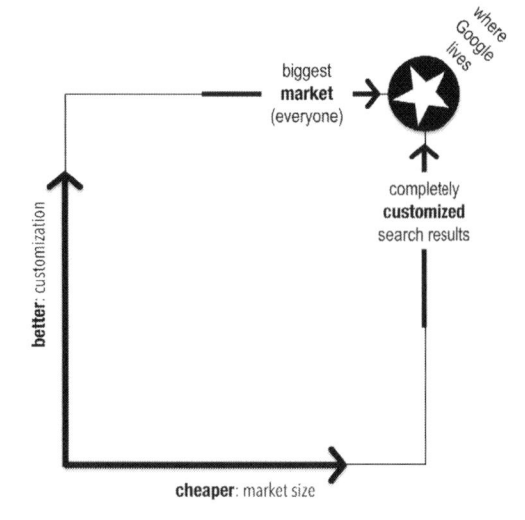

They're also free, which means that Google itself occupies the sweetest spot on the market map, the interesting sort of business Nirvana located in the upper right hand corner. Since no one has to pay to use this service, it can attract the largest possible customer base, and all results are entirely customized to the search terms you enter.

It takes only milliseconds, meaning that the search is completed in less time than it takes to type the search query into the search engine field. Google did this approximately 3 trillion times in 2018.[89]

Google's business model has created billionaires precisely because it's so well and uniquely positioned, and also because its leaders seem to fully understand the extraordinary position it occupies and are managing the firm to exploit and extend their significant advantage.

It's worthwhile to understand how this business model is different from a more conventional approach. In traditional business relationships, customers exchange money for goods, services, and experiences, but in the case of Google it's a triangular relationship that's much more complicated. As we saw above with all advertisers (and the billboard business), Google's revenue comes not from the search user customers who pay nothing (except data), but from their other customers, the advertisers, who pay money. Lots of it.

And so the entire menagerie of complementary services that Google has built around the search engine, Gmail, YouTube, calendaring, docs, maps, translate, photos, and all the rest, presently serve as drivers of search traffic, which in turn drives advertising revenue. This was not obvious at the beginning, but eventually it became clear, and dominant, with a massive 68% of the US search market.

Another company also occupying the sweet spot right next to Google is Facebook, likewise free to use and likewise a seller of advertising (and at present with a dubious ethical stance regarding your data and what it does with it)[90]. The price you pay as user is the "cost" of your data, and what it reveals about you.

Facebook's business model is also built entirely on the achievement of total customization, but in Facebook's case the customization is provided by you, the user. And billions of us are happy to participate, spending many hours to craft the online expression showing off who we are to the global Facebook community of 2.2 billion users. It's a creative economy business model.

Google also relies on us to customize, as we are the one who are creating the 180 million + web sites that Google then searches for us, for (almost) free. This profound partnership between content

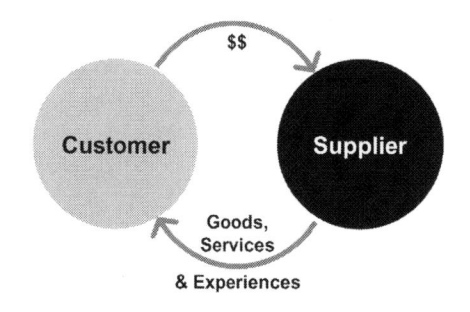

Conventional Business Model

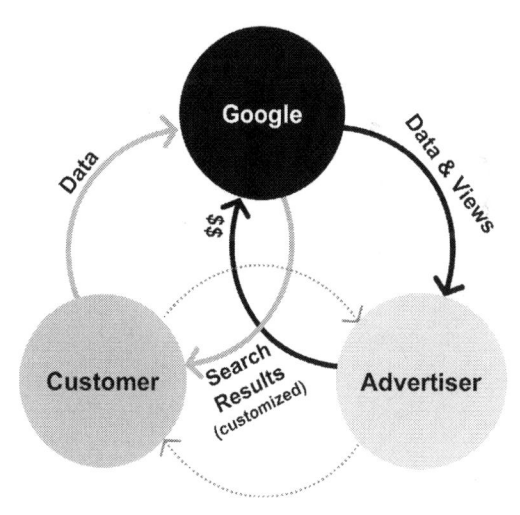

Triangular Business Model

creators (us), platform creators such as Facebook, and content locators such as Google and Bing, constitutes a hugely significant phenomenon for future business model innovators to understand, exploit, and further develop. It is here that we can anticipate many surprises in the future, particularly as computers become faster, more powerful, and less expensive.

Remember, though, that this doesn't mean that Google and Facebook will forever be entrenched as the exemplary occupants of the sweet spot. There is no end to the business factors that *could* become important in a future market, and which some other firm may master. Indeed, as I noted above, it's very often the case that when the key drivers of competition in a given market change, the old companies are pushed aside and new ones take their places as leaders. And this happens precisely because it's the new firms that master the new competitive factors first.

Now that we know how valuable the data are, and how important it is to build network effects into your business model, we will surely see new companies that leverage these factors taking a run at the leaders. Perhaps they will compete on privacy, which surely are weaknesses of Google and Facebook. Perhaps they will monetize the data of customers, paying you for knowledge about you. Perhaps they will leverage blockchains, or promote community, or develop new business models that effectively address climate change or inequality.

The Brand Bridge and the Experience

These last few pages have been all about the Means, the 50 areas identified above that you may be able to exploit in the pursuit of business model innovations. Elsewhere we've considered opportunities to innovate the business model by focusing on the brand, and we noted that first Nike and then Adidas have been experts at this, and that most other companies lag considerably, focusing on functional value and mundane stories rather than aspirational value and soulfulness.

To consider the opportunities that your brand offers, a Brand Audit is often in order, which considers the critical tacit factors that shape the attitudes and responses of customers, and attempts to clearly define what Jerome refers to as the "brand field," the complete ecosystem landscape in and around your brand. Designing that brand field and then implementing the design is what the art of soulful branding is all about.

And as we saw particularly with Disney and the extreme focus on what the customer experiences in every possible dimension, the experience itself is readily available for you to design. Walt Disney said repeatedly, "Everything speaks," which became an instruction to his designers not to overlook anything. And it's why Disney parks are so revered and so admired, and so difficult to copy.

It takes great patience, attention, and determination to craft an experience so authentic and yet so highly curated at the same time.

But it's certainly doable. Consider packaging design, for example. Decades ago Steve Jobs realized that Apple's packaging offered a great opportunity to initiate the customer's Apple experience by using the box to both tell and story and to provide instructions. So far from being a mundane and dismissive experience, now when you open up an Apple package you're greeted by messaging and information, rather than bits of messy styrofoam and a logistical mess.

In fact, the entire user experience was so important to Apple's success, and so poorly understood in the early days of the Mac, that Apple ended up writing and publishing a book of guidelines for software developers to explain to them why the Mac interface consisted of the elements it did, and how they should design their own software to utilize these elements in a way that would enable users to master their new programs without any instructions. The goal is "no user manual," and while that's elusive for more sophisticated tools, we've all seen how a child of less than a year old gravitates to a smart phone and can figure out how to use it in about a minute. That phone is the great grandchild of a Mac, and everything Apple learned along the way about interface design is all about the user experience, and it's now the standard not just for iPhones, but for all phones.

A friend who has young children recently told me an amusing story about his son, who at 3 years old was a proficient iPad user, and came upon a conventional laptop screen and immediately tried to use it by swiping his fingers as he would on the iPad. Nothing happened, and the boy looked at the laptop with a "What's wrong with this thing?" expression.

A great experience is like that – it makes everything else seem inadequate. And it can (and must) be designed as an integral part of your business model, whether we're talking about technology, packaging, theme parks, web sites, retail stores, industrial supplies, lumber, banking, or anything else.

So those are your three levers, the Means, the Story Bridge, and the Experience. Map your present and then design a better future. Today we don't know what those business models are, but we can be sure that astute innovators are preparing to exploit the technologies and the changes that are inevitably coming. This could be you, or your competitors; you choose.

Part 4: Step into the River

Chapter 30
TOOL #4:
THE VALUE LADDER

The business model map proposes that you can develop your business model in three directions, toward the top left and high quality differentiation, to the upper right toward the sweet spot, or toward the right and lower prices.

All three are valid business targets, and there are successful business models that occupy all of them. What the map suggests is that you have to choose, and after making that choice many of the other elements of your overall model will become clear.

That is, there are known formulas for how to compete successfully as a discounter, and quite different formulas for luxury goods. Make sense, right?

Maybe not.

Don't get drawn too far with this line of thinking, because the whole point of business model innovation is to turn these stereotypes around, to find ways to enhance the customer's experience that bend the established rules and provide enhanced value, and perhaps surprise and delight through the very experience of something new and different.

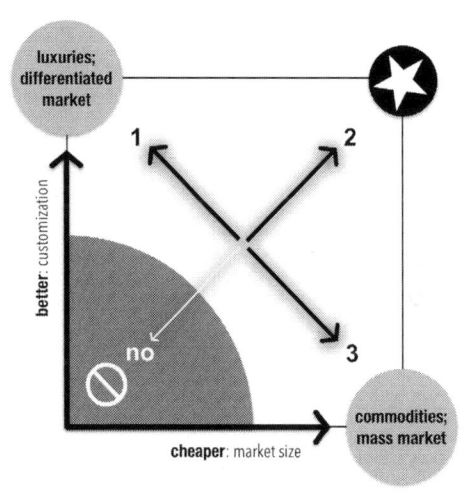

Three Strategic Options

245

To help you think about this we will to explore two different versions of another model, the Value Ladder.

In the first version, we see a conventional segmentation view of a four-tiered market. Taken from the customer's viewpoint, we see commodities at the bottom and differentiated goods and services at the top. The dashed line through the middle suggests a ceiling for commodity suppliers, above which they cannot go, and a floor for differentiated provider, below which they cannot successfully go. This is all pretty sensible and somewhat self-evident, although the framework is quite useful just because it helps us visualize important factors of any business model.

Conventional View: Value Ladder Model

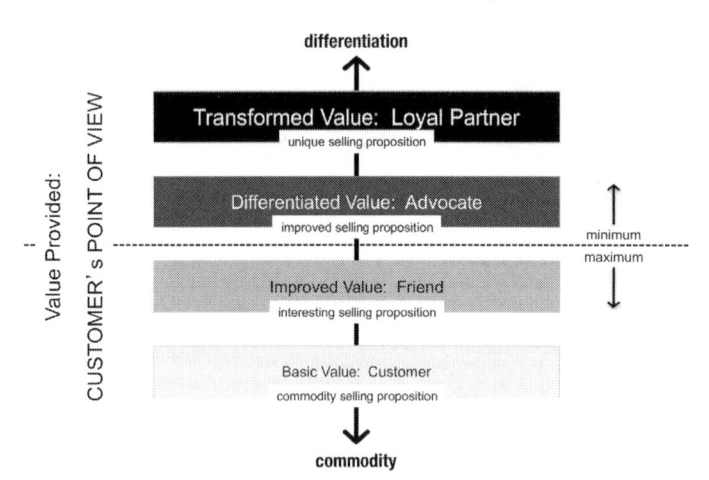

↑ differentiation

- Transformed Value: Loyal Partner — unique selling proposition
- Differentiated Value: Advocate — improved selling proposition
- (minimum / maximum)
- Improved Value: Friend — interesting selling proposition
- Basic Value: Customer — commodity selling proposition

↓ commodity

(Value Provided: CUSTOMER's POINT OF VIEW)

The second version (facing page) proposes that we rethink the model and twist the logic around to find new and useful business model value propositions. What, it asks, if a basic value provider, i.e., a discounter, could offer a transformed experience, and soar to the top of the ladder?

Conversely, what would it look like if a differentiated business model drew elements from the bottom and became a fervent discounter?

Well, we don't have to speculate about the first twist, about the discounter providing the differentiated experience. That's exactly the business model of both Amazon and Alibaba. Indeed, the essence of their model is providing a differentiated experience at huge savings. Who else offers 20% and free overnight delivery? Not long ago no one thought it even possible, but now it's entirely taken for granted.

And now you know why online retail is so attractive to Walmart – what a brilliant was to transform that often very unpleasant experience of shopping in a giant warehouse into the comfort of home? And to drive home exactly how much it's as good as Amazon (which it may or may not actually be...), Walmart spent millions of dollars on TV ads during the 2018 Christmas shopping season to show perfect suburban homes with Walmart's signature blue boxes waiting on the doorstep (instead of Amazon's), boxes so attractive that they didn't even need wrapping paper!

Ikea follows the same model, with its showrooms so nicely decorated as to make every piece of furniture and accessory irresistible even though the prices are so shockingly low that your cart ends up overflowing by the time you get to the checkout stand, even though you only came in for one itsy little thing.

Rethinking the Model

differentiation ↑

How can a transactional provider offer a differentiated experience?

Value Provided: CUSTOMER's POINT OF VIEW

no minimum ↑ ↓ no maximum

How can a differentiated provider successfully offer a satisfying commodity experience?

↓ commodity

Has any company successfully flipped the model the other way, and integrated commodity characteristics into a differentiated value proposition? That's a little more difficult to recognize, but you could make the argument that Apple's retail stores have done this with plain wooden tables, very simple store layouts, and the sales staff dressed in simple polos. The products are high end, but the stores are intentionally understated.

Costco's model is also a hybrid, a warehouse store where the work is done mostly by you, since the displays are just boxes plied on pallet racks towering to the ceiling; the differentiation is in the products themselves. (To make this clear, Costco also sells diamonds, and the diamond department is located just as you enter the store to make sure that you get the point that it's a high quality place, although this message is intended to be noted only on the unconscious level.)

The question that all this is intended to provoke is a simple but important one:

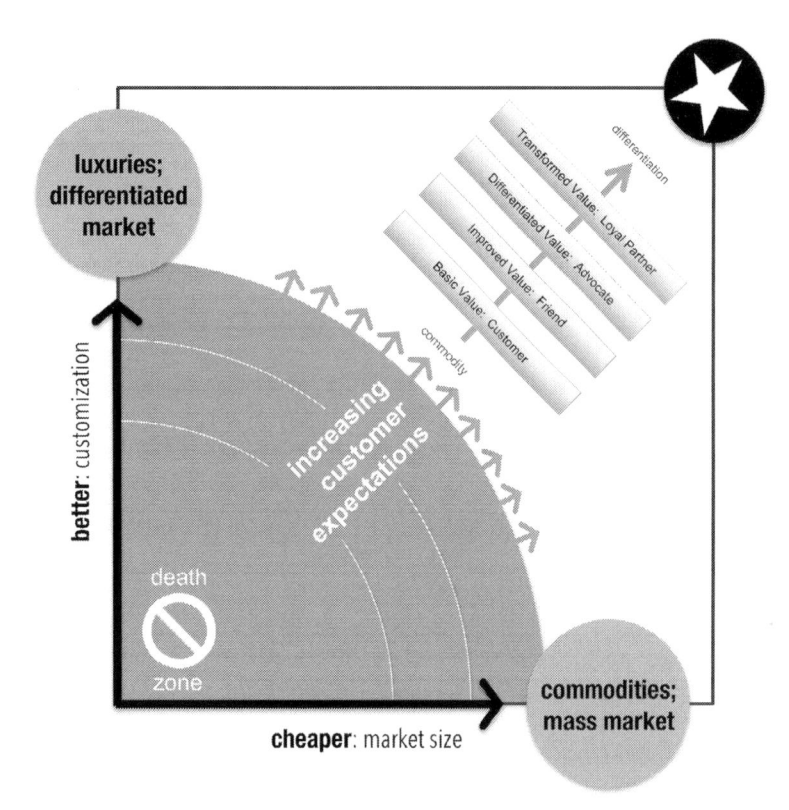

How can you alter the assumed rules of the game to devise business model innovations that move your value proposition into the "transformed" category, regardless of price?

Here's one more image to perhaps stimulate your thinking. Here we see that the value ladder ascends towards the sweet spot, and what's pushing it? It's customer expectations, which are always increasing, and thus shoving companies upward, while the death zone relentlessly expands and eats up those that don't continue to innovate their business models.

It's clearly a world of innovate … or die.

Part 4: Step into the River

Chapter 31
TOOLS #5 & 6:
THE CANVAS and the 10 TYPES

An innovative business model must function smoothly on many dimensions simultaneously. There's the experiential part, as well as the operational means of making the business function, and the branding story communications that articulate the value proposition to customers and engage in dialog with them. Since it all has to be fully aligned and completely consistent, it would be enormously helpful to be able to visualize it all in one picture.

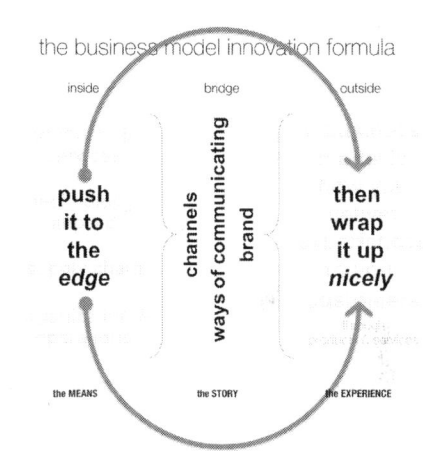

The Business Model Canvas

That's what a business model canvas does, a simple tool that innovators use the world over to design innovations.

The business model canvas was invented by Alexander Osterwalder and Yves Pigneur, and made famous in the book that they and 400 of their closest friends wrote, *Business Model Generation*.[91] Alexander received his Ph.D. studying business models (and he may have been the very first to do so), and what he achieved through his Ph.D. research was a clear understanding of a business model consisting of the nine key elements.

What he and his friends achieved by inventing the canvas was a very useful way to visualize the whole thing.

The canvas is a simple concept, a big piece of paper with nine boxes, one for each element of Alexander's business model framework:

> **Key Partnerships**
> **Key Activities**
> **Key Resources**
> **Cost Structure**
> **Value Propositions**
> **Customer Relationships**
> **Channels**
> **Customer Segments**
> **Revenue Streams**

The canvas is configured to express important relationships between these nine elements, and by using post-its on a poster-sized template you can play around with variations, which many people find to be a very productive way of being creative and purposeful.

the nine elements of the business model canvas

inside — bridge — outside

key resources
key activities
key partnerships
cost structure
} channels {
value propositions
customer segments
customer relationships
revenue streams

the MEANS — the STORY — the EXPERIENCE

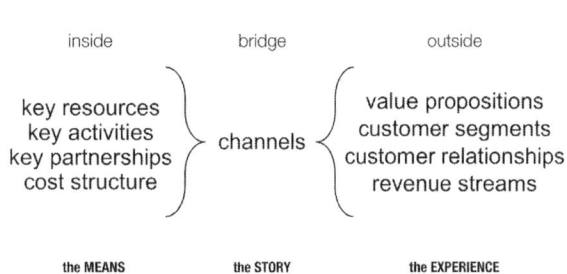

As you can see to the left and below Alexander's canvas template on the facing page, the nine elements he identified match up well with the three major categories we've used to express the business model warfare framework, with the "inside" factors on the left, the customer or "outside" factors on the right, and the channels in the middle.

The choice of the name "canvas" was very smart, as it nicely conveys the notion of a blank surface

Part 4: Step into the River

that's just sitting there and waiting for your brilliant ideas to come forth, just as a great painting by Picasso or da Vinci or Van Gogh emerges from the blank canvas – the initial, rough-sketched lines give way to base layers of paint, and then the refined and finished color fields and highlights that express true genius.

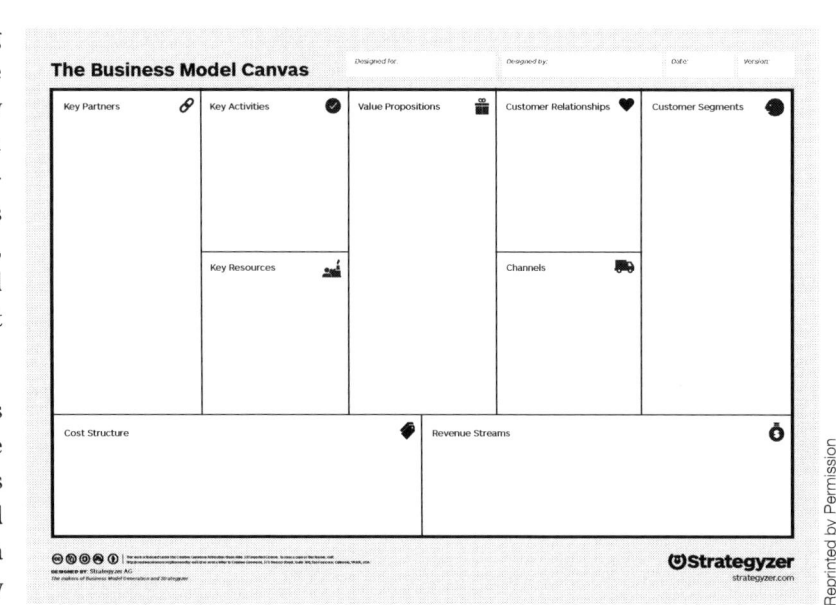

Designing a business or a business model is surely complex, and the capacity to effectively visualize this complexity is critical, and Alexander's insight that such a template could be so enormously helpful was right on the money.

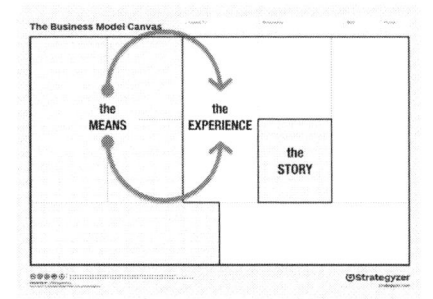

It's so important, in fact, that a major element in Japanese total quality process is called "the visual factory," wherein lots of information is displayed right there on the factory floor to enable the people at work to see what would otherwise be hidden among the whirring, stomping machines, to see the process flow and the productivity rates, and all the factors that they can affect and manage to achieve high performance and high quality.

The canvas is thus a clever, convenient, and templated way to organize information and model it at the same time.

You can download a free copy of the Business Model Canvas template, and get a lot of very good guidance and additional templates from Alexander's super helpful web site, Strategyzer:

https://strategyzer.com/canvas/business-model-canvas

The first business model canvas proved so useful that the concept has been adapted to address many types of business challenges, so now you see canvases and sketchpads with lots of different purposes, like "value proposition design," "disruption map," and "creative matrix," all of which are intended to make complexity more manageable by making it visual and promoting testing and experimentation.

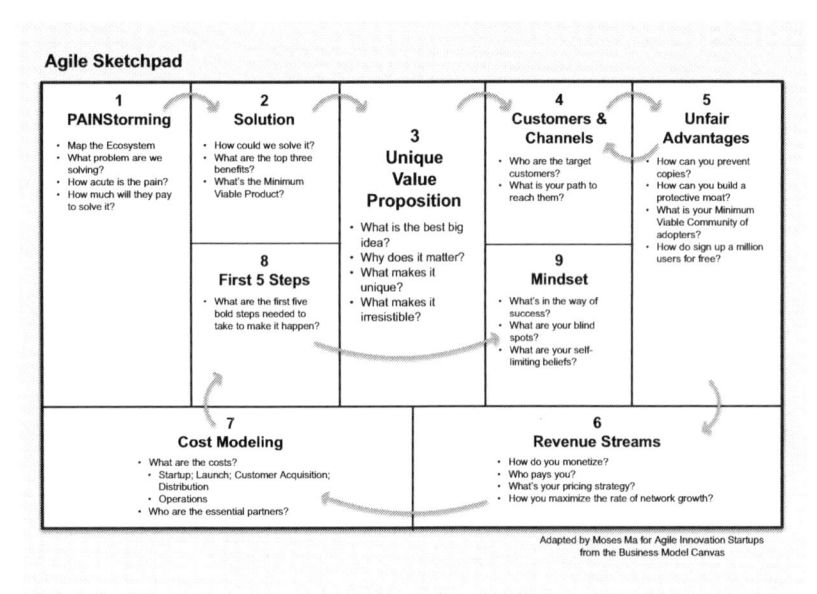

Our colleague Moses Ma, for example, developed a super useful variation on the canvas for Agile startups, the Agile Sketchpad, which begins by examining the customer's pain, and is specifically geared to help you find "unfair" competitive advantages for your business, and also help you to recognize and overcome psychological and mindset barriers that may stand in the way of your brilliant success.

Agile Sketchpad

1 PAINStorming	2 Solution	3 Unique Value Proposition	4 Customers & Channels	5 Unfair Advantages
• Map the Ecosystem • What problem are we solving? • How acute is the pain? • How much will they pay to solve it?	• How could we solve it? • What are the top three benefits? • What's the Minimum Viable Product?	• What is the best big idea? • Why does it matter? • What makes it unique? • What makes it irresistible?	• Who are the target customers? • What is your path to reach them?	• How can you prevent copies? • How can you build a protective moat? • What is your Minimum Viable Community of adopters? • How do sign up a million users for free?
	8 First 5 Steps • What are the first five bold steps needed to take to make it happen?		9 Mindset • What's in the way of success? • What are your blind spots? • What are your self-limiting beliefs?	
7 Cost Modeling • What are the costs? • Startup; Launch; Customer Acquisition; Distribution • Operations • Who are the essential partners?			6 Revenue Streams • How do you monetize? • Who pays you? • What's your pricing strategy? • How you maximize the rate of network growth?	

Adapted by Moses Ma for Agile Innovation Startups from the Business Model Canvas

Doblin's Ten Types

Ask any student of innovation how they organize the different types of innovation and they're probably ready to share their own categories.

Larry Keeley and his colleagues at Doblin, for example, have helpfully defined "ten types of innovation," and written a great book with that title.[92] It's a framework that many innovators have found very helpful in organizing their own innovation efforts.

The ten are:

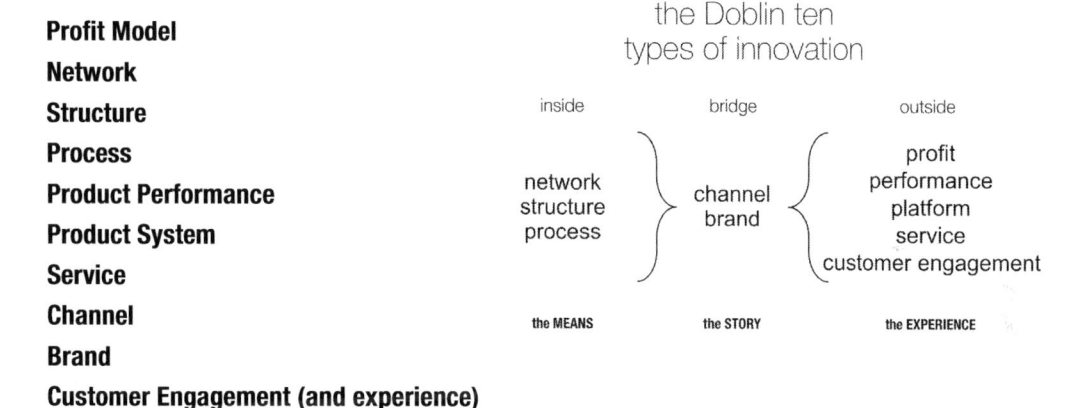

Profit Model
Network
Structure
Process
Product Performance
Product System
Service
Channel
Brand
Customer Engagement (and experience)

the Doblin ten types of innovation

inside	bridge	outside
network structure process	channel brand	profit performance platform service customer engagement
the MEANS	the STORY	the EXPERIENCE

As you can see, the Doblin ten also map well onto the basic business model warfare framework and Alexander's Canvas, which helps us to have confidence that the framework does indeed express something essentially important about business models and business model competition.

Doblin also developed a very cool card deck to help you apply these concepts creatively in your own business.

three variations on the business model innovation formula

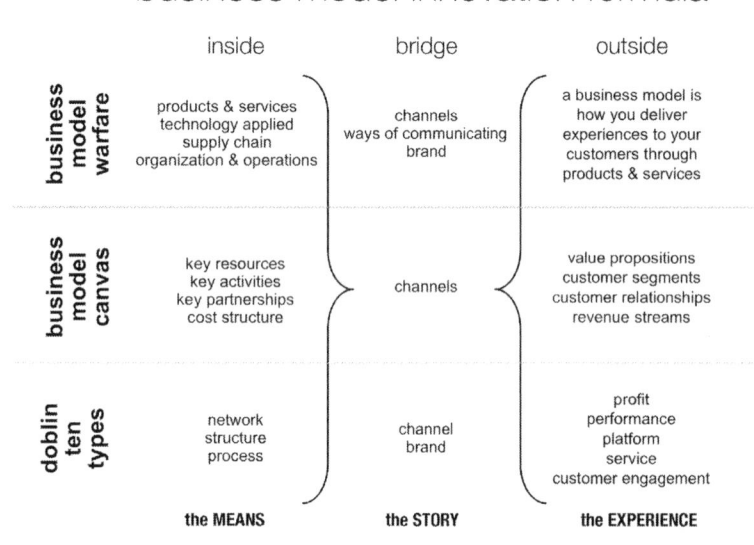

	inside	bridge	outside
business model warfare	products & services technology applied supply chain organization & operations	channels ways of communicating brand	a business model is how you deliver experiences to your customers through products & services
business model canvas	key resources key activities key partnerships cost structure	channels	value propositions customer segments customer relationships revenue streams
doblin ten types	network structure process	channel brand	profit performance platform service customer engagement
	the MEANS	the STORY	the EXPERIENCE

These are all variations on one important innovation theme, and as we see here, there is a broad consistency even as they show interesting differences. In all three approaches there is the outside (the experience), the inside (the means), and the bridge (the story), but which is most useful for you depends of course on the characteristics of your industry and your competitors.

Other Resources

Others have also explored these topics in very interesting and helpful ways. Clayton Christensen has written extensively about the character of industry disruption and the strategic errors that enable upstart firms to take advantage of missed opportunities that large companies so often overlook. His book *The Innovator's Dilemma*[93] is widely read. Another interesting view is offered by Adrian Slywotzky and David J. Morrision, whose book *Profit Patterns*[94] catalogs various strategies that companies have developed to earn profits in competitive markets. Patrick van der Pijl and his colleagues have written a very helpful book, *Design a Better Business,*[95] that also offers many great tools and templates.

No matter what frameworks and tools you choose to adopt, the goal is to think clearly about your firm's position and the ways you organize and innovate to achieve success in the future.

The underlying points remain the immediacy of market disruption, the inevitability of business model competition, and the utter imperative

Part 4: Step into the River

to innovate, to disrupt, before your competitors have the opportunity to disrupt you. Sketch some initial thoughts on this template. Where are your opportunities?

your business model innovation

inside
products & services
technology applied
supply chain
organization & operations

bridge
channels
ways of communicating
brand

outside
a business model is how you deliver
experiences to your customers
through products & services

push it to the *edge*　　　　　　　　　　　　　　　　**then wrap it up *nicely***

Sketch your first draft on this template.

Chapter 32
TOOL #7:
YOUR BUSINESS MODEL INNOVATION ACTION PLAN

what is a **business model**?

1. It's how you make money.
2. It's how you deliver *experiences* to your customers.
3. It's how you use products, services, technology, supply chain, and operations to compete.
4. It's how you differentiate your company.

Then why should you be scared?
Well, what if your competitor comes up with a better business model?
Then what?

A quick recap. Our exponentially-changing world is making the transition from an industrial economy to a much different digitalized one, a momentous shift that brings with it enormous complexity, great opportunities, and also great risks. We have explored many of the specific component of these shifts and considered how they aggregate into an overall one, and we have also recognized that all of this requires of us a new mindset, the capacity to cope with and manage change, as the days of stability are certainly no more.

In this book we've emphasized the importance of business models, the landscape of social, economic, and technological disruption, the imperative of leadership, and now we come to the critical action steps, designing your business model innovations. For it is through innovation, and innovation alone, that strategizing and planning and thinking come together into doing, into creating the new products and services and especially business models and systems that will enable sustained success.

Without innovation you're probably doomed; because of it you may well triumph.

Innovations embody that marvelously elusive yet curiously evocative quality of newness. They elicit excitement, intrigue, and sometimes inspiration. Innovation is the new and different *when it is also better*, when it expresses and provides something that did not previously exist. Such value can take many forms: innovation can yield a product or process, a policy, a technology, or a technique. It may benefit society rather than creating profit for a company, but whether for profit or for social good, in the end to qualify as an innovation, to be worthy, it must add value for someone or ones other than the creator: end users must benefit:

Innovation value is experienced and attributed by buyers and users, not by conceivers and makers.

It's true that some we label " innovations" are superficial and frivolous, fads and trinkets that don't at all deserve to be called innovative. But we admire those that are vital to who we are and how we live, a long and unforgettable list of tools that we rely upon daily: plows and seeds and cities, power plants and batteries, computers and telephones and iPhones, tractors and cars and airplanes, rockets and satellites and GPS, refrigerators, vaccines and medicines and fertilizers, water purifiers and antibiotics and anesthesia, and on and on the list goes.

Businesses that create innovations thrive, and nations that innovate often gain tremendous advantages, while those that fail to innovate may also fail outright, and disappear.

So how is innovation accomplished?

Innovation is a skill, and like every skill it can be studied and mastered. Innovation can also be managed, and indeed it *must* be managed since so much depends on it. For if it's not managed rigorously, then innovation occurs only as random luck, and who would think that random efforts are either sufficient or prudent?

The rigorous pursuit of innovation is guided by the knowledge that success requires us to balance the open-ended flow of creativity with prescriptive stages of disciplined inquiry. In its most robust form, innovation is a discipline that creates new possibilities for the future by structuring the inquiry into the unknown, which in turn creates new knowledge and new possibilities. It is driven from within by intrinsic aspirations and commitments, and guided from without by rigorous questioning, effective methods, and strong leadership.

So what's your action plan? The imperatives are:

1. **Understand change** through techniques such as trend tracking, disruption mapping, scenario planning, and technology roadmapping.

2. **Create business model innovations** using the map and the canvas and the sketchpad and the ten types, and any other tools that resonate with your way of thinking and your industry context.

3. **Experiment** each quarter. Put a SWAT team together for a three day exercise to develop alternative business models, and then test them not only in abstract and theoretical settings, but for real, with real customers. Do this through pop-up prototypes, test web sites, ethnographic research, and new brand identities. (Remember Bruno Palessi?)

4. **Take what you learn and apply it to your business. Quickly.**

CONCLUSION
WINNING THE WAR

1. Innovate the Business Model

Since business models are a more comprehensive way of understanding the character of competition, they must also become a focus of innovation itself. Relentlessly changing conditions mean that business models evolve rapidly, and business model innovation is therefore not optional. While innovations in any area within an organization may be important, innovations that pertain broadly and directly to the business model will be life-sustaining. Don't wait until it's too late.

2. It's the Experience

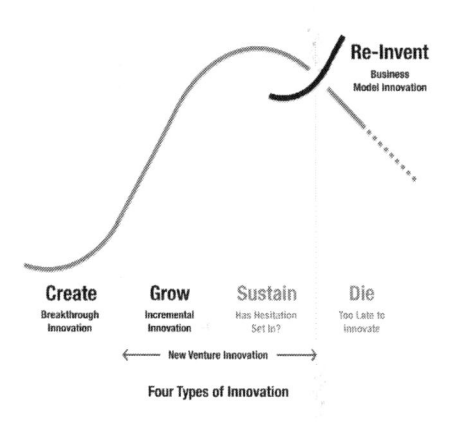

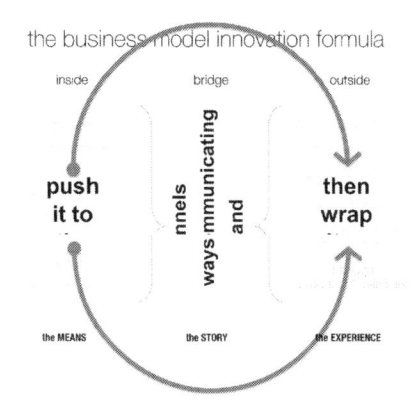

A "business model" defines a broad competitive approach to business, and articulates how a company applies processes and technologies to build and sustain effective relationships with customers by creating experiences for those customers. The experiences that customers have, and the relationships that companies build with customers, are the most critical factors. Creating them, understanding them, sustaining them, enriching them, and extending them are the critical attributes of success. Everything that is done must be in service to these relationships; they are the point; every successful business model earns some sort of competitive advantage to the extent that it serves successful relationships.

3. Price and Quality

However, any advantage may disappear overnight should a competitor devise a superior model, thereby displacing your company in the relationship with the customer. We can visualize that relationship by understanding the market as a two-dimensional map, on which we plot market size (i.e., price), and product/service customization. These two dimensions tell us a great deal about the value proposition underlying any business model.

Due to competitive forces, the life span of every business model is therefore limited, and due to the general unpredictability of change, its time frame is indeterminate. Leaders who have the good fortune to preside over a successful business model should never lose sight of the ephemeral nature of their advantages, and must focus not only on administering the (illusory) stability of today, but on preparing for or precipitating the inevitable changes of tomorrow, by understanding how costs can be lowered while customization is simultaneously increased.

The model also tells us that we must aspire to move upward and to the right, and that the upward creep of the dead zone is relentlessly chasing us that way. If we stop, the dead zone threatens to swallow us, as indeed it has done to so many failed business models.

4. Technology Is the Driver

Based on what we have discussed here, we gain further insight into how the pattern of company mortality operates as a real and significant phenomenon, and how it is often driven as a result of the acceleration of technology-driven change throughout the supply and demand economy.

Demand is enormously influenced by innovation – new technologies embedded in new products and services come into the market to significantly and decisively influence the fate of all market participants. As we are in an era of incredible and persistent technological innovation, we are forewarned that change is inevitable.

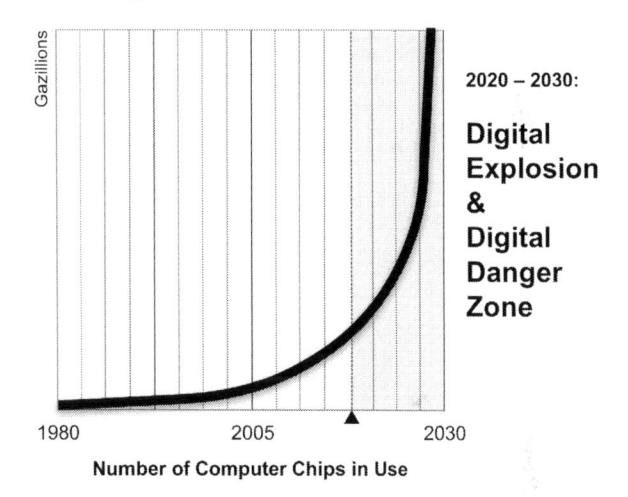

2020 – 2030:

Digital Explosion & Digital Danger Zone

Number of Computer Chips in Use

Supply innovation, that's what we do; *we* have to innovate, to apply these new technologies along with new insights in order to create the exceptional new experiences that our customers now expect.

5. The Upward Spiral

Improving performance through innovation and increasing stock price are both self-feeding cycles that create more favorable conditions for companies to develop and implement future innovations in three ways, by improving skill and performance, by enriching stock as currency for making acquisitions, and by lowering the overall cost of capital. Conversely, declining performance and a falling stock price can lead to a downward spiral that makes it progressively more difficult for companies to compete for attractive acquisition fodder, and which can also increase the cost of capital that could be invested in innovation-related activities such as R&D and product development. Get ahead and push farther ahead; get behind and fall farther behind.

It's also important to note that these positive feedback cycles can strike with lightning speed. A company can rise to the top or fall to the bottom in a stunningly short span. This is why, for example, social media monitoring is considered so critical, as a negative meme can infect the market in a matter of hours, and almost instantly erase billions in market capitalization (as it did with Tencent).

The data on company mortality show that even over the medium term, the majority of companies will become trapped in the downward spiral of increasing irrelevance, and one way or another most will disappear.

The immanence of this danger suggests that while leaders may be thinking and worrying about change and its impact on their companies, about competition and about competitive advantage, many have been doing so in a way that's simply not effective. Hence, we suggest that thinking about and enacting business model innovation may be a highly productive exercise for established businesses as it certainly is also for startups.

Conclusion

6. Winning Business Models

In summary, then, winning business models have these attributes:

1. They hit the **Sweet Spot** of **Quality** and **Price**
2. They push value creation to the **Edge of Possibility**
3. They tell a **Story** that's **Compelling** and **Soulful**
4. They sustain their relevance by evolving along with **Emerging Technologies**

The need for good thinking about business models is as important for new businesses as it is for old ones, and among the many examples consider the spectacular rise and equally spectacular collapse of Webvan, which squandered more than a billion dollars because its management team – including a renowned CEO who had formerly been the head of Andersen Consulting – was so confident in what they were doing, in their business model, that they invested hundreds of millions of dollars of capital in a business infrastructure even though market demand was completely unproven. They *believed* that they could make the business work, and fooled themselves into thinking that their belief was sufficient basis for betting massive capital on a business model that had never been fully tested. In the end, hundred-million-dollar warehouses were built but never used, never generating even a cent of return except as liquidated assets when Webvan went bust.

Thus, in spite of abundant talk about change, the temptation to build a business according to a fixed structure that is expected to endure for the long term remains strong. Never mind that the long term is completely unpredictable. Another way to say this is that any management approach that remains unrepentantly focused on stability and continuity, instead of on disruption and change, will be unpleasantly surprised in the end, and the end will probably arrive soon.

For these reasons it remains imperative to discuss managing for change as an absolute requirement, but many (most?) business leaders nevertheless still aren't very good at dealing with it. Recognizing change in the marketplace, anticipating, and adapting to its turbulent evolution, these are the challenges that confront all executives, for although we remember periods that seemed stable, they are in fact long gone and never to return.

As markets continue to evolve and competition becomes ever more demanding, engaging in Business Model Warfare therefore becomes not just an interesting possibility but a mandatory requirement. To survive and thrive, organizations must develop comprehensive innovation frameworks, and hopefully the perspectives offered here can help.

•••

In the end, when we look at the business world it's clear that the story of change and the change conspiracy are still the important stories to tell, and the process of leading an organization in the face of change remains the critical skill.

Ironically, a successful business model is often a trap. After struggling to find a way to create success, a firm finally lands upon a workable business model, a way of operating that attracts customers to buy its products and services. Transactions occur, and all is well. Attention then shifts to improving and perfecting this model, optimizing and scaling it, continuing to succeed and grow.

Sears grew this way, from an innovative startup to a national firm that

Conclusion

utterly dominated its industry. But then it stopped innovating, while Walmart (and Target, although less so) streaked past and redefined the terms of competition. A couple decades later along came Amazon, which streaked past all of them and re-redefined competition, and the whole thing starts all over and all retailers have to respond to Amazon and what Amazon embodies, the formulation of an entirely new and highly disruptive business model, that leverages new technology in a way that's awesome for customers, but brutal for competitors.

What's new, and why this whole conversation matters so much today, is the abrupt and now overwhelming impact of new technology that's just arrived or is about to, and the stunning abundance of new ways that technology will enable new business model innovations.

Business model innovators are already creating disruptions, and already achieving success in markets all over the world.

You see where this is going, right? When you fully understand what a business model is, why business model innovation matters so much to your future success, how to do it, and what to do about it in your organization, then you're on the path to success.

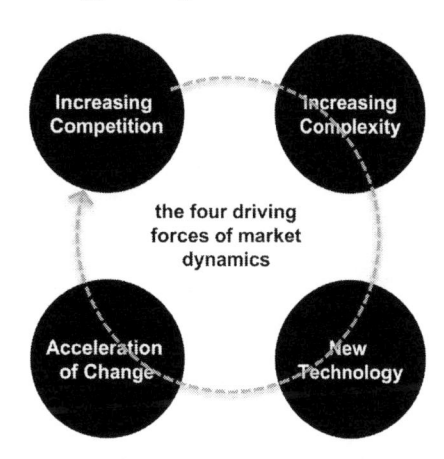

The "Change Conspiracy" — the four driving forces of market dynamics: Increasing Competition, Increasing Complexity, New Technology, Acceleration of Change.

It's war out there, and you'd better be ready ...

•••

Business Model Warfare

ABOUT THIS BOOK

The original version of this study was published as a white paper in 2004 with the gracious support of the Ackoff Center of the University of Pennsylvania, where I was at the time Senior Practice Scholar. It was one of the first detailed discussions that explored the topic of "business models," and it has been adopted and is still used in a many business schools. A revised version was published in *The Journal of Business Models* in 2014.

My sincere thanks to the late Russell Ackoff, and to John Pourdehnad and Bill Miller for their guidance and advice. Larry Keeley and Alexander Osterwalder were also most gracious and helpful with their support, as were Moses Ma, Po Chi Wu, and Jerome Conlon.

This book version takes all these ideas much farther and adds considerable depth and detail. Examples have been revised and many new ones added, but the core argument still appears to hold up nicely.

Indeed, there is no longer any dispute that business model innovation is one of the most significant of innovation's many useful forms, and I hope that the book convinces you to pay close attention to your own organization's business model, and be prepared to update or even transform it entirely, as our rapidly changing world makes the old ways obsolete even as it brings forth startlingly new possibilities.

NOTES

1. Richard Foster and Sarah Kaplan. *Creative Destruction*. Currency Doubleday, 2001. P. 14.
2. https://www.innosight.com/insight/creative-destruction/
3. Yuval Noah Harari. "Moving beyond nationalism." *The Economist: The World in 2019*. December 2018.
4. Andrew S. Grove. *Only the Paranoid Survive: How to Exploit the Crisis Points That Challenge Every Company*. Doubleday, 1996.
5. https://www.theringer.com/tech/2018/12/12/18136520/reed-hastings-netflix-hollywood-model-year-in-review
6. Adam Tooze. *Crashed: How a Decade of Financial Crises Changed the World*. Viking, 2018. P. 602.
7. https://www.scrapehero.com/many-products-amazon-sell-january-2018/
8. Theodore Levitt. *Marketing Myopia*. Harvard Business Review, 2008.
9. Walt Disney *Imagineering: A Behind the Dreams Look at Making More Real Magic*. Disney Editions, 2010.
10. *The Economist*. "Ubernomics: A hard bargain." November 3, 2018.
11. https://gbf.bloomberg.org/news/ford-motor-co-uber-lyft-announce-agreement-share-data-new-platform-gives-cities-mobility-companies-new-tools-manage-congestion-cut-greenhouse-gases-reduce-crashes/
12. *Motley Fool* https://www.fool.com/investing/2016/09/15/ the-real-reason-behind-fords-move-into-bike-sharin.aspx
13. *The Economist*, November 3, 2018.
14. *The Economist*, August 4, 2018.
15. *The Economist,* July 21, 2018.
16. *The Economist,* September 8, 2018.
17. Booz & Company. "Booz & Company Announce Its Ninth Annual Global Innovation 1000 Study." Oct 28, 2013. http://www.booz.com/cn/home/press/displays/2013-global-innovation-1000-cne
18. A small, but important footnote to the Xerox story is that at one time in its history the company was so successful and so dominant that it was literally forced by federal government regulators to license its technology to competitors. With this strange turn of events, utterly not of its own doing, the company's downward slide began. Hence, some blame for Xerox's demise does fall on misguided US government regulators.
19. Jerome Conlon, with Moses Ma and Langdon Morris. *Soulful Branding: Unlock the Hidden Energy in Your Company & Brand*. FutureLab, 2015.

Notes

[20] Langdon Morris. *The Agile Innovation Master Plan*. Innovation Academy, 2016.
[21] Don Wilson has contributed this insight, and many others that have substantially improved this work.
[22] Peter F. Drucker. *The Effective Executive: The Definitive Guide to Getting the Right Things Done*. Harperbusiness Essentials, 2006.
[23] https://www.salesforce.com/blog/2018/11/singles-day-stats-you-wont-see-anywhere-else)
[24] https://money.cnn.com/2017/12/12/news/companies/mall-closing/index.html)
[25] https://clark.com/shopping-retail/major-retailers-closing-2018/
[26] https://www.cnbc.com/2018/04/18/the-amount-of-retail-space-closing-in-2018-is-on-pace-to-break-record.html
[27] https://www.cleveland.com/expo/news/erry-2018/06/fbe79a56b79183/inside_an_amazon_fulfillment_c.html
[28] *The Economist*. "Money in your purse." December 5, 2018.
[29] https://www.washingtonpost.com/business/2018/11/30/they-had-us-fooled-inside-paylesss-elaborate-prank-dupe-people-into-paying-shoes/?noredirect=on&utm_term=.990e7cf6644f
[30] https://www.theguardian.com/artanddesign/2017/oct/01/bilbao-effect-frank-gehry-guggenheim-global-craze
[31] Adam Tooze. *Crashed: How a Decade of Financial Crises Changed the World*. Viking, 2018. P. 450.
[32] https://www.prnewswire.com/news-releases/general-motors-accelerates-transformation-300755112.html
[33] Saskia Sassen. "The Impact of the New Technologies and Globalization on Cities." *The City Reader*, Richard T. LeGates and Frederic Stout Editors. Routledge, 2016.
[34] *South China Morning Post*. https://www.scmp.com/news/china/article/1596367/shenzhen-losing-its-fight-against-pollution-main-rivers
[35] *The Economist*. "Schumpeter: Clout and Reach." December 1, 2018.
[36] *The Economist*. "Homing in." December 1, 2018.
[37] *The Economist*. "Icing on the cake." August 18, 2018.
[38] *The Economist*. "Staring down the barrel." December 8, 2018.
[39] http://www.climateaction100.org/
[40] https://www.eia.gov/state/rankings/?sid=CA#series/12
[41] *The Wall Street Journal*. "Talent Flocks to Big Cities." November 15, 2018.
[42] https://www.engadget.com/2018/12/21/google-former-ai-chief-apple-vp/
[43] *The Economist*. "Bartleby: Time to get in training." August 11, 2018.
[44] *The Wall Street Journal*. "Schools Get Fewer Overseas Students." November 13, 2018.
[45] *The Economist*. "Learning difficulties." July 21, 2018.

46. *The Economist.* "No secrets." December 15, 2018.
47. https://www.washingtonpost.com/news/global-opinions/wp/2018/03/27/chinas-new-surveillance-state-puts-facebooks-privacy-problems-in-the-shade/?noredirect=on&utm_term=.e93c85147998
48. *The Economist.* "Battery Farming." December 1, 2018.
49. http://www.lowesinnovationlabs.com/updates/
50. *The Economist.* "Hard-break hotel." December 15, 2018.
51. *The Economist.* October 27, 2018.
52. *The Economist.* October 13, 2018.
53. *The Economist.* "Waiting for Goodot" October 13, 2018)
54. W. Brian Arthur. "Competing Technologies, Increasing Returns, and Lock-In by Historical Events." *The Economic Journal*, March 1989.
55. *The Economist.* November 10, 2018.
56. Robert F. Service. "Chipmakers look past Moore's law, and silicon." *Science*, July 27, 2018.
57. *The Economist.* "The chips are down." December 1, 2018.
58. Kevin Freiberg and Jackie Freiberg. *Nuts!: Southwest Airlines' Crazy Recipe for Business and Personal Success*. Crown Business, 1998.
59. *The Economist.* August 4, 2018.
60. *The Economist.* August 18, 2018.
61. Kate Devlin. *Turned On: Science, Sex, and Robots*. Bloomsbury, 2018.
62. Ray Kurzweil. *The Singularity Is Near: When Humans Transcend Biology*. Penguin Books, 2006.
63. https://www.huffingtonpost.com/entry/taylor-swift-used-facial-technology-on-unknowing-fans-to-find-stalker_us_5c126ac9e4b002a46c14db45
64. Robert Chesney and Danielle Citron. "Deepfakes and the New Disinformation War: The Coming Age of Post-Truth Politics." *Foreign Affairs*, January/February 2019.
65. *The Economist.* "An old new world." January 5, 2019.
66. Victor J. Dzau, Marcia McNutt, and Chunli Bai. "Wake-up call from Hong Kong." *Science*, December 14, 2018.
67. https://www.engadget.com/2018/12/19/self-powered-electric-bandages-could-speed-up-healing/
68. *The Economist*, October 6, 2018
69. Noel M. Tichy and Stratford Sherman. *Control Your Destiny or Someone Else Will*. Currency Doubleday, 2993.
70. https://www.businessinsider.com/pharma-giant-gsk-signs-deal-with-pfizer-to-create-new-healthcare-leader-2018-12
71. *The Economist.* July 28, 2018.

Notes

72   Joseph Schumpeter, *Capitalism, Socialism, and Democracy*. Harper & Brothers, 1942, 1947, 1950. p. 84.
73   John Gall, *Systemantics: The Underground Text of Systems Lore*. 1986. P. 158.
74   Douglas K. Smith and Robert C. Alexander. *Fumbling the Future: How Xerox Invented, then Ignored, the First Personal Computer*. William Morrow & Company, 1988.
75   Russell Ackoff. *The Democratic Corporation*. Oxford University Press, 1994. P. 210.
76   Louis Gerstner. *Who Says Elephants Can't Dance*. HarperCollins, 2004
77   https://sproutsocial.com/insights/facebook-stats-for-marketers/
78   https://blog.bufferapp.com/psychology-of-social-media
79   https://www2.deloitte.com/us/en/pages/technology-media-and-telecommunications/articles/global-mobile-consumer-survey-us-edition.html
80   Scott Bedbury with Stephen Fenichell. *A New Brand World*. Penguin 2002, p.
81   *The Economist*. June 9, 2018
82   Richard Florida. *The Rise of the Creative Class, Revisited*. Basic Books, 2012.
83   https://www.3dnatives.com/en/3d-printed-house-companies-120220184/
84   https://www.forbes.com/sites/rachelarthur/2018/01/15/ai-ibm-tommy-hilfiger/#443a6b0378ac
85   William L. Miller and Langdon Morris. *Fourth Generation R&D: Managing Knowledge, Technology, and Innovation*. Wiley, 1999.
86   A minor but interesting detail is that Fords were originally brown, until a company engineer pointed out to Mr. Ford that black paint covered better and would therefore be less expensive. The point for Ford was thus not the color, but the principle of cost control. He understood well that lowering the cost of manufacture was the key to developing the market in the early years, but when this changed in the more mature market of the 20s, his company lagged as its business model lagged.
87   European Commission: https://ec.europa.eu/clima/policies/adaptation/how/sectors_en
88   It should be noted that Walmart's employment policies were and remain controversial, and one can argue that its success is based in part on its practice of under-paying its employees by manipulating the labor laws of the US. For the purposes of this discussion we leave that issue aside, but it's important to recognize the ethical issues associated with these practices. It seems likely that changes to Walmart's business model may be forthcoming as a result of either public pressure or unionization, both of which would bring some protections to tens of thousands of employees who at present lack much protection at all.
89   http://www.statisticbrain.com/google-searches/
90   Sue Halpern. "Apologize Later." *The New York Review*, January 17, 2019.
91   Alexander Osterwalder and Yves Pigneur. *Business Model Generation*. Wiley, 2010.

[92] Larry Keeley. *Ten Types of Innovation: The Discipline of Building Breakthroughs.* Wiley, 2013.
[93] Clayton M. Christensen. *The Innovator's Dilemma: When New Technologies Cause Great Firms to Fail.* Harvard Business School Press, 2016.
[94] Adrian Slywotzky and David J. Morrison. *Profit Patterns: 30 Ways to Anticipate and Profit from Strategic Forces Reshaping Your Business.* Times Business, 1999.
[95] Patrick van der Pijl, Justin Lokitz and Lisa Kay Solomon. *Design a Better Business: New Tools, Skills and Mindset for Strategy and Innovation.* Wiley, 2016.

INDEX

2

23andMe, 63, 65

3

3D Natives, 217
3D printing, 216, 217

9

9/11, 146, 199

A

AAC Microte, 112
AAdvantage, 146
Ackoff, Russell, 192, 267
Adcole Maryland Aerospace, 112
Adidas, 63, 64, 115, 197, 217
Advertising, 121
Aerion, 111
Aérospatiale, 110
Africa, 135, 232
agri-tech, 134, 135
AirAsia, 146
Airbus, 110, 269
Akers, John, 194, 228
Alibaba, 11, 22, 77, 78, 82, 139, 170, 246
Amazon, 9, 10, 19, 32, 33, 35, 59, 77, 78, 79, 80, 82, 121, 125, 126, 130, 131, 142, 170, 172, 181, 182, 186, 193, 200, 201, 222, 228, 237, 246, 247, 265
Amazon Prime, 82

Amazon Web Services, 82
American Airlines, 146
American Express, 132, 198, 208
Android, 49, 197
Angie's List, 203
Anna Karenina, 56
Anta, 115
AOL, 74
App Store, 130, 131
Apple, 10, 22, 26, 46, 49, 53, 59, 77, 98, 121, 130, 139, 170, 172, 175, 180, 181, 186, 188, 193, 197, 247
Argentina, 88
Arizona State University, 138
artificial intelligence, 57, 104, 154, 157, 159, 163, 204, 237
Aspen, Colorado, 89
Astrobotics, 112
Asura, 45
Auchan, 198
Australia, 106
Avis, 127
AXA, 96

B

Babbage, Charles, 150
Baidu, 11
Ballmer, Steve, 63
BBC, 98
Bezos, Jeff, 80, 81, 83, 202, 222
Bigelow Aerospace, 114
Bilbao, Spain, 88, 89
Bing, 242
biology, 160, 161

Biotech, 160
Bitcoin, 162
Black Friday, 78
Blackberry, 19
Blockbuster, 9, 19, 97, 129, 172, 193, 213
blockchain, 57, 162, 163, 164, 231
Blue Origin, 112
BMW, 44
Boeing 787, 31, 185
Bogota, Colombia, 114
Bolsonaro, Jair, 87
Booz & Co., 51
Bowerman, Bob, 208
Brazil, 87
Brexit, 44, 86, 87
Britain, 44, 87
British Aerospace, 110
Bruno Palessi, 83, 84, 258
Buick, 211
Business Model Canvas, 249
Business Model Generation, 249
Business Model Sketchpad, 252

C

Camp Mariana Paez, 114
Camp, Garrett, 114, 208
Canal+, 98
Carlson, Chester, 52
Carrefour, 198
chemistry, 160
Chevrolet, 239
Chicago, 198, 236
China, 11, 31, 44, 45, 77, 87, 91, 108, 122, 123, 159, 161, 170, 173

Chinese Academy of Sciences, 161
Christensen, Clayton, 254
Citi Bike Share, 41
cities, 135, 162, 257
Clear Channel, 127
Cleveland, Ohio, 79, 89
Climate Action 100+, 100
Climate Change, 230
cobalt, 109, 110
Coca-Cola, 187, 228
Comcast, 98
Compagnia Generale per lo Spazio, 112
computer chips, 137, 138, 139, 150, 151, 153, 155
computer code, 150, 153, 156, 162
Concorde SST, 110
Conlon, Jerome, 62, 267
consumer culture, 11
Containerization, 109, 116
Cook, Tim, 63
corn, 134, 135
Costco, 132, 248
Craigslist, 27, 131
Cray computer, 138
Creative destruction, 191
Creative economy business models, 217
creativity, 258
Credit Suisse, 83
CRISPR, 136, 160
Culp, Larry, 167, 222
Cyber Monday, 78
cybercurrency, 162

D

da Vinci, Leonardo, 152
DARPA, 122, 138
Deepfakes, 159, 163
Dell, 198, 199
Deloitte, 197
Democratic Party, 91
Democratic Republic of the Congo, 110

demographics, 102, 232
Design a Better Business, 254
Detroit, Michigan 89, 124, 193
Didi, 126
digital billboards, 137
digital diagnostics, 150
digital economy, 151, 156
Digitalization, 134, 135, 136, 138, 140, 142, 143
Disney, 22, 36, 37, 46, 49, 172, 256
disruption map, 252
Doblin, 253
Docutech, Xerox, 54, 55
Dollar Store, 235
Dragon Air, 146
drones, 135, 200, 237
Drucker, Peter, 73
Dubai, 91, 230
Dying to Survive, 45

E

EasyJet, 146
eBay, 131
Energy Industry, 99
English, 44
ethnography, 47
Etsy, 132
Europe, 43, 44, 122, 123, 146, 198, 232
European Commission, 104
European Union, 87, 94

F

Facebook, 10, 19, 103, 106, 121, 125, 130, 132, 159, 170, 196, 197, 217, 222, 241, 242
Facial Recognition, 156, 157, 159, 164
Farley, Jim, 16, 17, 71, 75, 189, 190
Fashion Institute of Technology, 218
Fedex, 19, 50, 181, 200, 205
Ferraro, Michael, 218

Fire (Amazon), 82
Firefly, 112
Flannery, John, 166
Ford, 17, 40, 41, 44, 124, 133, 189, 226, 227
Fortune 500, 13
Fourth Generation R&D, 223
France, 44, 198
Frankenstein, 152

G

Gameboy, 147
Gap, 201
GDPR (General Data Protection Regulation), 107
GE (General Electric), 52, 53, 166, 167, 169, 171, 180, 222, 227
Gehry, Frank, 88
Gerstner, Louis, 167, 194, 222, 227, 228
Giannandrea, John, 104
GM (General Motors), 19, 53, 174, 176, 180, 189, 190, 194, 226, 227, 239
GMO, 136
GoGoVan, 126
Goldberg, Rube, 34
Google, 9, 10, 19, 27, 28, 44, 59, 98, 102, 103, 104, 106, 121, 122, 125, 126, 130, 132, 139, 142, 175, 180, 186, 240, 241, 242
GPS, 38, 122, 134, 257
Great Depression, 124
Greece, 152
Greenland, 43
Grove, Andy, 18, 21, 71, 75
GSK (Glaxo Smith Kline), 169
Guggenheim Foundation, 88

H

Hackett, Jim, 40, 41
Haloid Company, 52
Hamtramck Assembly Plant, 90

Index

Harari, Yuval Noah, 14, 256
Hastings, Reed, 19, 23, 71, 99
Health care, 139
Hertz, 127
Hollywood, 97, 98, 128
Home Depot, 9, 12, 13, 19, 112, 181, 200, 201, 205
Honda, 205, 227, 239
Honduras, 31
Honeywell, 111
Hong Kong, 37
Houston, 144, 230
HP (Hewlett Packard), 199
Hulu, 98
human intelligence, 155
Hummer, 189

I

IBM, 52, 104, 167, 168, 169, 170, 171, 180, 188, 190, 194, 199, 208, 218, 222, 227
IED (Improvised Explosive Device), 179
Ikea, 109, 201, 235, 237, 247
India, 45
industrialization, 153
innovation, 257, 258
Innovator's Dilemma, The, 254
Instagram, 106
Intel, 18, 21, 227
International Space Station, 114
internet, 138, 151, 162
IoT (internet of things), 158, 163
iPhone, 38, 49, 51, 138, 171, 178, 193, 257
ispace, 112
iTunes, 130, 131

J

Japan, 16, 99, 174, 189, 193, 232, 251
JC Decaux, 127
JC Penney, 12, 13, 82
JD.com, 200
Jet Blue, 146
jet engine, 151
Jobs, Steve, 63
John Deere, 134
Jordan, Michael, 115, 197, 198
Journal of Business Models, 267
JPMorgan Chase, 94

K

Kalanick, Travis, 208
Keeley, Larry, 253
Kelleher, Herb, 207
Kindle, 82
King, Rollin, 207
Kinko's, 216
K-Mart, 12, 13, 34, 50, 173
Knight, Phil, 208
Kodak, 19, 52, 194, 228
Kurzweil, Ray, 155, 156, 160

L

Lampert, Edward, 66, 173
Lao Tzu, 221
LCD billboards, 44
Legg Mason, 80
Lehman Brothers, 19
Lenovo, 199
Levitt, Ted, 32
Lexus, 16, 239
LinkedIn, 106, 132, 170
Lockheed Martin, 111
London, 37, 105
Longhua River, 92
Los Angeles, 84, 129, 230
Louisiana, 101
Lovelace, Ada, 150
Lowe's, 82, 113
Lyft, 40, 126
lygus bug, 134

M

machine learning, 57, 104, 154
Macy's, 12, 13, 82
Maginot Line, 179
Maker Bot, 216
Malaysia, 31
McCarthy, Barry, 213
McDonald's, 152
Mercedes, 239
Metcalfe, Robert, 125, 126, 128, 188
Miami, 230
Microsoft, 10, 63, 74, 121, 128, 130, 170, 188
Miller, William, 223
MIT, 138, 152
Moon Express, 112
Moore, Gordon, 138
Morrision, David J., 254
Motivate, 40

N

NASA, 153
NBA, 149
Nebraska, 134
Netflix, 9, 19, 97, 98, 128, 129, 132, 172, 193, 202, 203, 213, 227
Netscape, 74
network effect, 136
New York, 37, 38, 39, 40, 41, 90, 102, 157
Nike, 49, 114, 193, 197, 198, 205
Nike Town, 64, 198
Nokia, 19, 51, 170, 171, 172, 174, 178, 193, 228
nonbiological intelligence, 155
North America, 16, 43, 82, 189
Northeastern University, 105
Novotel, 198
Numeracy, 150

O

Old Navy, 201

Oldsmobile, 19, 189, 190, 211, 228
Only the Paranoid Survive, 18
Oracle, 189

P

Pacific Gas & Electric, 101
Palantir, 140, 141, 204
Palessi (Bruno), 84, 85
Palo Alto Research Center (Xerox PARC), 54
Paris, 38
Payless ShoeSource, 83
Pepsi, 187
pesticides, 135
pharmaceuticals, 160
physics, 155, 160
Picasso, 235, 251
Pigneur, Yves, 249
Pittsburgh, 89
Pokemon Go, 149
Pontiac, 19, 189
Portland, 198
Porto Seguro, Colombia, 96
Positive feedback, 75, 76, 140, 262
Pourdehnad, John, 267
PPG, 53
Prefontaine, Steve, 197
Prius (Toyota), 198
productivity, 134
Profit Patterns, 254
Puma, 115
Pumpkin Space Systems, 112

Q

quantum computing, 57
Quicken, 95

R

R&D, 26, 51, 54, 55, 76, 170, 191, 262
Rate-My-Professors.com, 203
Red Hat, 170

Republican Party, 91
RFID chip, 149
RJR Nabisco, 208
robo-farming, 135
Robots, 9, 57, 135, 137, 138, 151, 152, 153, 154, 156, 231
Rocket Lab, 111, 112
rockets, 257
Rolling Stone Magazine, 156
Rometty, Ginni, 168, 222, 228
Rotterdam, 230
RyanAir, 146

S

S&P 500, 10, 13, 121
Saks Fifth Avenue, 26
Sam's Club, 132
Samsung, 11
San Antonio, 144
San Francisco, 40, 103, 104
Sassen, Saskia, 90, 91
satellite, 135
Saturn, 19, 189
Schultz, Howard, 208
Schumpeter, Joseph, 176, 177, 191, 221
Scion (Toyota), 16, 17, 19
Sculley, John, 63
Sears, 9, 12, 13, 19, 34, 50, 79, 81, 82, 168, 172, 173, 194, 228, 235, 236, 237, 239, 264
Seat Guru, 203
self-driving cars, 57, 137
Senegal, 32
sexbot, 154
Shanghai, 91, 158, 230
Shell Oil, 99
Shelly, Mary, 152
Shenzhen, 91, 92, 107, 108
shopping mall, 79, 83, 97, 143
Silicon Valley, 54, 123, 126
Singapore, 32, 91, 230
Singles' Day, 77, 78, 84

singularity, 154, 155, 156, 160, 164, 232
Sling, 98
Sloan, Alfred, 211
Slywotzky, Adrian, 254
Smart phones, 137
Softbank, 98
Sony, 19, 193
Southwest Airlines, 50, 59, 144, 181, 199, 205
SpaceIL, 112
SpaceX, 112
Spyce restaurant, 152
SST, 110
Standard Industrial Classification (SIC Code), 120
Stanford University, 138, 269
Starbucks, 9, 19, 26, 208
State Farm, 96
Strategyzer, 252
strawberry, 134
Sun Microsystems, 189, 190
Sweden, 32, 148
Swift, Taylor, 156, 157
Sydney Opera House, 88, 89

T

tacit knowledge, 47, 211, 223
Taiwan Semiconductor, 11
talkwalker, 204
Tao, 7
Target, 35, 81, 173, 201, 237, 265
taxi industry, 38, 50
TCP-IP, 163
Tencent, 11, 46, 98, 107, 262
Tesla, 150, 227
Texas, 144
The Economist, 122
Time-Warner, 74
Tokyo, 91, 189
Tolstoy, Leo, 56
Tommy Hilfiger, 149
Tooze, Adam, 20, 256
Total Oil, 100, 269

Toyota, 16, 23, 186, 189, 191, 198, 205, 211, 212, 227, 239
Toys R Us, 212
TripAdvisor, 114, 203
Twitter, 106

U

Uber, 9, 19, 37, 38, 39, 40, 42, 46, 50, 59, 126
Under Armour, 115
UnionLife, 96
United Airlines, 132
United Nations, 163
University of Illinois, 105
UPS, 50
US National Academy of Medicine, 160
US National Academy of Sciences, 161

V

Value Ladder Model, 246
value proposition design, 252
van der Pijl, Patrick, 254
Van Gogh, 235, 251
Verizon, 74
Viet Cong, 179
Vietnam, 31
Vikings, 43, 46
Virgin America, 146
Virgin Galactic, 113
Visa, 198, 205

W

Wagoner, Rick, 174, 176, 189, 239
Walkman, 147
Wall Street Journal, The, 77, 93
Walmart, 9, 12, 13, 19, 26, 33, 34, 35, 50, 59, 77, 81, 172, 173, 175, 182, 193, 201, 228, 231, 235, 236, 237, 239, 247, 265
Walmsley, Emma, 169
water, 135, 136, 257
Webvan, 263
WeChat, 107
Wells Fargo, 204
WeWork, 26, 96, 104
Whole Foods, 82, 201
whole system, 181, 182, 183, 184
World War I, 124, 227
WOW, 146
Wozniak, Steve, 63

X

Xerox, 19, 52, 53, 54, 55, 126, 175, 188, 190, 194, 228, 256
Xi Jinping, 46

Y

Yahoo, 74, 228
YouTube, 98, 241

Z

Zambia, 135
Zozo, 149
Zuckerberg, Mark, 21, 222

ABOUT THE AUTHOR

Langdon is an award-winning innovator and world-renowned innovation consultant, best-selling author, and acclaimed keynote speaker.

He is Senior Partner at *InnovationLabs*, where he leads the firm's global innovation consulting practice with a wonderful variety of clients in business, government, and non-profits; and President of *FutureLab Consulting*, a technology and blockchain incubator.

Recent clients include: Accor, Airbus, Bayer, France Telecom/Orange, ING, Ingersoll-Rand, Kaiser Pemanente, Leidos, L'Oreal, National Board of Medical Examiners, Stanford Health Care, Total Oil, UNICEF, US Navy, US Coast Guard, and many others.

He is recognized as one the world's leading thinkers, writers, and consultants on innovation, and his original and ground-breaking work has been adopted by corporations and universities on every continent.

He is also:
- Board member of the prestigious *International Association of Innovation Professionals*, and Chair of its Conference, *Innova-Con*.
- Associate Editor of the *International Journal of Innovation Science*.
- Director of *Innovation Academy*, a world-renowned innovation training group.
- Co-Chair of the Innovation Council at *RedTeam Engineering*.
- Member of the *USA Technical Advisory Group (TAG)* for ISO 56000, the new global standard for innovation management now under development.

Many of his books are best-sellers, and most are standard business, strategy, and innovation references globally.

InnovationLabs offers exceptional workshops, trainings, and consulting in Business Model Innovation and indeed in all facets of innovation.

FutureLab offers consulting and training on blockchains.

Please contact us for more information.

You can learn more at www.innovationlabs.com and www.futurelabconsulting.com

Made in the USA
Las Vegas, NV
03 May 2022